Women, Violence, and the Media

WOMEN, VIOLENCE, AND THE MEDIA

Readings in Feminist Criminology

Edited by

Drew Humphries

Northeastern University Press

BOSTON

Published by University Press of New England

HANOVER AND LONDON

Northeastern University Press
Published by University Press of New England,
One Court Street, Lebanon, NH 03766
www.upne.com
© 2009 by Northeastern University Press
Printed in the United States of America
5 4 3 2 1

Library of Congress Cataloging-in-Publication Data
Women, violence, and the media : readings in feminist criminology /
edited by Drew Humphries.
p. cm. — (The Northeastern series on gender, crime, and law)
Includes bibliographical references.
ISBN 978-1-55553-703-6 (pbk. : alk. paper)
1. Women—Crimes against.   2. Violence in women.   3. Rape in mass media.
4. Sex in mass media.   5. Violence in mass media.   6. Feminist theory.
I. Humphries, Drew.

HV6250.4.W65W6616 2009
362.88082—dc22   2008049862

Book design by Dean Bornstein

University Press of New England is a member of the Green Press Initiative.
The paper used in this book meets their minimum requirement
for recycled paper.

CONTENTS

TABLES

PREFACE

Two goals guided the development of *Women, Violence, and the Media*. One was to develop a collection that would help readers to think more clearly about women's experiences of violence; the other was to organize it so that readers would begin at step one and progress by degrees toward a reflective, critical approach to media representations. It struck us that the Preface would be a good place to pull together all the bits and pieces that otherwise seemed to get lost.

But first, a digression. The collection raises issues of concern to college readers. Sexual violence is a fact of life for too many college students; it traumatizes victims and interrupts college careers, temporarily and permanently. Because popular culture, including the media, tends to encourage victim blaming, students may find the collection useful in challenging their tendencies to blame victims and, perhaps more importantly, for survivors of violent attacks to avoid the erroneous conclusion that they may be responsible. Moreover, many college students are headed toward careers in the very agencies—criminal justice, health, and social services—responsible for dealing with violence by and against women. An initial step in learning to approach women in crisis is to acknowledge and put aside gendered biases discussed by the contributors to this collection. A second step is to understand the role that justice, health, and service professionals may play in interfacing with the media and how they can work with journalists to improve the accuracy and the quality of media representations of violence and women.

A second digression allows us to talk about media trends that bear on the collection and its concerns. High-profile cases are examined in several chapters and reflect shifts in the organization of electronic media. Network news has given way to cable networks such as CNN and Court TV, which require a constant stream of news stories in order to fill the airwaves twenty-four hours a day, seven days a week. As Court TV's coverage of the O. J. Simpson case demonstrated, an ongoing, larger-than-life crime attracts and retains a sizable audience and provides content to fill the airtime. Over the last several decades, other highly publicized cases (e.g., the Scott Peterson case and that of Susan Smart) have turned a second wave of domestic and family violence into epic tales about women and violence. These cases offer unique opportunities to investigate gendered constructions of violence.

In addition, television has had to adjust to women in the labor force and their role in purchasing the household items advertised on commercial networks. The television industry has responded by casting women in leading roles as professionals. Cable networks such as Lifetime have taken the additional step of catering to an all-female audience. These changes resonate throughout the offerings of television, and scholars have examined them for new kinds of gendered assumptions.

The last set of media changes reflected in the collection concerns globalization, the "interconnectedness" of persons, processes, and institutions, across national boundaries and from one region to another. U.S. news services bring ethnic cleansing (in Bosnia, Rwanda, and Darfur) into the domestic market, but reports are selective, emphasizing some insurgencies or civil wars and disregarding others. Moreover, television programs developed in one country are exported to other nations: A popular TV series, *Prime Suspect*, and the reality-based monthly program *Crimewatch UK* are both produced in the United Kingdom for English-speaking audiences. *Prime Suspect* has been imported and aired in full on the Public Broadcasting System, where its status as a quality mystery has earned it a loyal following. In contrast, *Crimewatch UK* has remained in Britain: U.S. viewers watch *America's Most Wanted*, a home-grown version of reality-based programming. Finally, the Internet has decentered the distribution of news. An on-line version of a newspaper, the *Star*, published in print form in Bangladesh, reaches far-flung expatriates with news of home, gives voice to resistance, and provides a refuge from censorship. In one way or another, these changes provide background for readings encountered in *Women, Violence, and the Media*.

Now let's return to the main point, the bits and pieces about teaching and the critical thinking skills this collection aims to foster. From the outset, readers must keep in mind that *real violence* and *media representations of violence* are not the same thing. The distinction is not as obvious as some might suppose. Much of what everyone "knows" about crimes of violence comes from watching television, playing video games, or going to films. Some may be aware of the difference, but few have reflected on the secondhand nature of this knowledge.

For purposes of discussion, *real violence* is defined legally, and information about it comes from systematic data collected by government agencies or social science surveys. Although it appears to be a stable feature of life in the United States, what many think about violence has changed over time. Sexual assaults have been added to forcible rape as a measure of sexual violence. From homicide has emerged the concept of intimate homicide. Similarly, intimate partner violence has its roots in assault. These crimes exemplify women's experience of violence, linked as they are by the relationships among intimates, family, friends, and acquaintances.

Media representations are based on real violence, but they have been shaped by other processes. The news judgments of journalists, literary conventions that define subgenres, and publishing standards for mainstream texts all reshape real violence into represented violence. Manufacturing is an analogy used by scholars to describe the effects of these decisions. If real violence is like the raw material, then represented violence looks more like a car coming off the assembly line than the metals used in its construction.

Critical thinking also involves the ability to discern different systems of thought and to recognize, weigh, and respond to their underlying assumptions. Part I of this volume, "Gendering Constructions: Women and Violence," introduces students to four gendered assumptions that influence media representations, and the individual chapters illustrate the ways in which these assumptions shape media images of violence. One method of assessing recognition skills is to ask students to identify the assumptions in different media contexts. Students tend to respond more enthusiastically to visual images (e.g., films or TV news or dramas) than to print news (e.g., newspapers or magazines). When using visual media in a group setting, it is important to clarify the learning goals beforehand and require students to commit their ideas to paper.

The capacity to formulate issues and make arguments requires more complex critical thinking skills. If an issue is something people argue about, then it has at least two sides, and people who care about the issue advance arguments based on a logical series of claims about reality. Finding an issue that students would care about was a challenge, but because life and death matter to us all, Part II, "Debating the Issues: Femicide and Sexual Terrorism," focuses on the killing of women by men because they are women. Students are introduced to the dispute about femicide in the United States and then are asked to consider violence against women in a cross-cultural or global context. To advance their own arguments, students may need guidance in breaking down competing definitions of the problem and in keeping track of its manifestation in other parts of the world. The key comparison involves: (1) the *reality* of violence against women in the United States, Bangladesh, Bosnia, and Rwanda and (2) the *representation* of femicide and sexual terrorism by U.S. and foreign media outlets, including news and entertainment. A position would necessarily entail discussion of the realities of violence and the selectivity of media representations.

In reading Part III, "Changing the Image: Feminist Critics and Criticism," readers are likely to find change a more accessible topic than criticism. Consequently, the section begins with straightforward examples of change. Chapter 6, for instance, looks at news sources and news images: If the quality of news images is related to reporters' sources, then substituting a high-quality source for another is an appropriate change. In this, suggestions for change follow logically from research or feminist analysis. In addition, this section presents three other models of criticism: scholars working toward a critical stance, critics challenging oppressively gendered terms of a debate, and researchers testing the limits of feminist thinking on victim blaming. An introductory essay provides background material that will help readers with the styles of argumentation used by the contributors.

On a final note, I would encourage students to use the collection as a resource for media projects of their own. The chapters give details about data sources, research strategies, and qualitative analyses. The contributors have asked a variety of questions about media representations, connecting violent images to gender inequality, change, globalization, and broader cultural conversations. In doing this, they have drawn from different data sources, either news (print or television) or entertainment (i.e., the police procedural, black film, or women-in-jeopardy films). Note that the chapters describe electronic data sources and sampling strategies. One can identify a population, select a sampling strategy, and draw a sample quickly and efficiently. I would also encourage students to pay attention to what the contributors have written about coding, the value of multiple coders, and the use of coding instruments. In addition, qualitative analyses characterize the collection: Many are based on grounded theory, where themes are pursued until the point of saturation, and others are based on content analysis, where particulars (e.g., demographics and crime types) are coded and presented as frequencies. It is not enough to report content; one strives to relate media representation to broader issues. At the end of this volume, the Selected Readings section describes and lists some recent contributions to the field.

ACKNOWLEDGMENTS

I would like to express my gratitude to Susan Caringella for her support at every stage in the preparation of this volume. From the articles we edited for *Violence Against Women* (February 1998) to the discussions we have had about this project, Susan's intellectual and moral support has kept this project on track. I would also like to acknowledge Gray Cavender for his sage advice at several key points.

To Claire Renzetti, editor of the series on Gender, Crime, and Law, I say thank you. I am also grateful to the University Press of New England and its able editorial staff, including Phyllis D. Deutsch, Helen Wheeler, Hal Henglein, Barbara Briggs, Harry Huberty, Christine Hauck, Deborah Forward, Sherri Strickland, and Sarah L. Welsch.

Two contributors wish to acknowledge previously published work. "Making Sense of a Female Malady" by Deborah Jermyn (Chapter 11, this volume) draws on her 2007 book *Crime Watching: Investigating Real Crime TV*, published by I. B. Tauris and Palgrave Macmillan. Lynn S. Chancer's 2005 book *High Profile Crimes: When Legal Cases Become Social Causes*, published by the University of Chicago Press, is the basis for "Victim-Blaming through High-Profile Crimes" (Chapter 12, this volume).

My colleagues at Rutgers-Camden provided encouragement, and Sherry Pisacano helped in ways too numerous to list. I am indebted to my husband, Daniel Tompkins, and to my daughter, Victoria Tompkins, for believing in the value of this project.

INTRODUCTION
Toward a Framework for Integrating Women, Violence, and the Media

This collection is concerned with questions that arise at the junction of women, violence, and the media. What does it mean to be a woman? How do we begin to think about violence? And what do women's experiences with violence look like through the lens of the media? In an effort to explicate the theoretical commitments that shape *Women, Violence, and the Media*, this introduction offers an account of feminist perspectives on gender and emerging concepts of violence along with an eclectic approach to the media and media representations. In the latter part of the chapter, the theoretical choices that define the collection are summarized and related to its organization.

Feminist Approaches to Gender

This collection takes a feminist approach to women, violence, and the media. Here, the principles and the debates that have shaped the perspective are reviewed. In talking about women, feminists begin from the premise that gender constructions organize identity, social participation, and the standards for judging self and others. According to West and Zimmerman (1987, p. 129), social constructions take form as a set of attitudes, practices, and "doings" that reflect basic social arrangements and that function to legitimate inequalities based on gendered social structures. Building on this basic insight, Daly and Chesney-Lind (1988) enumerated five elements that distinguish feminist perspectives on gender from other modes of inquiry. First, gender is a "complex social, historical, and cultural product" that "is related to, but not simply derived from biological sex differences" (Daly & Chesney-Lind, 1988, p. 504). Second, gender orders social life and social institutions in fundamental ways. Next, gender and the relationships it defines are the basis for constructs of masculinity and femininity, which are organized such that male power

· I ·

gives men dominion over women. Fourth, the views of men that rationalize the subordinate position of women are embedded in "systems of knowledge" and in the processes that produce them. Daly and Chesney-Lind's final point concerns the focus of feminist analysis. In a world that gives men "natural" authority over women, the task of feminist analysis is to challenge this presumption by making women "the center of intellectual inquiry" (Daly & Chesney-Lind, 1988, p. 504). The fourth and fifth principles, as well as inclusive definitions of gender, are important guideposts in understanding the approach taken in this collection.

Feminist perspectives evolved in the context of intellectual debate over the root causes of inequality, the role of race, ethnicity, and social class in feminism, postmodernism, and the study of masculinities. One of the first sets of debates arose over the origins of gender inequality. Feminists took a variety of positions, focusing on either the role of discrimination, the class basis of society, or patriarchy in subordinating women. Liberal feminists, for example, urged legal reforms that would ease women's access to education and employment. Marxist and socialist feminists linked female emancipation to the destruction of capitalist society, although socialist feminists recognized that patriarchy coexisted with capitalism. Radical feminists took the position that emancipation depended on the eradication of patriarchy itself. As it turned out, the substance of these debates was less important to the recent history of feminism than the white, middle-class scholars and activists who advanced a conception of gender and womanhood that mirrored their own experience.

Taking issue with a white, middle-class concept of gender, black feminists made the case that the experience of black women was central to the feminist project (Collins, 2000; hooks, 2004) and advanced the notion of intersectionality; that is, race and gender are a dual system of identity that shapes and is shaped by social class experience (Collins, 2004; hooks, 2000). The push for inclusiveness came from third world and postcolonial feminists, who focused on women's struggles in relation to developed countries and postcolonialism—in effect, globalization—which figures in the discussion of femicide in Part II of this volume.

An emphasis on the diversity of women's experiences brought feminism closer to the growing intellectual movement called postmodernism. The characteristics of postmodernism that concern us are the recognition that there are multiple realities and a multiplicity of truths, both of which

introduce considerable ambiguity into social inquiry a
tion of gender. Multiple realities and truths make gend
ambiguous construct, although it retains some theoret
of the interplay between oppression and resistance and betw
and human agency (Connell & Messerschmidt, 2005).

A useful approach to investigating multiple systems of oppression is found in the work on hegemonic masculinity and emphasized femininity by Connell (1987). In a recent reformulation, Connell and Messerschmidt (2005) describe hegemonic masculinity as "the pattern of practice (i.e., things done, not just a set of role expectations or an identity) that allowed men's dominance over women to continue" (Connell & Messerschmidt, 2005, p. 832). Practiced by elites, hegemonic masculinity allows for subordinated masculinities, explaining the range of variations, and it serves to legitimate the global subordination of women, explaining the pervasiveness of gender inequality. The term "hegemonic" refers to the means by which men practice masculinity. Although it may entail coercive force, hegemony is more closely associated with persuasive practices of social reproduction. In their reformulation, Connell and Messerschmidt conceptualize the relationship between hegemonic and subordinate forms as one of reciprocal influences, accommodation or co-optation. They also draw attention to the subordinate position of hegemonic or "emphasized femininity" in relation to masculinity. "Gender is always relational, and patterns of masculinity are socially defined in contradistinction from some model (whether real or imaginary) of femininity" (Connell & Messerschmidt, 2005, p. 848). In other words, the practices in which women take part and that ultimately perpetuate female subordination mirror practices that sustain male dominance.

The concept of gender allows us to focus on women in relation to men and male dominance. In carrying out the practices associated with masculinity, men reap the benefits of authority, whereas the practices that define femininity press to marginalize women. The approach assumes multiple forms of oppression (based on race, ethnicity, class, and sexual identity) and recognizes that the practices of masculinity and femininity are specific to social context. It leaves open the question of whether women are complicit in the arrangements that shape their lives and makes provision for the possibility that women resist subordinating features of femininity. The point is that the conceptualization allows for change either from subordinate men pushing back against hegemonic masculinity or from the resistance of angry or courageous women striking out on their own.

Intimate, Family, and Acquaintance Violence

Most criminology students should be able to list the offenses that the FBI designates as violence. They are homicide, forcible rape, aggravated assault, and robbery, although forcible rape was not added to the list until the 1950s. Less apparent than the list might suggest, however, is the fact that what most people believe to be violence has changed significantly over the last several decades. Now, the official listing of criminal violence also includes intimate partner violence, family violence, and sexual assault. The National Crime Victim Survey (NCVS) distinguishes between *rape* and *sexual assault*[1] and uses both categories in measuring sexual violence. Rape is "forced sexual intercourse," but the NCVS recognizes physical and psychological coercion. It involves penetration, but includes penetration by a foreign object. And it recognizes heterosexual and same-sex rapes. Sexual assault includes a wide range of victimizations—unwanted sexual contact that is separate from rape. Rape and sexual assault both include attempted and completed attacks. The Centers for Disease Control (CDC) defines *intimate partner violence* (IPV)[2] as "the intentional use of physical force with the potential for causing death, disability, injury or harm," and the CDC goes on to describe behaviors that IPV includes: "Physical violence . . . includes, but is not limited to, scratching; pushing; shoving; throwing; grabbing; biting; choking; shaking; slapping; punching; burning; use of a weapon; and use of restraints or one's body size, or strength against another person." But the Bureau of Justice Statistics defines IPV[3] more narrowly as homicides, rapes, assaults, and robberies committed by intimates; that is, by current or ex-spouses or current or ex-girlfriends or boyfriends. Intimates are distinguished from other family members, acquaintances, and friends. The term "*family violence*"[4] refers to other family members (e.g., mothers, siblings, or uncles) who have killed or assaulted other members of the family.

The attention given by officials to newer crimes reflects the impact of the women's movement, the movement against rape, and the struggle against domestic violence and battering. Danger is no longer equated with a stranger poised to attack women; instead, the women's movement has driven home the point that those most likely to pose a risk are a woman's intimates, family members, friends, and acquaintances. As such, violence is understood to take place in or near the home and as women go about daily activities, commuting, visiting friends, or staying home. Thus, a common element in these crimes is that violence shatters the perceived safety of the home and violates the fundamental trust established through the bonds of intimacy, marriage, parenthood, or friendship.

When it comes to estimating this kind of violence, readers have to be aware that there are significant problems in the measurement instruments.[5] Nonetheless, it is plain that, since the 1990s, violence has declined in the United States,[6] but "females are substantially more likely to be killed by an intimate than male[s]."[7] Of course, females kill former or current intimate partners (spouses or boyfriends), and these crimes also violate basic trusts. It is important, however, to keep two things in mind. First, female-on-male homicides are relatively infrequent. Most homicide victims and perpetrators are males. Two-thirds of the homicides involve male-on-male killings. Of all homicides, less than 10% involve female-on-male murders.[8] Second, since 1976, the number of men killed by women in intimate homicides has dropped dramatically,[9] and the greatest decline, that for black males, has been attributed to an improvement in emergency responses in minority communities and to high incarceration rates for African American males (Websdale, 2001, as cited by Alvarez & Bachman, 2006). Even so, questions still arise about female-perpetrated intimate killings. Do women take the offensive? Or are they more likely to kill in order to defend themselves or their children? Although one cannot provide an answer, it is worth reviewing the source of confusion. The Conflicts Tactics Scale (CTS) is a measurement instrument used in social science surveys to estimate the extent and nature of domestic violence (Strauss & Gelles, 1990). The instrument distinguishes between minor forms of violence (pushing or shoving) and severe violence (being beaten with a weapon). In surveys, respondents are asked whether they have ever used these tactics. Results show that women are as likely to use them as men, but the CTS has been criticized for failing to distinguish between defensive and offensive use of such tactics and therefore for wrongfully inflating the prevalence of female-on-male violence (as discussed by Alvarez & Bachman, 2006).

In contrast to the equivocal status of females who kill intimates, available data provide a clear picture of the women who face violent attack by intimates, family, and friends. According to NCVS surveys, women residing in low-income households face higher risks of rape or sexual assault than women in households with higher incomes, although the 2005 survey found no differences in victimization rates across all income groups.[10] Furthermore, black women are at higher risk for nonlethal intimate partner violence than are white women.[11] In the context of nonlethal intimate partner violence, minority women, especially Native American women, have higher victimization rates than white women (11.1 per 1,000 population age 12 and older compared with 4.3). Poor women, those living in households with an annual income of less than $7,500, have higher rates of IPV victimization (12.7 per 1000 population age 12 or older) than women living in households with higher annual incomes. In contrast, white women, who face a higher risk of death at the hands of an intimate than do black women, are the exception to the rule that rape or sexual assault or IPV are among the costs borne by women for being poor and belonging to minority groups.

Feminists have interpreted much of this violence as a form of social control inflicted directly or culturally by men on women. Brownmiller (1975) was one of the first to make the argument that rape or the implied threat of rape functions to keep women in their place, second and subordinated to men. In a practical sense, rape functions in this way every time a woman opts to stay home, where she sees herself as safe, instead of going out alone at night. "Take Back the Night" marches organized by feminists take aim at these self-imposed restrictions, but perceived threats of stranger danger and the anticipated menace of public space find reinforcement in popular culture. But do intimate partner violence and family violence function in similar ways? Belknap (2001) points out "that the fact that some men victimize some women serves to control most females' lives through at least some degree of fear" (Belknap, 2001, p. 214). But fear is no more generic than women are. For black women, fear involves a history of rape and slavery, the experience of a sexist and racist justice system, and cultural acceptability of black male violence (Collins, 2000, pp. 146–148). By reading Naffire's *Feminism and Criminology*, one begins to appreciate the power of the cultural discourse that links fear, vulnerability, and femininity with male prepossession, authority, and masculinity (Naffire, 1996, Chapter 4).

So far, the discussion has focused on "real" violence, that is, violence that is both legally defined and institutionally recognized by labels such as intimate homicide and data-collection systems such as NCVS. As the discussion moves toward media representations, it is important to understand that real intimate, family, and acquaintance violence differs dramatically from media-represented violence.

An Eclectic Approach to the Media

This collection has been influenced by studies on the production of media images, especially news images, and by feminist work on media representations. Production processes demonstrate differences between real and represented violence.

The Production of Media Images

Most contributors to this volume focus on media content (i.e., the pattern of images revealed by systematic analysis) but interpret findings based on the premise that the meaning of content is revealed in the decisions that are made in the course of producing it (see Fishman, 1980; Gitlin, 1980; Scaggs, 2005). The premise undercuts any notion that individual sexist men (or women) deliberately construct images that demean women, supporting instead an understanding that media images are gendered as the result of routine judgments institutionalized in journalism curricula, literary conventions, and publishing standards. These judgments are captured by the concepts of newsworthiness, literary convention, and publication standards.

Newsworthiness is a term that sums up the wisdom of the craft of journalism, and it has been fully described in the newsmaking literature (Chibnall, 1977; Fishman, 1980; Schudson, 2003). In deciding among potentially newsworthy incidents, journalists select those they think are the most likely to appear in the paper or on local or national newscasts. The list of potentially newsworthy characteristics compiled by Chibnall (1977) applies specifically to crime news. Immediacy, drama, authoritative source, novelty, titillation, conventionalism, personification, and simplification make the difference between an ordinary event and a newsworthy incident. Breaking news lends a sense of immediacy. Violence provides drama, and because police record such incidents, journalists have an authoritative source. Departures from real crime patterns as suggested by extremely young or elderly victims establish novelty, and bizarre or voyeuristic details heighten novelty. Titillation is satisfied by sexuality (e.g., rape or sexual assault, prior sexual abuse, and sadistic or serial homicides). Balanced against titillation and novelty are the reassuring symbols of conventional order: the girl next door or another example of domesticity. Incidents or people whose circumstances stand for larger social issues add to the appeal of storylines. And incidents that easily fit into simplifying devices (e.g., mad or bad women) add to the newsworthiness of an incident. It is important to recognize that newsworthiness is selective for infrequent, atypical incidents. Surette (1998) refers to this pattern as the "law of opposites," suggesting that what appears in the news is the opposite of what occurs in reality.

The literary conventions that define the police procedural (the subject of Chapters 2 and 8 in this volume) have been described as misogynistic. In the police procedural, antipathy toward women is expressed by the fate of female characters: They are killed, maimed, degraded, or otherwise exploited. Meanwhile, the main plot features a cynical lone detective and tracks his efforts as he finds and apprehends devious, dim-witted, or demented killers (Scaggs, 2005). Feminists have debated whether the form can accommodate women in other than sexually objectified roles. *Law and Order*, the workplace drama examined by Humphries in Part I, features professional women who match the audience demographic—salaried women who control the family's purse strings. They are, however, buried under the show's professional brand of masculinity, in which the real drama—what one actor called "killing the bull"—takes place between the lead district attorney and the chief suspect (Stein, 2006). A more successful integration of women is provided by writers for the British series *Prime Suspect*, the mystery studied by Adelman, Cavender, and Jurik in Part II. Over the course of the series, detective inspector Jane Tennison, played by Helen Mirren, has outwitted overtly sexist colleagues and wily bureaucrats, sacrificed a personal life for the job, and solved—often through female sensibilities—every case assigned to her. With the exception of her battle against sexism, she is modeled on masculine detectives, who also lack a personal life, follow hunches, and battle the brass to solve cases (see Cavender & Jurik, 1998, 2004).

Academic publishing recognizes a wide range of scholarship, including mainstream and specialty contributions. The use of these terms is problematic, however, because "mainstream" and "specialty" publications reflect a dominant area of study defined implicitly by male scholars and another subordinated one defined quite explicitly as female. In the topical area of violence, for instance, two recent texts[12] attend to the major violent felonies (homicide, aggravated assault, forcible rape, and robbery) with one or two chapters on forms of violence affecting women (sexual assault, intimate partner violence, intimate homicide, stalking, and gender-motivated hate crimes). Texts constructed in this manner appeal to the broadest audience and tend to increase adoptions by college professors charged with teaching broadly defined and sizable survey courses. However, the masculine construction of criminology has come under fire as the number of female and feminist criminologists has increased dramatically over the last 30 years. It is now commonplace to find gender-, crime-, or justice-related courses. These courses have created an independent market for relevant texts.

Feminist Approaches to Media Representations

The discussion now turns to several recent studies that illustrate two very different approaches to analyzing gendered constructions in the media. The first approach focuses on women, the second on men. The first poses questions about the interplay between feminism and changing media representations.

In Dow's book *Prime Time Feminism* (1996), she asks how television programming has contributed to cultural conversation about feminism since the 1970s. Here, television programming is understood as a medium that interprets social change and manages cultural beliefs. The social transformation at issue was the consolidation by women of gains in education and employment. Television responded to these changes by introducing female-led series, ranging from *The Mary Tyler Moore Show* to a westernized medical show like *Dr. Quinn, Medicine Woman*. The closest Dow comes to crime or violence is in her discussion of the *Dr. Quinn* series. She argues that the female lead models a "liberated woman," but whatever instability one might see in the rise of professional women, they are managed by the strategic use of nostalgia, the appeal to a mythic past when women nurtured and cared for men. Thus, Dr. Quinn's version of the "liberated woman" mixes feminist gains, eases postmodern uncertainties, and appeals to the postfeminist declaration that everyone is equal and that no further action need be taken.

In *Redesigning Women*, Lodz approached female-led series as sites where "the meanings of modern femininity are forged, fought over, and understood" (Lodz, 2006, p. 35). In the stories told by network series like *Law and Order* or *E.R.*, women are naturalized as professionals. They are lawyers, doctors, or police officers first and women second. In these roles, white, middle-class women easily balance work and home to get on with the business of catching criminals or sewing up patients. All in all, the professional woman has become so much a part of network television that Lodz warns scholars to avoid the trap of thinking of these roles as "progressive" (Lodz, 2006, p. 164). Instead, she argues that by portraying women as professionals, these stories document the arrival of equality and announce, quite erroneously, the end of feminist struggle.[13]

A second approach to gender focuses on males and masculinity, defining violence as a male preserve. One example uses TV representations of rapists to understand the effects of feminism on television (Cuklanz, 2000), and the other sets out to make the gendered (masculine) nature of media violence visible (Boyle, 2005).

The main question in *Rape on Prime Time* (Cuklanz, 2000) is whether TV representations of rape (covering the years 1976–1990) had changed in response to feminist antirape campaigns. Cuklanz focuses on the "basic plot rape" to compare rapists, detectives, and victims across two time periods. In early plots, detectives exemplify effective masculinity, rapists carry the burden of ineffective masculinity, and victims are peripheral to the central male-on-male relationship. Competence, volatility (wildness), freedom, compassion, and caring for women are the hallmarks of effective masculinity, and detectives display them as they work rape cases and as they show superior understanding of women and their feelings about rape (Cuklanz, 2000, p. 77). In reporting this, Cuklanz makes the point that this kind of detective wards off feminist criticisms about the police response to rape. Ineffective masculinity is epitomized by rapists, who are strangers, unknown to the other characters, and who are psychologically damaged, evil, extreme in their violence, or committed to repeating their behavior (Cuklanz, 2000, pp. 68–72).

In later plot rapes, detectives are still competent, volatile, free, and still explain rape to victims, but victims have speaking roles and articulate their feelings and trauma. In this new mix, detectives have complex relationships with colleagues and rape victims and spend time discussing issues, emotions, and feelings. Rapists, however, are acquainted with victims or even date them and appear normal to other characters. Aside from traditional attitudes toward women and a need for control, there is little to explain the brutal violence that these men use against women they know. Overall, the most dramatic changes occur with respect to date rape and acquaintance rape. Desirable traits of hegemonic masculinity (competence, volatility, and freedom) are a constant: Compassionate detectives are the ones who put the rape in context for victims.

Like Cuklanz, Boyle examines violence along with masculinity, but an important piece of Boyle's argument in *Media and Violence* (2005) is that female violence (offending and being victimized) is visible as gendered, whereas male violence is not. Hence, Boyle sets herself the task of uncovering the stratagems by which news reports obscure the gendered nature of *male* violence in sexed crimes (Howe, 1998). In a section on British tabloids, Boyle discusses male-perpetrated sexual murders as expressions of a perverse masculinity combining "misogyny, transcendence, and sadistic sexuality" (Boyle, 2005, p. 64). In cases like those of Jack the Ripper or the Ripper of Yorkshire, these men are cut off from the rest of society, they spew out misogyny in word and action, and they enjoy sadistic pleasures implicit in male domination. When it comes to representing such killers in press accounts, Boyle argues that "other things" obscured the role of masculinity. Most notably, excitement and the cleverness of Jack the Ripper effaced masculinity. Male journalists, letterwriters, hangers-on, and would-be killers laid claim to insider knowledge and told an enticing tale about the killer's "evasion, detection, and cunning" that erased "the [masculine] reality of what the killer [did]" (Boyle, 2005, p. 66).

Other things also obscure the gendered and sexed nature of rape and pedophilia. In the case of rapists, Boyle argues that the media tend to emphasize *interracial* rapes (black rapist and white victims), and as a result, the news narrative is about race and racism, as in the Central Park jogger case. Sexual obsession obscures masculinity and drives the discourse about pedophilia to such an extent that the perpetrators are widely perceived to be beyond rehabilitation. So what advantage, one might ask, accrues from reshaping the construct to include masculinities? For Boyle, the answer to this question turns on the perpetrator's subjectivity and agency. Sexual obsession condemns the pedophile to repeat his actions. Locating those actions in the context of masculinities, however, allows for the possibility that pedophiles may opt for alternate masculinities that offer less damaging expressions of sexuality.

Theoretical Choices and the Organization of this Volume

Taken together, the theoretical choices reflected in this collection can be restated in summary form. First, the chapters express a commitment to keeping women at the center of inquiry, with the understanding that class, race, ethnicity, immigration status, and national or cultural origin are among the impersonal forces that position women with respect to men and violence.

Second, the collection approaches officially defined violence as a social construction, subject to change, and focuses on definitions of intimate and acquaintance violence, among other forms, that have become institutionalized over the last several decades. In the United States, datasets include the National Crime Victim Survey as well as a number of social science surveys. In other areas of the world, UN-sponsored surveys provide usable measures of domestic violence. Although recognizing that official surveys like these tend to underreport violence against women, the contributors nonetheless use these data as indicators of "real" violence in contrast to media representations.

Third, this volume tends to take an eclectic approach to the media and media representations. In drawing on production studies, some contributors trace gendered assumptions about violence to judgments about newsworthiness or literary conventions. Others, however, address media representations in relation to cultural debates about gender and race, inequality, or justice-related themes (e.g., the fear of crime and victim blaming). Taken together, the collection contributes to an understanding of the role that media representations play in defining and reinforcing gender inequality and other forms of inequality.

In comparison with recent feminist analyses of media representations, the collection's focus on women comes closer to the work of Dow and Lodz. In this respect, one can legitimately ask whether the female focus of this inquiry ignores questions of masculinity and violence. The book was not conceived as an examination of masculinity; nonetheless, contributions address relational aspects of gender, and many chapters can be interpreted in light of masculinities and femininities. In respect to criminology, the topical significance of violence brings the volume closer to the work of Cuklanz and Boyle. Justice and law, however, provide a more important backdrop for criminologists than do the cultural issues addressed in the work of Cuklanz and Boyle.

The volume begins with the basic tools of feminist analysis and moves on to consider the intertwined forms of gender oppression (intersectionality). From there, it addresses the prospects for changing representations of women and violence. As such, it is divided into three parts.

The purpose of Part I, "Gendered Constructions: Women and Violence," is to demonstrate how one goes about identifying media assumptions that make it appear as if it were natural to second-guess women and target them for discrimination. Linked to the pioneering work on gender and media content, Part I explicates some of the framing devices that persist in shaping contemporary media products. These include distinctions between good girls and bad girls and between female domesticity and male work. When these distinctions are used to frame women's experiences of violence, they also tend to stereotype women, misrepresent risk, encourage victim blaming, and trivialize male motives. In addition, Part I attends to media representations that combine gender, race, ethnicity, and social class and that encourage some audiences to idealize white, middle-class women as well as to demean poor women and women of color. Although Part I focuses on conventional media, Chapter 4 considers college textbooks and the status of women's issues in one area of academic publishing.

Part II, "Debating the Issues: Femicide and Sexual Terrorism," examines the issues of intersectionality and global media markets. It uses U.S. debates about femicide and the media's treatment of mass murder incidents as the starting point for an exploration of the way foreign media handle violence against women. In a failed state like Bangladesh, the news about local attacks on women can be read as evoking fear and reinforcing harsh restrictions on women. A journalistic tradition of witnessing violence and injustice, however, challenges Bangladeshi leaders who would ignore problems of any kind. When it comes to ethnic cleansing, geopolitics play a role: Newspapers in the United States gave far less attention to and provided fewer details about wartime sexual violence in the African country of Rwanda than in European Bosnia. A closer, albeit fictional look at ethnic cleansing is rendered by an episode produced for the British TV series *Prime Suspect*, which aired on PBS in the United States. In a tale characterized as progressive moral fiction, American viewers are given the opportunity to reframe two ordinary London murders as part of the horrific legacy of ethnic cleansing in Bosnia.

Efforts to change the way the media present women is the focus of Part III, "Changing the Image: Feminist Critics and Criticism." What actions might lead the media to more accurately represent women's experiences of violence? Contributors offer two kinds of answers. One concerns sources and writers: Domestic violence experts, for example, can be singled out as news sources that offer a more helpful view of victims and the risks they face than police sources that stress the inevitability of domestic homicides. The second answer concerns criticism. The technique of "positive redescription" is described as broadening the context in which female victimization is perceived. Another kind of criticism offers readers a model for how they might enter the arena of public debate: A critic reclaims the integrity of female images, tarnished in British debates about the fear of crime. And finally, in challenging notions about victim blaming, another critic encourages readers to see it as an unintended consequence of the two-sided framework of debate that itself reflects the organization of criminal trials.

Contributions to this volume stand as a sound basis for learning to use the tools of feminist analysis, understanding some of the complexities associated with media representations, and gaining an appreciation for the ways in which scholars have sought to improve the representation of women. I have included Selected Readings, a brief essay about emerging trends along with a list of recent scholarship. Readers interested in knowing more about the authors will find short biographies in the final section Contributors.

NOTES

1. For definitions of rape and sexual assault, see Bureau of Justice Statistics (2005, July 7), Criminal Victimizations in the U.S. Statistical Tables Index (Definitions). Retrieved March 31, 2008, from http://www.ojp.usdoj.gov/bjs/abstract/cvus/definitions.htm#rape_sexual_assault.

2. See the definition of intimate partner violence at Centers for Disease Control (2007, September 27), Intimate Partner Violence Prevention—Scientific Information (Defi-

nitions). Retrieved March 19, 2008, from http://www.cdc.gov/ncipc/dvp/IPV/ipv-definitions.htm.

3. See S. Catalano (2007, December 19), Intimate Partner Violence in the U.S. Retrieved February 14, 2008, from http://www.ojp.usdoj.gov/bjs/intimate/ipv.htm.

4. See Note 3.

5. The difficulties inherent in estimating violence against and by women are well known. The Uniform Crime Reports and the National Incident Based Reporting System are collected by law enforcement agencies and represent the crimes that people report to the police or those that the police have discovered. Consequently, these reflect the reporting behavior of citizens. The National Crime Victimization Surveys (NCVS) tap into unreported crime, which makes them a better source than police reports for estimating violence. Another police source, the Supplemental Homicide Reports (SHR), is considered the gold standard of measurement because deaths are confirmed by the medical examiner and because information about victims, offenders, and circumstances is linked to the homicides. The NCVS is frequently used to measure non-lethal partner violence, rape or sexual assault, and violence committed by other family members, but these data present two difficulties. First, low prevalence is a problem, especially for rape or sexual assault, which raises questions about demographic comparisons. Second, NCVS uses narrow definitions and, some say, inappropriately vague screening questions, which result in low estimates of violence. Social science surveys that broaden definitions and use behaviorally specific screening questions tend to produce higher estimates. For an overview of the measure of violence, see Reidel and Welsh (2002, Chapter 2) and Alvarez and Bachman (2008, Chapters 1 and 5).

6. Bureau of Justice Statistics (2007, August 8), Serious Violent Crime. Retrieved January 3, 2008, from http://www.ojp.usdoj.gov/bjs/glance.htm#Crime.

7. Bureau of Justice Statistics (2007, December 9). Homicide Trends in the U.S. (Intimate Homicide). Retrieved February 10, 2008, from http://www.ojp.usdoj.gov/bjs/homicide/intimates.htm.

8. Bureau of Justice Statistics (2007, December 9). Homicide Trends in the U.S. Retrieved February 10, 2008, from http://www.ojp.usdoj.gov/bjs/homicide/gender.htm.

9. See Note 5 for intimate homicide.

10. See Statistical Table 14, Victimization Rates for Persons 12 Years and Older by Type of Crime and Household Income, from the National Crime Victim Surveys, 1996–2005. Retrieved February 5, 2008, from http://www.ojp.usdoj.gov/bjs/abstract/cvusst.htm.

11. See Bureau of Justice Statistics (2007, December 9), Homicide Trends in the U.S. (Intimate Partner Violence in the U.S. Chart: Nonfatal Intimate Partner Violence, by Gender and Race, 1993–2005). Retrieved March 31, 2008, from http://www.ojp.usdoj.gov/bjs/intimate/victims.htm#race.

12. The texts include *Criminal Violence* (Reidel & Welsh, 2002) and *Violence: The Enduring Problem* (Alvarez & Bachman, 2006).

13. The critique of second-wave, or liberal, feminism offered by Lodz is based on objections to the narrow legalistic strategy (e.g., equal access to education and employment), and acceptance of the broader position outlined by bell hooks that would eradicate domination in all its forms (sexism, racism, economic injustice) and would support the principle of self-determination over imperialism, economic expansion, and materialism.

REFERENCES

Alvarez, A., & Bachman, R. (2006). *Violence: The enduring problem*. Thousand Oaks, CA: Sage.

Belknap, J. (2001). *The invisible woman: Gender, crime, and justice* (2nd ed.). Belmont, CA: Wadsworth/Thomson Learning.

Boyle, K. (2005). *Media and violence: Gendering the debates*. London: Sage.

Brownmiller, S. (1975). *Against our will: Men, women and rape*. New York: Simon and Schuster.

Cavender, G., & Jurik, N. C. (2004). Policing race and gender: An analysis of *Prime Suspect 2*. *Women's Studies Quarterly, 32*, 211–230.

———. (1998). Jane Tennison and the feminist police procedural. *Violence Against Women, 10*, 10–29.

Chibnall, S. (1977). *Law and order news*. London: Tavistock.

Collins, P. H. (2004). *Black feminist thought: Knowledge, consciousness, and the politics of empowerment* (2nd ed.). New York: Routledge.

Connell, R. W. (1987). *Gender and power: Society, the person and sexual politics*. Stanford, CA: Stanford University Press.

Connell, R. W., & Messerschmidt, J. W. (2005). Hegemonic masculinity: Rethinking the concept. *Gender and Society, 19*, 829–859.

Cuklanz, L. M. (2000). *Rape on prime time: Television, masculinity, and sexual violence*. Philadelphia: University of Pennsylvania Press.

Daly, K., & Chesney-Lind, M. (1988). Feminism and criminology. *Justice Quarterly, 5*, 497–538.

Dow, B. J. (1996). *Prime time feminism: Television, media culture, and the women's movement since 1970*. Philadelphia: University of Pennsylvania Press.

Fishman, M. (1980). *Manufacturing the news*. Austin: University of Texas Press.

Gitlin, T. (1980). *The whole world is watching: Mass media in the making and the unmaking of the New Left*. Berkeley: University of California Press.

hooks, b. (2000). *Feminist theory: From margin to center*. Cambridge, MA: South End Press Classics.

Howe, A. (Ed.). (1998). *Sexed crime in the news*. Sydney: Federation Press.

Lodz, A. D. (2006). *Redesigning women: Television after the network era*. Urbana: University of Illinois Press.

Naffire, N. (1996). *Feminism and criminology*. Philadelphia: Temple University Press.

Reidel, M., & Welsh, W. (2002). *Criminal violence: Patterns, causes, and prevention.* Los Angeles: Roxbury.

Scaggs, J. (2005). *Crime fiction.* London: Routledge/Taylor and Francis.

Schudson, M. (2003). *The sociology of news.* New York: W. W. Norton.

Stein, J. (2006, July 16). This season, it's law & reorder. *New York Times*, Section 2, pp. 1, 30.

Strauss, M., & Gelles, R. (1990). *Physical violence in American families: Risk factors and adaptations to violence in 8,145 families.* New Brunswick, NJ: Transaction Press.

Surette, R. (1998). *Media, crime, and criminal justice: Images and realities* (2nd ed.). Belmont, CA: West/Wadsworth.

Websdale, N. (2001). *Policing the poor: From slave plantation to public housing.* Boston: Northeastern University Press.

West, C., & Zimmerman, D. H. (1987). Doing gender. *Gender and Society, 1,* 125–151.

PART I

GENDERED CONSTRUCTIONS
WOMEN AND VIOLENCE

Part I introduces readers to gendered constructions of violence. "Gendered" refers quite specifically to masculine assumptions used by the media to characterize women's experiences with violence. The constructions in question are discernible in daily news reports, television dramas, films, and textbooks, and they reflect and reinforce complex social, historical, and cultural judgments about violence and its relationship to women. When women run into trouble as victims or as perpetrators, the media invoke a common set of assumptions that reporters, scriptwriters, and others use to valorize or demonize women, depending on the circumstances. These assumptions are based on (1) a sexualized dichotomy between good and bad women, (2) a distinction between the social worlds of women and men, (3) the compounding influence of race, ethnicity, and social class identities on stigmatizing processes, and (4) the gendered construction of knowledge in disciplinary fields of study. These assumptions shape gendered constructions of women as both victims and perpetrators.

Good versus Bad Women

"Sexual history" is a shorthand term implying that women who have a "certain kind" of sexual history are less worthy of fair treatment than those who do not. The distinction, however is outdated as women in the United States become sexually active in their teens (National Survey of Family Growth, November 25, 2005). The difference between sexual tolerance and the media construction of bad women, thus, requires explanation. The assignment of women to marriageable and sexually available categories reflects masculine prerogatives. Feinman (1986) labels marriageable women as Madonnas and bad women as whores, whereas Benedict (1992) and Boyle (2005) use the terms virgin and vamp to convey the same sexualized dichotomy. Although the distinction has outlived its usefulness, it remains a cultural resource, available when needed to simplify complex phenomena such as gender and sexuality. Media outlets use the distinction as a simplifying device to position women with respect to violence. Bad women should expect to be victimized. The media maintain an illusion that good girls have privileges and protections that eroticized bad girls are justly denied.

The distinction is readily apparent in media representations of rape victims, many of whom are blamed for their own attacks. When women are raped, sexualized questions of provocation "naturally" arise, the assumption being that the victim wanted it, deserved it, or lied about it. Similar questions arise when the context is date rape, although the male defense in date rape turns on miscommunication, the assumption being that he misread the situation or that the woman was insufficiently clear about her intentions (Boyle, 2005). Victim blaming, a corollary of the distinction between good and bad women, is gendered; it gives men an edge in the court of public opinion and frequently in criminal court as well.

It is important to keep in mind that the good girl/bad girl distinction is relational. Women (good or bad) are defined in relation to men whether men and masculinities are overt features of the construction or not. What is missing is often as important as what is present. For example, in Chapter 1 of this volume, Meloy and Miller describe an unusual balance in news themes that idealized Laci Peterson and demonized her killer, her husband, Scott Peterson. More typically, violence is gendered as female because the construction omits references to men or masculinity. Representations of evil or threatening women stand alone, as in the cases of Susan Smith and Andrea Yates, both of whom were at the center of high-profile cases about infanticide. The role of the men in their lives is obfuscated or made insignificant by transgressive women who killed their children.

Home and Work

The division of the world into male work and female domesticity is difficult to see in the United States, where the entry of women into the labor force has altered traditional family arrangements. Female-headed households, dual-career families, and common-law arrangements have pushed aside two-parent households financed by a single breadwinner (Ferree, 1990). These changes have been mirrored in television programming. Taylor (1989) tracked family representations in early television, noting that family situation comedies (*The Lucy Show*) gave way to the workplace family as exemplified by *The Mary Tyler Moore Show* in the 1970s. In a follow-up study, Lodz (2006) related changing images of women on television to the growing importance of females in the television audience. Because television executives believed white, upper-income women controlled household spending, women were courted as an important audience demographic. The introduction of mixed-gender casts, workplace dramas, female-led series, and women's cable networks, studied by Lodz (2006, Chapter 1), all reflect the importance of the new female audience to the companies that rely on television programming to sell products.

Crime dramas in which female characters played police, attorneys, and judges reflected many of these changes. In them, the ethos of equal-opportunity feminism limited scripts to exploring the difficulties women faced in juggling their work and professional lives and to examining the impact of family on professional men (Lodz, 2006, p. 148). By the turn of the twenty-first century, professional women had become so much a part of television programming that Lodz (2006) cautioned against interpreting their presence as progressive. Indeed, she argues that the success of professional women on television conveys the counterproductive impression that the feminist struggle is over.

As for violence, television programming kept apace with the growing concern about violence committed by intimates, friends, and acquaintances. In her study of rape in prime-time crime shows, Cuklanz (2000) shows a shift from stranger rapists to acquaintance rapists and from hard-boiled detectives to effective investigators capable of empathizing with victims. Humphries' study of the construction of female killers on *Law and Order* finds that murder is also an intimate or family affair and that its dynamics are powerful enough to domesticate the traditionally male world of work. As such, the subordination of women and their subsequent empowerment are important but tacit themes that appeal to women who watch *Law and Order*.

Privilege and Marginality

Issues of marginality that are addressed by contributors to this volume revolve around representations of race and ethnicity more than those of social class. This is not because class is unimportant in determining the circumstances of one's social life, but rather the volatile mix of minority status and white racism pushes aside considerations of wealth and power. The unresolved tensions that make race an exploitable issue for the media cannot be overlooked when examining race as a social construction shaped by social, historical, and political forces. National network news uses racial stereotypes to define black communities as separate from exclusive white communities to which black athletes, entertainers, or victims of discrimination have access (Entman & Rojecki, 2000; Hoynes, 2003). Moreover, in an analysis of news coverage of the effects of Hurricane Katrina in New Orleans, blacks were referred to as "refugees" and "looters," whereas similar behavior by whites earned them the label of "evacuees" engaged in "food finding" (Sommers et al. 2006).

When it comes to women, however, the exclusionary processes are more complicated. Following the lead of Patricia Hill Collins, one can talk about "controlling images," stereotypes about black women that make "racism, sexism, poverty, and other forms of injustice appear to be natural, normal, and an inevitable part of everyday life" (Collins, 2004, p. 69). Mammy and the black matriarch are two controlling images that objectify black women. The mammy embodies white stereotypes about the positive role played by black domestics in affluent (white) families, whereas the black matriarch embodies white stereotypes about the negative, even crimogenic, role that black women play in poor (black) families (Collins, 2004, pp. 72, 75). From a white perspective, the "goodness" of the mammy is that she socializes black children in the kinds of accommodations required by whites, and the "badness" of the black matriarch is that she fails in mothering her own children, who in turn commit crimes, leave school, and fail to get jobs. Both stereotypes objectify black women by a white standard that allows white society to ignore the low wages and long hours imposed on domestic workers (hooks, 2000, p.15) and to overlook the quality of schools, health care, and public safety in low-income areas. With respect to sexuality, stereotypes about black women do not fall into the good-girl category described above (Young, 1986, as cited by Belknap, 2001; Young, 2001). White society eroticizes black women and women of color (DeFour, 1990; hooks, 2000), representing them as jezebels, whores, and "hoochies" (Collins, 2004, p. 81). Hispanic women are presented as "hot-blooded," and Asian women are labeled as "sexpots" (DeFour, 1990).

Bailey (Chapter 3, this volume) examines these and other stereotypes in Hollywood films directed by both white and black filmmakers. She argues that, historically, white filmmakers have restricted black actresses to stereotypic roles (e.g., mammy, jezebel, and the tragic mulatto) that reinforced white expectations about black women. She goes on to argue that the recent films made by black filmmakers anchor violence in the structure of inequality at the same time they restrict black actresses to stereotypic roles, blaming "ineffectual mothers" for the loss of their sons to crime, gangs, and the street. While Bailey goes on to consider color-blind casting as a means to improve the career prospects for black actresses, she emphasizes the continuing impact of stereotypic film roles in the real world on employers' attitudes toward black women and women of color in the wider job market.

Gender and Knowledge

An important feminist principle is that "systems of knowledge" reflect masculine understandings of the world and that these systems legitimate the "natural" authority of men and the subordination of women (Daly & Chesney-Lind, 1988, Flavin, 2004). For some researchers, this means exposing underlying masculine assumptions in what appears to be neutral knowledge. For example, Susan Estrich (1987) argued that appellate decisions in rape cases reflected the kind of "playground rules" that equate harm with physical injury and that overlook the effects of fear and intimidation on questions of victim consent. By limiting legal redress and exposing women to danger, "playground rules" disadvantage women. For other scholars, what passes for neutral knowledge defines female knowledge as peripheral and non-Western epistemology as superstition (Bailey, 2005; Zack, 2000). In criminology, successive feminist critiques point to the effects of masculine assumptions on errors about female offenders, one-sided explanations of crime, and skewed samples (Daly & Maher, 1998; Naffire, 1996; Smart, 1989).

Gendered knowledge figures in this collection in two ways. In Chapter 4 of this volume, Snyder illustrates the pattern of omissions, underrepresentation, and marginalization of violence with regard to the representation of women found in a sample of mainstream college textbooks about media and violence or crime. It is clear from Snyder's chapter that scholars have an uphill struggle in mainstreaming feminist approaches to women, violence, and the media. In the second case, which appears in Part III of the collection, Deborah Jermyn argues in Chapter 11 that the standards by which women's fears of crime were made to appear irrational expressed male, not female, experiences of violence. Generally speaking, the violence men experience includes things such as assault or robbery. By contrast, the violence women experience includes crime plus the daily affronts that may be shrugged off but accumulate to the level of a "culture of peril" (Schlesinger, Dobash, Dobash, & Weaver, 1992). Taking this culture into account, women's fears are entirely reasonable, according to Jermyn.

Masculine assumptions about women's experience with violence are remarkably persistent across different mass media outlets. Despite changes in the understanding of violence, sexual morality, domesticity, marginality, and narrow parameters of knowledge, we continue to find masculine assumptions expressed in the news, on television, in film, and in college textbooks. The chapters in Part I provide ample illustrations of the ways in which they reinforce and occasionally update gender inequalities.

Keep in mind that gendered constructions reflect complex social, historical, and cultural judgments about both violence and women. As such they are neither true nor false; they simply offer and reaffirm the tacit oversimplified ways of thinking about complex problems. All other things being equal, few would condemn a woman on the basis of sexual history. Many readers, however, would pause, single out an eroticized detail from a news story, and use it to "explain" a woman's violent behavior or to "question" a victim's role in sexual assault. Without thinking, readers participate in the processes that reproduce inequality. A more analytic way of formulating the same question might be to ask, "What judgments are embedded in this social construction, and why do they lead me to think in terms of a single titillating detail?" Posing questions like this leads readers in an entirely different direction.

In Chapter 1, "Words that Wound," Meloy and Miller review press accounts of several high-profile criminal cases to unravel the complex ways in which the good girl/bad girl distinction functions. First, the "good girl" establishes the standard, which has a white, middle-class, suburban undertone, according to Meloy and Miller. In the Peterson case, the idealization of the murder victim (pregnant Laci Peterson) is matched by the demonization of her killer (her husband, Scott Peterson), who rejected fatherhood for the fast-lane life of a single man. Second, other women do not measure up to the Laci Peterson sort of idealization. The press gave scant attention to the case of Evelyn Hernandez, the victim of another intimate homicide. Her story—the murder of a poor, immigrant woman who carried the unborn child of a married man—was too far removed, in income and ethnicity, from the idealized white, middle-class standard to be newsworthy. In the next two highly publicized cases, Meloy and Miller show that gender transgressions can pile up. Susan Smith killed her two sons in order to pursue a romance, and press reports stressed that she had had prior affairs and may have been the victim of sexual abuse. Like Scott Peterson, who favored romance over parenthood, the combination of a trivial motive and horrific violence led Meloy and Miller to label these killings as "crimes of convenience." The difference, however, is that extramarital affairs fall within the limits of masculinity, whereas the affairs of married women violate gender standards. The situation is different for Andrea Yates, who complied with the vows of marriage but broke down and killed her children under the pressure of postpartum depression and the demands imposed on her by a fundamentalist Christian husband. In this egregious case, infanticides make her husband's indifference a secondary concern.

The home versus work distinction is a subtle framing device in many television dramas and comedies. Typically, the distinction reinforces masculine control of the world of work, but not always. The media have the power to reshape some of these images, although it is usually a good idea to question whether a particular change necessarily undermines inequalities. In Chapter 2, "The Construction of Murderers," Humphries raises this question. She surveys episodes of *Law and Order*, a popular crime drama modeled on police procedures, in an effort to identify the terms on which the show has integrated female characters who kill. If the professional women who dominate workplace dramas are shown as balancing the demands of work and home, then how might female killers, who also appeal to female audiences, find a niche? According to Humphries, *Law and Order* typically locates murder in the domestic sphere, where female characters, and many men as well, are motivated to kill by tensions arising from the family, romance, and gendered inequalities. In this sense, the show domesticates homicide, but there is a second point. Exposure of the killer is played out against the backdrop of a trial or plea-bargained justice, where a reoccurring tension, a sense of gender injustice, finds expression as aggrieved women testify against and settle old scores with partners and intimates charged with murder. Moreover, *Law and Order* places female killers in a highly stratified world and distributes justice accordingly. Despite *Law and Order*'s reputation for even-handed justice, Humphries makes an argument for discrimination: Smart, relatively affluent, white female characters may get away with murder, whereas their poor or minority counterparts, who rely on self-defeating male characters to commit crimes, are easily convicted. In between these two extremes, the women who kill are based on old-style stereotypes (e.g., self-effacing, emotionally unstable, or impressionable women).

Representations of women and violence have ramifications beyond the media, as suggested by Bailey in Chapter 3, "Screening Stereotypes." Bailey offers a sweeping critique of racial stereotyping and its marginalizing effects on black actresses in the Hollywood film industry. She reviews older film roles that embodied white expectations about women of color. "Mammy" roles were among the few open to black actresses, and in emphasizing self-sacrifice and black women's loyalty to white families, Bailey wonders about their effect on how whites perceive real-life black women. She also considers film roles that embody the views of black filmmakers about black women. In these films, progressive directors related violence to structural realities but faulted black mothers for failing to protect young men from the violence of the streets. In other film genres, Bailey argues that tough gal and female action roles combine and caricature older stereotypes. Faced with limited opportunities, Bailey concludes by considering the advantages and disadvantages of color-blind casting for the careers of black actresses in Hollywood.

In Chapter 4, "What about Women?," Zoann Snyder closes Part I of this volume by surveying college textbooks adopted by professors who teach courses on the media and violence or crime. Topics such as sexual assault, domestic violence, and intimate homicides, which reflect significant changes in thinking about what constitutes violence, should be reflected in mainstream college textbooks. They are, however, ignored, underrepresented, or marginalized as specialized topics, according to Snyder (see also Flavin, 2004). The realities of textbook marketing are such that books with a potential mass audience are a better commercial venture than texts with a specialized audience. Mass audiences, however, are a function of the organization of academic disciplines, which historically have been defined by male scholars. Feminist-inspired scholarship in most disciplines tends to appear in specialty journals and to be published by presses whose editorial boards have feminist commitments and cater to a narrow market. These are the publication realities that scholars face in mainstreaming feminist scholarship on women, violence, and the media (Flavin, 2004). And they are reflected in Snyder's second point, namely that further progress in this field depends on feminist, not mainstream, scholars.

Taken together, the gendered constructions function to perpetuate and reinforce gender, race, and social-class inequalities. They do so in the following ways. First, the pattern of omissions, underrepresentation, and marginalization found in mainstream media and crime or violence textbooks reflects the gendered organization of academic disciplines and publishing that makes the specialty, some would say secondary, status of feminist scholarship appear natural or inevitable. Second, racialized stereotypes continue to be implicated in the discrimination against black actresses: Secondary roles available to them reflected first white and more recently black male filmmakers' equivocal perceptions of African American women. Third, even though workplace dramas such as *Law and Order* feature competent female characters in professional roles, their counterpart, the female killer, is fully domesticated, and with a few exceptions, she conducts herself in a manner that reinforces demeaning stereotypes. And finally, in exploiting good girl/bad girl themes, journalists oversimplify complex domestic situations and in the process sexualize violence, trivialize motive, and add layers of stigma without clarifying the meaning of violence or its relationship to the lives of women who face the risks of real violence.

REFERENCES

Bailey, A. (2005). Review of the book *Women of color and philosophy*. *Hypatia, 20*, 220–226.
Belknap, J. (2001). *The invisible woman: Gender, crime, and justice* (2nd ed.). Belmont, CA: Wadsworth/Thomson Learning.
Benedict, H. (1992). *Virgin or vamp: How the press covers sex crimes*. New York: Oxford University Press.
Boyle, K. (2005). *Media and violence: Gendering the debates*. London: Sage.
Centers for Disease Control (2005, November 25). *National Survey of Family Growth*. Summary. Retrieved April 3, 2008, from http:www.cdc.gov/nchs/about/major/nsfg/abclist-shtm#sexualactivity.

Collins, P. H. (2004). *Black sexual politics: African Americans, gender, and the new racism* (2nd ed.). London: Routledge.

Cuklanz, L. (2000). *Rape on prime time: Television, masculinity, and sexual violence.* Philadelphia: University of Pennsylvania Press.

Daly, K., & Maher, L. (1998). Crossroads and intersections: Building from feminist critique. In K. Daly & L. Maher (Eds.), *Criminology at the crossroads: Feminist readings in crime and justice* (pp. 1–17). New York: Oxford University Press.

Daly, K. & Chesney-Lind, M. (1988). Feminism and Criminology. *Justice Quarterly, 5,* 497–538.

DeFour, D. (1990). The interface of racism and sexism on college campuses. In M. A. Pauludi (Ed.), *Ivory power: Sexual harassment on campus* (pp. 45–52). Albany: State University of New York Press.

Entman, R. M., & Rojecki, A. (2000). *The black image in the white mind: Media and race in America.* Chicago: University of Chicago Press.

Estrich, S. (1987). *Real rape.* Boston: Harvard University Press.

Feinman, C. (1986). *Women in criminal justice* (2nd ed.). New York: Praeger.

Flavin, J. (2004). Feminism for the mainstream criminologist: An invitation. In P. J. Schram & B. Koons-Witt (Eds.), *Gendered (in)justice: Theory and practice in feminist criminology* (pp. 68–94). Long Grove, IL: Waveland Press.

Ferree, M. M. (1990). Beyond separate spheres: Feminism and family research. *Journal of Marriage and the Family, 54* (4), 866–884.

hooks, b. (2000). *Feminist theory: From margin to center.* Cambridge, MA: South End Press.

Hoynes, W. (2003). Race and representation [review essay]. *Qualitative Sociology, 26* (2), 281–284.

Lodz, A. D. (2006). *Redesigning women: Television after the network era.* Urbana: University of Illinois Press.

Naffire, N. (1996). *Feminism and criminology.* Philadelphia: Temple University Press.

Schlesinger, P., Dobash, R. E., Dobash, R. P., & Weaver, C. K. (1992). *Women viewing violence.* London: British Film Institute.

Smart, C. (1989). *Feminism and the power of law.* London: Routledge and Kegan Paul.

Sommers, S. R., Apfelbaum, E. P., Dukes, K. N., Toosi, N., & Wang, E. J. (2006). Race and media coverage of Hurricane Katrina: Analysis, implications, and future research questions. *Analyses of Social Issues and Public Policy, 6* (1), 39–55.

Taylor, E. (1989). *Prime time families: Television culture in postwar America.* Berkeley: University of California Press.

Young, V. (1986). Gender expectations and their impact on black female offenders and victims. *Justice Quarterly, 3,* 305–327.

Young, V. D. (2001). Women, race, and crime. In S. L. Gabbidion, L. T. Greene, & V. D. Young (Eds.), *African American classics in criminology and criminal justice* (pp. 169–176). Beverly Hills, CA: Sage.

Zack, N. (Ed.). (2000). *Women of color and philosophy.* Malden, MA: Blackwell.

CHAPTER I

WORDS THAT WOUND

Print Media's Presentation of Gendered Violence

Michelle L. Meloy and Susan L. Miller

News stories about female victims, offenders, and criminal justice profes-sionals permeate our culture and shape our perceptions of them. When reporters dissect criminal incidents, they rely on well-worn clichés and stereotypes associated with men and women and work these gendered as-sumptions into news accounts about victims and offenders. Unfortu-nately, little attention has been paid to how the media frame gender and violence despite numerous studies that show that the media are one of the most powerful influences in shaping public perceptions about crime and victimization (Chermak, 1995; Lipschultz & Hilt, 2002). To help rectify the deficit, we discuss how gendered assumptions work their way into news reports and then we identify gendered assumptions about victims and offenders in several high-profile cases.

Americans devote a large portion of their leisure time, about 40%, to consuming and interfacing with the media. This time exceeds that spent reading, visiting with friends and family, or being outdoors (Ryan & Wentworth, 1999). Although some individuals may experience crime or violence directly, most Americans look to the media as the primary story-teller (Chermak, 1995). Not surprisingly, there is a direct correlation be-tween the time individuals spend consuming mass-media information and their "buy-in" or acceptance of its images and stereotypes (Ryan & Wentworth, 1999). In other words, the media frame how and what we view as social problems, what we define as good or bad or as acceptable or unacceptable, and who we label as criminal offenders or legitimate vic-tims. More specifically for our purposes, the media frame how women's experiences with crime and victimization are presented to the public (Jewkes, 2004).

When we compare the media's presentation of crime with more objec-tive sources of data, several things are clear. The media exaggerate crime compared with its actual occurrence. The media misrepresent who is primarily at risk of becoming a victim of violence and tell a false story about who is most dangerous (Meyers, 1997; Ryan & Wentworth, 1999). Distortions and misrepresentations like these are built into the process of newsmaking. As reporters scan events, looking for what is newsworthy, they sort according to established criteria. Events must be serious in nature (Chermak, 1995), have sensational components and crime elements (Benedict, 1992), involve prestigious victims[1] (Benedict, 1992) or notorious offenders (Meyers, 1997), and match the relevance to and interest of the viewing audience (Chermak, 1995). The more a crime incident exemplifies these tenets (e.g., violent and high-risk situations), the more likely it is that a reporter will write it up as news, ignoring other considerations such as accuracy or balance (Benedict, 1992; Daly & Chasteen, 1997; Grover & Soothill, 1996; Johnstone, Hawkins, & Michener, 1994; Pritchard & Highers, 1997).

The selection of newsworthy events and the framing of those events are not arbitrary processes; instead, they rest on the decisions of reporters, journalists, and their supervisors operating within the print media's hierarchy. Men outnumber women as reporters. They hold most of the high-level and high-visibility positions within the news and media industry and thus possess the authority to direct news agendas (Chermak, 1995; Meyers, 1997). As a result, the working assumptions that male journalists have about gender, including ideas about female victims and offenders, play a role in the selection of events and in the framing of those events. Such working assumptions might be called a "masculine perspective."

Feminist scholars argue that male journalists, relying on a masculine perspective, suffer from a failure to see gendered violence as the significant social problem that it is (Meyers, 1997). Others have noted that the failure to see is part of a broader system of domination: "The concept of male power is interwoven throughout all interpersonal male–female interactions, constituting a structural dimension of society in which violence against women and other demonstrations of male power act to reproduce and maintain male dominance and female subordination" (Hanmer & Maynard, 1987, p. 3).

The masculine perspective that we are describing tends to underreport male-on-female violence while highlighting the atypical event: extreme acts of violence by or against women. Most crimes against women and most of the crimes committed by women are considered ordinary and

\

common from a masculine perspective. They rarely becor.
Up to 95% of all reported crimes against women do not recei
attention (Caringella-MacDonald & Humphries, 1998). Th
matic example of underreporting is the media's failure to report
of domestic battery;[2] yet, battering is the *most* common form of
and injury to women (Buzawa & Buzawa, 2003). When a case ..o-
mestic abuse is reported in the newspapers, it stands out for its extremity,
usually involving rape or murder (Zalin, 2003).

In addition to selecting newsworthy events, reporters and journalists
craft the news story itself, constructing the images that so affect public
perceptions. Vivid language, a capacity to personalize events, and a thor-
ough knowledge of the audience are necessary to write the news. But at
the same time, newswriters are required to adhere to the rules of objectivity, balance, and neutrality. Journalistic conventions and basic rules of
fairness can be discerned in the news they write, but so, too, can their
working assumptions about gender and violence.

Journalistic neutrality, for example, relies on a "nothing but the facts"
approach to description (Benedict, 1992), but an observer should be alert
to when the "facts" give way to interpretative frameworks. Descriptors are
the words or phrases that journalists use to characterize victims or offenders in the stories they write. They locate the significant actors in a
moral universe that is readily understood by an audience. Subtle differences in the manner in which victims or offenders are described can have
far-reaching consequences. Furthermore, research conducted by Henley,
Miller, and Beasley (1995) found that in news stories written in the passive voice about violence against women, male readers (but not female
ones) attribute less victim harm and less offender responsibility, and both
male and female readers become more accepting of abuse. Additional research by Lamb and Keon (1995) found that when articles imply that
women share responsibility for men's violence against them, reader attitudes toward punishment for the batterers were more lenient.

Effective descriptors connect a news story to the audience's basic
understanding of crime and violence. Americans' tendency to blame victims can have far-reaching implications for how the public will perceive
the event.[3] Blaming female crime victims functions in several ways. First,
it offers an explanation that focuses on individual deficiencies, that is, the
victim did or failed to do something that caused the victimization. In ad-

dition, victim blaming reinforces gender norms that tell women to restrict their activities in order to avoid increased risk of victimization. Second, victim blaming is part of a moral universe in which characterizations of guilt or innocence are associated with a sexualized dichotomy; that is, with contrasting images of "good girl" and "bad girl" (Karmen, 1984; Russell, 1984; Russo, 1997). Third, victim blaming easily accommodates other highly charged distinctions, including social-class location, race, and ethnicity, as well as immigration status (Cavender, Bond-Maupin, & Jurik, 1999).

Our research addresses the nature of gendered themes that shape news accounts about women and violence. We are interested in how they might vary depending on whether a woman is a victim or an offender and whether the case is a high- or low-profile news story.

The Present Study

This is an exploratory study designed to identify the major gender themes in newspaper coverage of violent crime. The four cases selected for study illustrate principles of newsworthiness: They involve dramatic violence, a personal focus, and offer opportunities for exploitation as national stories. Note that attention to dramatic violence reduces the coverage given to ordinary crimes that threaten women and, in doing so, also distorts the assessment of danger and risk. In addition, the circumstances surrounding the four cases place women at the center of attention, providing a set of news accounts in which gendered themes may be observed. Although the study is descriptive, less attention to one case provides a natural opportunity to compare high- and lower-profile news stories. That the cases also involve female victims and offenders allows us to compare gender themes as they relate to these roles. Two cases examined in this study involve the murder of pregnant women, both of whose bodies were dumped into San Francisco Bay. Laci Peterson's case created a media frenzy, but the print media gave limited attention to the death of Evelyn Hernandez in much the same circumstances. In the second two cases, the women in question, Susan Smith and Andrea Yates, killed their children. The resulting press coverage made both crimes high-profile cases.

Newspaper accounts were identified by searching the media components of Lexis-Nexis Academic Sources. The search involved approximately 260 newspapers from across the country and yielded 180 news accounts for the Laci Peterson case, 22 for the Evelyn Hernandez case, 168 for the Susan Smith case, and 270 for the Andrea Yates case. In high-profile cases, we limited the number of local and national papers and sampled within them to generate a sample small enough for qualitative analysis but large enough to pick up variations.

In coding data from news accounts, we focused on victims or offenders, collecting demographic data because social class, ethnicity, and race had to be considered potential factors in explaining variations. We also distinguished between descriptors and themes. Descriptors are words and phrases that described the women and other actors. Themes, especially gender-based ones, emerged, as we noticed similarities among the descriptors used repeatedly to frame women. Issues of offender responsibility and victim blame were important to our assessment of the data, although data collection focused on descriptors. Our intention was to identify the major themes and how specific themes corresponded to an actor's responsibility or blame. To that end, we read each article in its entirety and kept track of descriptors and emerging themes as grounded theory suggests (Slobogin, 2003). We then reread the articles to ensure that emergent themes accurately captured the articles' content (Strauss, 1987). Saturation was achieved when both authors agreed that no new conceptual themes emerged from the articles (Krueger, 1994).

Themes that appeared in at least 30% of news articles about a case were included in the analysis. Relative frequencies were computed for gender and other themes and are presented as the main findings for each of the four cases. Findings are presented in two sections, one devoted to victim themes, the other to offender themes.

Findings on Female Victims of Violence
Newspaper Themes Related to the Laci Peterson Case

On December 24, 2002, Scott Peterson reported that his wife, Laci Peterson, who was eight months pregnant, was missing. He told authorities that he had been fishing and did not miss his wife until he returned later that evening, Christmas Eve. When authorities learned that Scott Peterson was having an affair with Amber Frye, they confirmed that he was a suspect in his wife's disappearance. Scott denied any involvement in the case and said he had no personal knowledge about his wife's whereabouts. Police located Laci Peterson's badly decomposed body and later the remains of her unborn child, Conner, in San Francisco Bay, near the place where Scott had told authorities he had gone fishing. They arrested Scott Peterson and charged him with two counts of first-degree murder. While on bail, Peterson fled; when police arrested him near the California–Mexico border, he had dyed his hair to conceal his identity and carried enough cash to make a getaway. On November 12, 2004, Peterson was convicted on both counts of first-degree murder and was subsequently sentenced to death.

Laci Peterson sets the standard for a "blameless victim" based on finding that the news reports idealized her as a perfect woman and demonized her husband as having betrayed her and their life as a perfect couple. More specifically, the four themes that emerged in our review of the 180 newspaper articles about the case were ideal woman, evil husband, pretrial publicity/trial coverage, and perfect couple.

THE PERFECT WOMAN

Laci Peterson epitomized traditional notions about what women should do with their lives. Throughout the coverage of this case, she was described approvingly as domestic, as a stay-at-home wife and homemaker, as feminine, as a mother, as pregnant, as a schoolteacher, and as attractive. The following example, which characterizes the perfection as lifelong, is typical:

> In her typical American hometown, she was the girl next door, the high school cheerleader and softball player who went off to college and returned years later in a story book marriage . . . .
> The expectant mother . . . [and] substitute teacher . . . [who] was scheduled to give birth to a boy—already named Conner . . . was walking the family dog, McKenzie, at a nearby park when she disappeared on Christmas Eve. (*Chicago Sun-Times*, January 26, 2003a)

Other descriptors that justified the idealization included perfect daughter, devoted wife, beautiful, [part of an] attractive couple, great housekeeper, excited expectant mother, [person] dedicated to being the best mother and wife, [looking forward to a] long-awaited pregnancy, [a person who] loved to cook, best friend, and everyone's friend.

Ceremonies honoring her memory treated her death as a "national tragedy":

Thousands of people locked hands and wept during a nationally televised packed church service to honor Laci Peterson on what would have been her 28th birthday nearly three weeks after her badly decomposed body washed ashore along with the remains of her unborn son. . . .

[Laci] Peterson's story has touched so many Americans . . . .

[N]ine of [Laci] Peterson's closest girlfriends wept as they took turns at the lectern remembering the avid gardener and cook. (*Houston Chronicle*, May 5, 2003)

Amid tragedy, the press and public celebrated her domesticity, finding solace in the fact that a young wife from California's Central Valley so clearly exemplified traditional womanhood and domesticity. No one should be so murdered, let alone a white, middle-class woman, protected by affluence and sheltered in the suburbs. She was by all accounts an impeccably "innocent" murder victim.

EVIL HUSBAND

The characterization of Scott Peterson as an "evil husband" appeared in 70% of the stories reviewed. It is based on descriptors that raise disturbing questions about basic features of his character. The language includes adulterous [person], cheater, liar, untrustworthy, [a person who could justify] leaving a pregnant wife alone on a holiday, and selfish. In nearly every instance where Scott Peterson was mentioned, the characterizations were negative. Consider a passage from a news article about his relationship with Amber Frye:

One of the snapshots [of Peterson and his girlfriend, Amber Frye] shows a grinning Peterson, sans wedding ring, patting Frey on the buttocks during an outing. Another has Frey, wearing a shimmering red dress, sitting on Peterson's lap as he wears a Santa Claus hat. (*Boston Herald*, May 11, 2003b)

A neighbor recounts a long list of lies and questionable behavior that confirm suspicions about Scott:

He was immersed in an affair with a Fresno massage therapist, Amber Frye, who, in the weeks before Laci's disappearance, had discovered that Scott Peterson was lying about being widowed and single . . . Laci's sister . . . told police she was surprised to learn that Peterson went fishing out of town the day before Christmas. She testified that he told her he was playing golf. . . .

"The fishing; he's not too upset [about Laci's disappearance]; his eyes are cold. Him going to San Diego, dyeing his hair, $10,000 in cash on him—that's not what someone does when their wife dies," says a neighbor. (*Los Angeles Times*, November 19, 2003)

The uniformly negative descriptors are unusual, suggesting that the defense failed in disseminating a positive portrait of Scott Peterson. But there is more: Scott's dreadful behavior as a husband and soon-to-be father points to a darker, sinister side of marriage in which a husband's longings and his secrets might lead him to kill the person who trusts him most, his wife.

PRETRIAL PUBLICITY AND MEDIA INTEREST

Roughly 40% of the articles reviewed speculate about the extraordinary media interest in this case. This category was operationalized by references to issues such as fair trial, jury prejudice, change of venue, and extensive media reporting, but due process aside, the press coverage also characterized this case as a "slam dunk" for the prosecution. The following excerpt speaks to media saturation:

Eleven days of testimony in the preliminary hearing was picked apart and hyped on cable TV shows nationwide. . . .

A resident and newspaper columnist stated that she was glued to 24-hour cable TV talk shows [covering the Peterson case] throughout much of the past year. "How much evidence do you need? The handwriting is on the wall with an arrow pointed at his [Scott's] head. (*Los Angeles Times*, November 19, 2003)

Saturation, of course, had consequences for Mr. Peterson's right to a fair trial, and the theme makes it clear that the court protected his rights.

Citing extensive media coverage and public demonstrations against accused killer Scott Peterson, a judge ruled that Peterson can't get a fair trial in his wife's hometown and ordered a change of venue.

Geragos [Peterson's defense attorney] argued in court papers that Peterson has been demonized by the media. Geragos said arguments that the trial should remain in Modesto "can be boiled down to the old adage, 'Sure, we can give him a fair trial. Then we will take him out and hang him.'"

The depth of pretrial animosity . . . is obvious. (*Los Angeles Times*, January 9, 2004)

So many articles had been published that we had difficulty narrowing our search criteria to accommodate the search limit of the Lexis-Nexis Academic Sources. The coverage had contaminated the jury pool in Fresno as the court granted a change of venue. Ultimately, it is impossible to know whether coverage affected the new jury pool or, if it did, whether it tipped the verdict toward guilty.

PERFECT COUPLE

The "perfect couple" was identified as a theme in 30% of the articles we examined. It was operationalized by referents such as a fairy tale, romance, love affair, attractive couple, and college graduates/sweethearts. The following excerpts from news stories illustrate the representation of the couple as "all-American":

> This case was portrayed as an American tragedy, with Laci Peterson's smile beaming from photos and videos. The expectant parents seemed like the All-American couple until Scott Peterson's mistress surfaced and he admitted having an extramarital affair. (*Chicago Sun-Times*, October 29, 2003b)
>
> Clearly, Laci and Scott have mesmerized the media, cyberspace, and much of America with their picture perfect life. Yet there's little usual here save this: the nearly full-term child murdered, too, the soccer-mom-to-be victim in her Range Rover, and, last but not least, the bracing good looks of the alleged killer. . . .
>
> Would we "care" as much were the couple less attractive, less white, less familiarly middle-class as they exchanged wedding vows to a string quartet? No, we wouldn't. (*Boston Herald*, April 27, 2003a)

In the early stages of the case, the Petersons came to epitomize the cultural ideal for marital and economic success. They were a young, white, and physically attractive couple, both of whom were college educated. They prospered as members of the middle class and stood on the threshold of family building. As the image of a perfect couple crumbled and the sordid details of the murder emerged, the case touched the public in an intimate way. It may have stirred anxieties about the safety of women in marriage, or it may have served as a cautionary tale for errant spouses. The harrowing and well-documented fall from a state of perfection enthralled the public.

Newspaper Themes Related to the Evelyn Hernandez Case

In May 2002, just months after the disappearance of Laci Peterson, Herman Aguilera reported as missing his girlfriend, Evelyn Hernandez, who was nine months pregnant with his child, and her five-year-old son, Alex. Aguilera was married to another woman during his relationship with Hernandez. He told authorities he had last seen his girlfriend on April 30, 2002, the day before she was believed to have vanished with her son, when they went shopping for bedroom furniture for Alex. A few days after her disappearance, Evelyn's wallet was found near her boyfriend's house. Evelyn's torso was later found floating in San Francisco Bay. Her body was eventually identified through DNA testing. Alex's body was never recovered. Although police indicated that Aguilera was a suspect in the case, no arrests have been made. Limited media attention characterized this case until the Scott Peterson defense team claimed there was a connection between the murders of Evelyn Hernandez and Laci Peterson.

We analyzed the 22 newspaper articles devoted to the Hernandez case. The results show that three themes characterized news coverage: single motherhood, an affair and out-of-wedlock pregnancy, and the tie-in to the Laci Peterson case.

SINGLE MOTHERHOOD

The first theme, single motherhood, was mentioned in 21 of the 22 articles (95%). Note how Evelyn Hernandez is described in the following examples:

> Friends and the sister of a pregnant San Francisco woman whose body was found in the bay held a memorial Friday and pleaded for help in finding her missing 5–year-old son.
>
> With the San Francisco Bay Bridge as a backdrop, about 20 mourners conducted a special ceremony in honor of Evelyn Hernandez. The 24-year-old single mother disappeared a year ago with her son, Alex, one week before she was to deliver a baby boy. (*San Francisco Chronicle*, May 3, 2003)

> Hernandez, a 24-year-old single mother, disappeared in May 2002 with her son, Alex, one week before she was to deliver a baby boy. Part of her torso and maternity clothing were found July 24, 2002 on the San Francisco side of the bay. The boy was never found. (*Long Beach Press-Telegram*, June 20, 2003)

"Single motherhood" may be an objective description of Hernandez's situation, but it hardly stands as neutral. Instead, it has to be seen as a heavily freighted term that draws attention to Hernandez's sexual or marital history. Its systematic use as a descriptor compromises any claim that she might have had to being a "legitimate" victim.

SEXUAL AND REPRODUCTIVE HISTORY

The next major theme identified in the Hernandez articles concerns the illicit circumstances of her pregnancy. She was nine months pregnant with her married boyfriend's child. Her affair with Aguilera and pregnancy were mentioned in nearly half of the 22 articles. The following examples provide an illustration of how this issue was presented in the newspaper articles:

> The also-pregnant Hernandez and her 5-year-old son—yet to be found—vanished May 1, 2002. Her torso only, still clad in maternity blouse, was discovered three months later in the same San Francisco Bay [as Laci Peterson]. . . .
> To be sure, there are differences [between the two cases]. . . . Apparently, when you're a single mother originally from El Salvador whose unborn child was conceived in a relationship with a married man—Hernandez's situation—the story loses some of its luster. (*Copley News Service*, April 22, 2003)

> Hernandez's wallet was found a few days after she disappeared, in a gutter. . . .
> The wallet was found within two blocks of where Hernandez's married boyfriend and the father of her unborn child, Herman Aguilera, worked at a limousine company and as a mechanic for United Airlines. . . .
> Aguilera's attorney . . . said that his client had done everything he could to cooperate with police and was "deeply saddened by the news of his close friend." (*San Francisco Chronicle*, September 4, 2002b)

If the single mother label failed to raise questions about Evelyn Hernandez's sexual history, an out-of-wedlock pregnancy clearly relegates her to the category of illegitimate victim.

In the articles, few passages refer to the police investigation or to the legal status of the victim's boyfriend, Herman Aguilera. He is considered a suspect in the case, but the police had not made an arrest when we completed data collection. The lack of progress in the case is surprising. After the disappearance of Hernandez, her wallet had been found near Aguilera's residence. In addition, the fact that women are more likely to be killed by their male intimate partners than any other person (Bureau of Justice Statistics, 2004) should have focused the investigation on Aguilera. Although the investigation may have been stalled from lack of evidence or witnesses, the police were not pressured by national media exposure. If media exposure provides incentives for police to aggressively pursue cases, then reasons for the lack of media attention in the Hernandez case require appraisal.

PETERSON AND HERNANDEZ CASES COMPARED

In nearly 60% of the articles (12 out of 22), news accounts compared the Peterson and Hernandez cases. Both murders were committed by the same killer, according to Scott Peterson, but the thematic focus points to something else. The comparisons concern inequities in media coverage, the critical edges of which were not lost on Evelyn Hernandez's friends and relatives, or reporters. For instance:

> Friends and relatives have noted that Hernandez's case received far less media attention than Laci Peterson's disappearance. One woman . . . held a sign with a picture of Alex [Hernandez's 5-year-old son] that read, "Where is Alex? Wasn't this investigation important?"
> "There's three victims here" [responded a homicide detective]. (*San Francisco Chronicle*, May 3, 2003)

> Hernandez's killing received little attention in the news until her family complained about the flood of coverage in the Peterson case as the Hernandez investigation languished, with the father-to-be considered a primary suspect in both cases. (*Alameda Times-Star*, July 10, 2003)

The circumstances of the Peterson and Hernandez murders were similar. In both cases, the crimes were atrocious, involving the murder of pregnant women by intimate partners and the disposal of their bodies in San Francisco Bay. One could argue that the Hernandez crime was a greater atrocity in that it involved the apparent abduction and murder of the victim's five-year-old child, Alex. Obviously, the seriousness of the crime is not the determining factor in deciding which story might attract attention. If seriousness had been decisive, the Hernandez case would also have been at the center of media frenzy. There are, however, other possibilities.

Consider the social identities of the two victims. As a white, middle-class suburbanite, Laci Peterson had the demographic profile on which reporters could credibly construct an identity as an innocent victim. She epitomized traditional family virtues (e.g., she was perfect as daughter, wife, and expectant mother). One would not normally question the veracity of a person with this sort of social identity. On the other hand, Evelyn Hernandez's profile raises questions. She was a Hispanic woman from an uncertain background and was unmarried, yet she had one child and was pregnant with another by a man married to someone else. Viewed through the lens of the double standard, Evelyn Hernandez's profile comes far too close to the image of a "bad" girl to prevent reporters from posing questions about victim responsibility.

Findings on Violent Female Offenders
Newspaper Themes Related to the Susan Smith Case

On November 4, 1995, Susan Smith was arrested for drowning her two young sons. While the boys were strapped in their car seats in the rear of the vehicle, Susan submerged the car in a lake. For nine days prior to her arrest, Susan claimed that she was carjacked by an unknown black male. She pleaded with the kidnapper on national television to return her boys safely. Then, she confessed to the crimes. Although she was eventually convicted on two counts of first-degree murder, she avoided a possible death sentence when the jury spared her life and sentenced her to life in prison. Throughout the trial, the media reported on Susan's prior sexual abuse by her stepfather and her recent sexual relationships with several men other than her estranged husband, and they speculated that she killed the children because they hampered her dating life.

A comprehensive reading of 168 newspaper articles on Susan Smith's case discovered three primary themes: her sexual history, the potential mitigating effects of mental illness, and the aggravating circumstances related to her character defects. Taken together, promiscuity and self-centered cunning counted more than prior abuse in making Susan Smith only slightly less deserving of punishment than Scott Peterson.

SEXUAL HISTORY

Roughly three out of four newspaper articles in the sample (130 out of 168) made some reference to Susan Smith's sexual history. Here, her active sex life was often presented in a salacious and judgmental manner. The following excerpts provide illustrations as to how the media associated the offender's crimes with her sexuality:

> Susan Smith's nervous paramour [Thomas Findlay] cast doubt today on charges that she killed her children to pursue their romance, saying Smith's anguish actually stemmed from a recent affair with her own stepfather.
>
> In a day filled with dramatic testimony, Smith sat blank-faced as witnesses took the stand and painted a conflicting portrait of the 23-year-old defendant as a vixenish adulteress, a lovesick secretary, an abused child, a frightened wife, a skillful liar and a doting mother. (*Washington Post*, July 20, 1995)

> She [Smith] . . . had an affair with a co-worker of her husband, David Smith, an assistant manager at a Union grocery. She had had an affair with the same man before she was married, when she was trying to make another lover, a 40-year-old married man, jealous.
>
> When Findlay broke up with her just days before she killed her children, she told him she had slept with his father [J. Carl Findlay]. (*Wilmington Star-News*, July 9, 1995).

Such accounts may seem to recount the facts of Susan Smith's history. But far from being neutral, the reports provide ample support for prosecutors who contended that Smith killed her children to pursue extramarital affairs. Her sexual history was fairly extensive, predating the killings, and the contemporaneous affair may not have been a motivating factor in the killings. Coverage of her promiscuity weakened the defense attorneys' ability to rebut the prosecution's assertions about Smith's motive or to develop a storyline that she was a good mother despite a troubled past.

MENTAL ILLNESS AND MITIGATION

Approximately 60% of the newspaper articles concerned Susan Smith's mental instability, and they cited childhood abuse, being "sick," and a desire to be a good mother to her sons.

> Psychologists wanted to send Susan Smith to a psychiatric hospital for treatment of depression and other problems when she was just 13-years-old, but her family refused to cooperate. . . .
>
> If she had gotten help earlier, Smith, now 23, might not have drowned her sons. . . .

Smith's mental evaluation was released by Circuit Judge Howard . . . .
Smith suffers from severe depression. (*Post and Courier* [Charleston, SC],
July 11, 1995)

"We all felt Susan was a really disturbed person," said one of the jurors,
"We all felt that giving her the death penalty would not serve justice." (*Atlanta Journal and Constitution*, July 29, 1995).

Although the portrait of Susan Smith as a deeply troubled, sexually
abused young woman failed to alter the guilty verdict, it apparently provided grounds for mitigation during the penalty phase of the trial. The
jury opted for imprisonment, not death.

CHARACTER DEFECTS

References to a deeply flawed and blameworthy character constitute a
third theme. Susan Smith's character flaws were a factor in 50 of the 168
articles (30%). They included the terms evil, monster, liar, bad mother,
heartless, selfish, and racist. The following examples illustrate the general
tone of these articles:

In the 23 years she lived in [Union] . . . Smith developed a dual persona,
almost as distinct as a split personality. And that fractured image . . . has
become the centerpiece of her murder trial . . . .
   "It does seem like she is two people, like a split personality, and one of
them is evil," said [a local resident]. . . .
   Her history suggests a dark side, that she was not always the victim.
People who have known her for years describe her as manipulative and deceitful and capable of ending her children's lives to improve her own. It is
that possibility . . . that sickens people the most in Union. (*New York Times*,
July 9, 1995)

Having sex with four men in one month (including a young man and his
father), murdering two children while saving herself, using alibis to conceal her crimes all speak to character defects that go well beyond her being
severely depressed. (*St. Petersburg Times*, August 4, 1995)

Although character defects were used less frequently than other references, they were so emotionally charged that it is difficult to avoid the observation that they helped the prosecution. A manipulative and deceitful
person may be capable of ending her children's lives to improve her own
life, and this portrait of Susan Smith more than justified guilt.

Newspaper Themes Related to the Andrea Yates Case

On June 20, 2001, Andrea Yates, a stay-at-home mother suffering from postpartum depression, called 911 and then her husband, Russell Yates, to report that she had drowned their five young children in the bathtub, claiming that it was the only way to save their souls and ensure their admittance to heaven. On March 12, 2002, the jury rejected the claim that she was not guilty by reason of insanity and convicted Andrea on two counts of capital murder (the state only filed charges on two of the five deaths). The jury had recommended that Yates be sentenced to life in prison in lieu of receiving the death penalty. Details regarding Andrea's long-term and pregnancy-related mental illnesses were the focal points of the investigation, news coverage, and trial. In a surprising turn of events, in January 2005, the First Texas Court of Appeals reversed the conviction of Andrea Yates and ordered a new trial. The state's expert psychiatric witness had testified that Yates decided to kill her children after watching a *Law and Order* television episode in which a woman killed her children and was found not guilty by reason of insanity. Research revealed that no such episode ever existed. In a second trial, Yates was found not guilty by reason of insanity.

A review of 270 newspaper articles about Andrea Yates revealed four themes: profound mental illness, secondary victimization, parental irresponsibility, and religious fundamentalism. News coverage was similar across geographical regions, although we detected greater sympathy for her plight in the sources from Texas, where the incident occurred. Given the punitive and retributive criminal justice ideology that is often associated with Texas, this was a surprising finding.

MENTAL INSTABILITY

The first major theme, mental illness, was mentioned in all of the 270 articles we reviewed (100%). It comprised references to postpartum depression, postpartum psychosis, suicide attempts, hospitalizations, hallucinations, visions, insanity defense, psychiatrist, and psychotropic medications. References to Yates's psychological state stressed profound deterioration and its connection to the trial. In the first example, the reporter appears to make the case for an insanity defense:

Videotaped interviews with Andrea Yates show her emerging from psychosis in the months after she drowned her children in their bathtub, a psychiatrist testified.

In a tape played in court before the defense rested [its legal case], a disheveled Yates was asked to recall her thoughts and emotions the day of the drowning. Yates cried, rocked in her chair, paused and eventually said: "I don't remember."

In a second tape made last month, Yates looks well-groomed and bright-eyed. "I'm a little more aware of what's going on," she can be heard saying.

The stark difference from the first tape, made five weeks after the drownings, is due to the treatment Yates is receiving . . . . Yates was so sick . . . the day she drowned her children . . . that she was incapable of determining her actions were wrong. (*Milwaukee Journal Sentinel*, March 8, 2002)

After the trial, another reporter noted that although the insanity defense failed to avoid a guilty verdict, the jury recognized the extent of Yates's illness, opting for a life sentence instead of the death penalty:

The same jury that convicted Yates of capital murder in less than four hours took only 35 minutes to rule out the death penalty. That suggests, if not second thoughts, then an understanding that this mentally ill woman was not a vengeful and calculating Medea, but an individual in the thrall of the demons of psychosis.

Ms. Yates' history of mental illness suggested that, while she might have answered "yes" if she had been asked if killing one's children was a crime, she thought killing them to save them from Satan was a lesser evil. (*Pittsburgh Post-Gazette*, March 19, 2002)

The well-documented history of Andrea Yates's mental illness provided a focal point for the story. Research demonstrates that associating mental illness with maternal filicide is a common practice (Simpson & Stanton, 2000). According to this research, when women kill their children, it is almost always the result of extreme psychological conditions. Because the topic of maternal filicide is such a dark, taboo, and rare event, it nearly always meets the newsworthiness criteria discussed in the opening pages of this chapter and frequently captures newspaper headlines.

SECONDARY VICTIMIZATION

The second major category to emerge from the newspaper articles was the secondary victimization of Andrea Yates, something that made her a sympathetic offender. This theme appeared in nearly 70% of materials reviewed and involved references to the lack of medical insurance, a family history of mental illness, her father's death, a belief that her actions were saving her kids, a belief that she could not save herself, a belief that she did not have control over her actions, and the lack of support from family and friends. Although many passages recount the cruelty of Yates's crimes (see *Alameda Times-Star*, March 17, 2002), the next one acknowledges that others had a hand in aggravating her condition.

> I am sorry that there is no way to put her husband behind bars. He knew his wife needed medical help. He knew she had been treated for postpartum depression. He was right there consenting to bringing five children into the world. . . . He had a responsibility to seek help for his family. (*Washington Post*, March 17, 2002)

Andrea Yates's crime was also attributed in part to the failure of the medical and legal systems to effectively treat and protect her. Her case demonstrates the problems that need to be addressed:

> Andrea Yates' capital murder conviction may help medical and legal experts better understand mental illness, a National Institute of Mental Health official said. . . .
> Yates [was] a diagnosed schizophrenic who claimed insanity in the drowning of her five children. . . .
> Yates' case is a tragedy but may have a positive effect on the courts, legislatures and the public when it comes to "how we approach severe mental illness in the court system. . . . "
> When a mentally ill person is found responsible for a criminal act, society also must question itself . . . [the official] said he thinks society and the mental health system failed Yates and her children.
> "We should have been trying to save her life 10 years ago" [he said]. "Just the cost of this trial alone could have paid for her mental health intervention." (*Associated Press State and Local Wire*, March 13, 2002)

Recall that women are most likely to receive social support when their behavior is consistent with gendered norms. By most accounts, Andrea lived a life that conformed to the ideal of the "good girl": Prior to having children, she was a nurse; later she became a stay-at-home wife and mother, she homeschooled her children, and she was religious, in addition to being a caretaker to her ailing father. Reporters had a lot to work with in representing her story in a positive light. We empathize easily with Yates's plight, whereas we blame Susan Smith based on the "bad girl" story that dominated press reports.

PARENTAL RESPONSIBILITY

In 37% of the 270 newspaper articles reviewed on the Yates case, parental responsibility was called into question for both Andrea and Russell Yates. Fewer news items (20) blamed Andrea Yates, while far more (80) blamed her husband. Designators included admonishments by doctors not to have additional children, descriptions of Andrea Yates as a bad mother, references to an absentee father and husband, and other labels, such as evil, monster, denial, or selfish husband. Insofar as news articles held Andrea Yates responsible, they described the murders as grisly chores or blamed her for having too many children:

> The Texas woman drowned her five small children with a ghoulish precision, as if the deaths were chores checked off on a horrific to-do list. . . . (*Oregonian*, March 15, 2002)

> A prosecutor, in final arguments to bolster his request for a guilty verdict, blamed Andrea Yates for having a fifth child after she had been diagnosed as being mentally ill. (*Cox News Service*, March 19, 2002)

Accounts took Russell Yates to task for leaving his troubled wife alone and for disregarding advice to limit the number of children in his family:

> Shortly after Andrea Yates was convicted . . . [the district attorney] said his office was looking into whether her husband had any culpability [in the drownings]. . . . [P]rosecutors have questioned why Russell Yates left his wife alone with the children given her history of mental illness, including hospitalizations, depression and attempts at suicide. (*St. Louis Post-Dispatch*, June 15, 2002)

What is Russell Yates' responsibility in this tragedy? He should have known better.

He is a computer specialist at NASA, so it is a stretch to excuse him on the basis of ignorance.

Should a loving and concerned husband and father continue to have [more children with] a maximally stressed and emotionally fragile wife? . . .

Mr. Yates told Andrea he "wanted a basketball team first," then they'd "talk about a girl."(*Sarasota Herald-Tribune*, July 4, 2001)

According to some reports, mothers who kill their children are significantly less likely to receive the death penalty than murderous fathers,[4] despite the fact that Bureau of Justice Statistics data (1976–1999) indicate that mothers and fathers kill their children in nearly equal numbers.[5] This finding, and others, indicates that crimes of maternal filicide may be primarily influenced by "chivalrous" treatment (i.e., women receiving more lenient sanctions based on their sex) by the criminal justice system.

RELIGION

The final theme in the Andrea Yates case was religion and its role in her troubles. Religious references were found in nearly 30% of the newspaper articles reviewed and included words such as Satan, hell, heaven, evangelical Christian, church, preachers, and god-like. The fundamentalist sect that the Yates family followed required women to be good mothers and rise above satanic influences or make the ultimate sacrifice.

Andrea read the Bible and carried "on correspondence with an evangelist who kept reminding her to be a good mother in order to raise good kids" (*Post Standard* March 22, 2002). She went along with the preacher's belief that society corrupts and that "it is too late to undo society's damage to a child by age 14" (*New Mexico Daily Lobo*, March 1, 2002). A psychiatrist later testified that Andrea "believed she had been marked by Satan and the killing her children was the only way to save them from hell" (*New Mexico Daily Lobo*, March 1, 2002). She had come to believe that she had "ruined her children so much" that by killing them, she would save one from growing "up to be a serial killer" and another from becoming "a mute gay prostitute" (*Grand Rapids Press*, July 20, 2006).

In effect, religious themes added to the developing view of Andrea Yates as a person more victimized than victimizing. Her religious beliefs may offer insight into how she viewed her situation and the alternatives she had. It may also help explain why the media presented this case in a more compassionate light and why the public was so willing to forgive Yates, even in a traditionally conservative and punitive state like Texas.

Discussion and Conclusion

The four cases discussed have offered a unique opportunity to identify the sorts of gender themes that shape media representations of intimate violence. Following prior research, we began from the gendered premise that those who conform to the traditional norms and expectations of what it means to be a good woman and mother or a good man and father can generally anticipate rewards, and when they are the subject of news stories, they can also expect to be characterized respectfully or compassionately. In contrast, those who deviate from these standards can anticipate sanctions, formal or otherwise. When gender deviations coincide with criminal violence, the combination raises additional questions about defendants. Our findings suggest that the premise is overly simplistic. The consequences of conformity and deviation are far less certain than what the premise led us to expect.

First, the rewards of conformity may be symbolic, ambiguous, or even counterproductive for women caught up in violence. The murder of Laci Peterson was a stark reminder that physical safety is not an automatic reward. And although her idealization as a perfect wife and mother may comfort some, her status as an innocent victim contrasted with an evil husband, adding to the commercial value of the story. Nor was Andrea Yates, who delivered on her religious commitments, spared the madness that led her to kill her children or legal judgment against her.

Second, women who deviate from gender standards may escape severe punishment even when violence is extreme. A South Carolina jury convicted Susan Smith, a promiscuous and cold-blooded manipulator, on murder charges. But in recognizing prior abuse, the jury saved Smith's life just as a Texas jury had saved the life of troubled Andrea Yates, who had honored her marital vows. Furthermore, the murder case of Evelyn Hernandez remains open. But a few things are clear. No reasonable person would attribute her death to her sexual or reproductive history as described by the press. And second, the limited attention given to the murder of Evelyn Hernandez by the police and the press reflected the political and social disregard for justice at the margins, in this case among immigrants from El Salvador. On the other hand, socially conservative proponents of family values and the elimination of legal abortion had a vested interest in only one case. That Laci Peterson's unborn child also perished at her husband's hand was instrumental in making the killing of an unborn fetus an offense eligible for the death penalty.

Third, the only person for whom the consequences of transgressing gender norms held true is Scott Peterson. He received the death penalty for murdering his wife and unborn son. His murderous act may better be classified as a "crime of convenience"; that is, an atrocious crime that the press and prosecutors link to trivial motives, increasing the perceived gravity of the offense. It was inconvenient for Scott Peterson to have a pregnant wife while having an affair and wanting a carefree bachelor lifestyle. In the absence of mitigation (that is, themes such as mental instability), one had to assume that the construct crime of convenience had a role in the jury's decision to impose the death penalty. Furthermore, crimes of inconvenience might apply to other cases. It was inconvenient for Susan Smith to have two young children when she was dating men who were only interested in having a good time. But in this case, the defense had established mental health as a creditable basis of mitigation during sentencing. It may have also been inconvenient for Herman Aguilera, the main suspect in the murder of Evelyn Hernandez, to have a pregnant mistress while married to another woman. But without an arrest and trial, motive, trivial or otherwise, would not be an issue.

In understanding our findings, it is important to point out that high-profile cases are managed in part by media specialists who spin the news in order to influence the jury pool. Such managers and the attorneys they work with are likely to use gender themes opportunistically to advance a profile that benefits the client whether the client is the defense or the prosecution. Prosecutors and defense attorneys have strong interests in disseminating their theories of the case and making sure that details such as the defendant's motive are picked up by reporters and relayed to the public. More often than not, the prosecutor prevails, but balance in journalism means covering both sides in a trial. In addition, the sentencing phase makes news imagery all the more important. In capital cases, as those examined in this study show, an accumulation of news characterizing a defendant one way or another has the potential to influence a non-sequestered jury's assessment of mitigating and aggravating factors.

In addition to the legal system, the findings may well reflect the power of social class, ethnicity, and race to define events and people. One cannot rule out race and ethnicity in distinguishing between high- and low-profile cases. Laci and Scott Peterson were seen as the "all-American couple," race being an unstated, but nonetheless glaring, reality in the social identities created for them by the press. Evelyn Hernandez, as an El Salvadoran, did not reap the racial benefit. Andrea Yates benefited from being white and not on welfare, and though she had too many children, she was not painted with the same brush that a black welfare mother with too many kids might be. The photographic image of Susan Smith's angelic white boys was forever seared into the nation's consciousness. The media shied away from Smith's claims about a black killer perhaps because the press had been soundly criticized for the media frenzy that had surrounded claims by white Charles Stuart that a phantom black man had killed his pregnant wife in Boston.

Fourth, the media's presentation of the four cases tends to highlight the sensationalized and titillating nature of the murders. For instance, rather than putting Scott Peterson's violence in the context of intimate partner violence and rather than discussing the fact that women are at greatest risk of being harmed or killed by someone close to them (not strangers), the media causes alarm by portraying atypical crimes as the norm. As Jane Caputi says, "The murders of women and children . . . are not some inexplicable evil or the domain of 'monsters' only" (Caputi, 1993, p. 7). Husbands and paramours kill their wives and mistresses all the time. And people who suffer from depression and child sexual abuse do desperate things. The media would do well to remind readers of these truths.

A fifth related point is that the media often fail to relate crimes to broader remedial efforts. The Laci Peterson case was used to make killing an unborn child a crime. The Andrea Yates and Susan Smith cases had the potential to be used as vehicles for advancing public education about violence and mental health legislation. Andrea Yates suffered tremendously from postpartum psychosis, and yet nothing was done. Susan Smith was a victim of childhood incest (by her stepfather) and never received counseling. Although news coverage exploited many aspects of these cases, it fell miserably short of relating individual problems to systemic difficulties or to the changes that might alleviate them. Journalists continue to rely on gender stereotypes and to sensationalize sexually prurient details. Even with the influx of feminists into journalism, traditional newspaper coverage of the "crime beat" may remain wholly masculine, but the alternative press might reflect a different kind of coverage. It would be fascinating to compare how themes found in daily press reports compare with those in news weeklies such as *Time* and *Newsweek* (that can do more in-depth coverage) and more progressive outlets like the *Village Voice* and the *Nation*. Finally, crime reporters who follow the conventions of journalism and focus on individuals are by necessity going to ignore larger social forces that shape the attitudes and behavior of the people they write about, the victims and the offenders. By ignoring the structural context of criminal behavior, the media let fundamental institutions of society off the hook.

NOTES

1. The more socially valuable and important a victim is, the better the crime story and the more likely that the story will become news. As long as victim attributes continue to influence the newsworthiness of a story, the choice of overemphasizing some victimizations and underemphasizing others will have little to do with the real danger certain crimes present to the public and more to do with the social status of the victim and/or the perpetrator.
2. A notable exception to this occurred during the O. J. Simpson murder trial. When the media learned that Nicole Brown Simpson, prior to her murder, had been a victim of domestic abuse during her marriage to O. J., it catapulted the topic into the national spotlight in an unprecedented way. The media attention to domestic violence was probably deemed newsworthy and relevant more because it involved a black celebrity with a white wife than the well-documented fact that abused women are most likely to be killed by the abuser *after* they leave the relationship (Belknap, 2001). Furthermore, research finds that the media are more likely to report on domestic violence cases that result in a homicide (Family Violence Prevention Fund, 2003).
3. Euphemistic or neutral language is typically used when gender and violence are discussed for crimes such as rape and battering. According to the Media Report to Women (1994), language choices shape the way readers interpret and react to news-

paper stories about the murder and rape of women by their husbands, ex-husbands, or boyfriends. Journalists talk about these crimes as "love triangles" or situations where "love turns bad" rather than focusing on the criminal aspects of the incidents.

4. As stated in the *Courier-Mail* [Global News Service], August 2, 1995: Americans don't execute mothers, p. 15, (byline: S. Roberts).

5. As stated in the *San Francisco Chronicle*, February 23, 2002a: An unfathomable crime: Parents who slay their kids, p. A1 (byline: Elizabeth Fernandez).

REFERENCES

Alameda Times-Star. (2002, March 17). Cruelty beyond belief.

———. (2003, July 10). Peterson lawyer's request denied; Investigators not allowed into files of another missing woman's death.

Associated Press State and Local Wire. (2002, March 13). In wake of Yates' verdict some call for legal, medical reforms (byline: Pam Easton).

Atlanta Journal and Constitution. (1995, July 29). "Giving Susan death won't serve justice," p. A1 (byline: Chris Buritt and Jack Warner).

Belknap, J. (2001). *The invisible woman: Gender, crime, and justice.* Toronto: Wadsworth.

Benedict, H. (1992). *Virgin or vamp: How the press covers sex crimes.* New York: Oxford University Press.

Boston Herald. (2003a, April 27). Mattapan's horror ignored in Laci land, p. 16, (byline: Margery Eagon).

———. (2003b, May 11). Sunday briefing: Mistress is hero in Laci case, p. 2.

Bureau of Justice Statistics. (2004). Trends in homicide: Intimate partner violence. Retrieved June 14, 2004 from www.ojp.usdoj.gov/bjs/.

Buzawa, E., & Buzawa, C. (2003). *Domestic violence: The criminal justice response.* Thousand Oaks, CA: Sage.

Caputi, J. (1993). The sexual politics of murder. In P. Bart & E. Moran (Eds.), *Violence against women: The bloody footprints* (pp. 5–25). Newbury Park, CA: Sage.

Caringella-MacDonald, S., & Humphries, D. (Eds.). (1998). Women, violence, and the media. *Violence Against Women, 4,* 3–113.

Cavender, G., Bond-Maupin, L., & Jurik, N. C. (1999). The construction of gender in reality crime TV. *Gender and Society, 13,* 643–663.

Chermak, S. (1995). *Victims in the news: Crime and the American news media.* Boulder, CO: Westview Press.

Chicago Sun-Times. (2003a, January 26). Husband of missing woman denies affair, p. 20.

———. (2003b, October 29). Prosecutors to reveal clues that point to Scott Peterson, p. 40 (byline: Brian Melley).

Copley News Service. (2003, April 22). Why do the media focus on some murders, not others?

Courier-Mail (Global Wire Service). (1995, August 2). American's don't execute mothers, p. 15 (byline: S. Roberts).

Cox News Service. (2002, March 19). What about Russell Yates (byline: Ana Pecina Walker).

Daly, K., & Chasteen, A. (1997). Crime news, crime fear, and women's everyday lives. In M. Fineman & M. McCluskey (Eds.). *Feminism, media and the law* (pp. 235–248). New York: Oxford University Press.

Family Violence Prevention Fund. (2003). Intimate partner violence goes underreported in California newspapers. Retrieved June 14, 2004, from http://endabuse.org/programs/display.php3.

Grand Rapids Press. (2006, July 20). Yates thought kids would end up in hell, p. A4.

Grover, C., & Soothill, K. (1996). A murderous underclass: The press reporting of sexually motivated murder. *Sociological Review, 44* (3), 398–415.

Hanmer, J., & Maynard, M. (1987). Introduction: Violence and gender stratification. In J. Hanmer and & M. Maynard (Eds.), *Women, violence and social control* (pp. 1–12). Atlantic Highlands, NJ: Humanities Press International.

Henley, N. M., Miller, M., & Beasley, J. A. (1995). Syntax, semantics, and sexual violence. *Journal of Language and Social Psychology, 14* (1–2), 60–84.

Houston Chronicle. (2003, May 5). Birthday service honors Peterson; thousands pack church in California, p. A3 (byline: Juliana Barbassa).

Jewkes, Y. (2004). *Media and crime*. Thousand Oaks, CA: Sage.

Johnstone, J., Hawkins, D., & Michener, A. (1994). Homicide reporting in Chicago dailies. *Journalism Quarterly, 71*, 860–872.

Karmen, A. (1984). *Crime victims: An introduction to victimology*. Monterey, CA: Brooks/Cole.

Krueger, R. A. (1994). *Focus groups: A practical guide for applied research* (2nd ed.). Thousand Oaks, CA: Sage.

Lamb, S., & Keon, S. (1995). Blaming the perpetrator: Language that distorts reality in newspaper articles on men battering women. *Psychology of Women Quarterly, 19*, 209–220.

Lipschultz, J., & Hilt, M. (2002). *Crime and local television news*. Mahwah, NJ: LEA.

Long Beach Press-Telegram. (2003, June 20). S.F. officials: No cult link in Laci case.

Los Angeles Times. (2003, November 19). Judge finds cause for Peterson Trial; Modesto neighbors see no reason for surprise in the way the spotlighted case developed.

———. (2004, January 9). The state: Peterson trial will be moved; Judge order a change of venue from Stanislaw County over extensive media coverage.

Media Report to Women. (1994). Choice of language shapes views. *Media Report to Women, 22* (2), 1.

Meyers, M. (1997). *News coverage of violence against women: Engendering blame*. Thousand Oaks, CA: Sage.

New Mexico Daily Lobo. (2002, March 1). Yates: wife downplayed illness; husband outlines lifestyle of family before kids drowned.

Milwaukee Journal Sentinel. (2002, March 8). Tape suggests Yates emerged from psychosis, p. A10.

New York Times. (1995, July 9). Mother who killed: Loss, betrayal and a search for a fairy tales life, p. 16 (byline: Rick Bragg).

Oregonian. (2002, March 15). Death penalty wrong in Yates case, p. B10.

Pittsburg Post-Gazette. (2002, March 19). Compassionate contribution; a jury convicts Andrea Yates, then spares her life, p. A10.

Post and Courier (Charleston, SC). (1995, July 11). Smith needed treatment at age 13, report reveals, p. A7.

Post Standard (Syracuse, NY). (2002, March 22). Where was husband as Yates fell apart, p. A13 (byline: Virginia Hoppe).

Pritchard, D., & Hughes, K. D. (1997). Patterns of deviance in crime news. *Journal of Communication, 47,* 49–67.

Russell, D. (1984). *Sexual exploitation: Rape, child sexual abuse, and workplace harassment.* Beverly Hills, CA: Sage.

Russo, A. (1997). Lesbians, prostitutes, and murder. In M. Fineman & M. McCluskey (Eds.), *Feminism, media and the law* (pp. 249–266). New York: Oxford University Press.

Ryan, J., & Wentworth, W. (1999). *Media and society.* Boston: Allyn and Bacon.

San Francisco Chronicle. (2002a, February 23). An unfathomable crime: Parents who slay their kids, p. A1 (byline: Elizabeth Fernandez).

———. (2002b, September 4). Torso in bay is identified: DNA matches that of missing pregnant mom, p. A17 (byline: Jaxon Van Derbeken).

———. (2003, May 3). Woman, whose body was found in bay mourned, p. A12 (byline: Henry K. Lee).

Sarasota Herald-Tribune. (2001, July 4). "The mother was 'drowning,'" p. A14.

St. Louis Post-Dispatch. (2002, June 15). Nation and world briefs: District attorney clears Russell Yates in deaths, p. 29.

St. Petersburg Times. (1995, August 4). The abuse of children too often goes unreported, p. A19.

Simpson, A., & Stanton. J. (2000). Maternal filicide: A reformulation of factors relevant to risk. *Criminal Behavior and Mental Health, 10,* 136–147.

Slobogin, C. (2003). The integrationist alternative to the insanity defense: Reflections on the exculpatory scope of mental illness in the wake of the Andrea Yates trial. *American Journal of Criminal Law, 30,* 315–341.

Strauss, A. (1987). *Qualitative analysis for social scientists.* Cambridge: Cambridge University Press.

Washington Post. (1995, July 20). Former lover says Susan Smith had affair with stepfather, p. A3, (byline: Tamara Jones).

————. (2002, March 17). What about Mr. Yates, p. B8.

Wilmington Star-News. (1995, July 9). Trial to focus on Susan Smith's identity, pp. A1, A8 (byline: Rick Bragg, New York Times News Service).

Zalin, L. (2003). *Stress on the press: Reporters alone in dealing with trauma.* Dart Center for Journalism and Trauma. Retrieved June 14, 2004, from www.dartcenter.org/articles/special/stress_on_press2.

CONSTRUCTING MURDERERS
Female Killers of Law and Order

Drew Humphries

Law and Order is an award-winning drama organized around the investigation and prosecution of homicide cases in New York City. Its engaging formula has made the series a significant presence in NBC's lineup of evening shows for nearly two decades. Week after week, the show—a police procedural—follows a team of detectives and prosecutors as they hunt down suspects and hold killers accountable. Although its popularity can be attributed to crime and justice themes, its power to attract and hold a female audience is at odds with the misogynist assumptions built into the classic police procedural. To explore this apparent contradiction, we turn our attention to the social construction of killers, a typification that deserves more attention than it often gets. Killers are, after all, the raison d'être of crime dramas: Murder is the pretext for the hunt, and punishment provides moral certainty. There are more than law and order symbols involved, however, as the social construction of female killers should reflect feminist gains. What is at issue is the extent to which *Law and Order* may have overcome the genre's masculine ethos and the degree to which it may have also incorporated feminist sensibilities that would appeal to a female audience.

We begin with a discussion of the police procedural and *Law and Order*'s departures from genre conventions. Next, we address the social construction of killers, the impact of mystery on character structure and transformation, and female killers. Research procedures and findings occupy the middle portions of the chapter. The last section discusses the implications of the female killer for reconciling the apparent contradiction between a female audience and a misogynist genre.

Law and Order as Police Procedural

The police procedural is a literary subgenre that begins after a murder has taken place and that strives to present a realistic picture of what police actually do in the course of an investigation. Accordingly, *Law and Order* episodes begin with the discovery of a corpse and take the audience through a homicide investigation. It concentrates on a team of law enforcement professionals: seasoned homicide detectives (e.g., detective Lennie Briscoe, played by Jerry Orbach) and hard-driving prosecutors (e.g., Sam Waterston's executive assistant district attorney (EADA) Jack McCoy). Critics have cited the genre as hypermasculine (Scaggs, 2005). Some have also asked whether the police procedural can accommodate women in any meaningful sense (Klein, 1995). In its first season, *Law and Order*'s all-male, ensemble cast tended to confirm doubts.

At the end of the first season, however, NBC's president, Warren Littlefield, met with Dick Wolf, the show's creator and executive producer, and told Wolf to add women to the cast. The all-male cast had failed to attract women, and Littlefield wanted to expand the audience beyond its original base. According to published accounts of the meeting, Littlefield told Wolf, "Professional, well-educated women want to see themselves depicted on the screen faithfully and realistically" (Strachan, 2006). Wolf heeded the advice and replaced Robert Brooks and Dann Florek with two actresses—S. Epatha Merkerson as Anita Van Buren, a black police lieutenant, and Jill Hennessy as assistant prosecutor Claire Kincade—according to Strachan (2006). Ratings went up, and increases were attributed to female cast members (Courrier & Green, 1999). Since then, other women have circulated through the ensemble cast, including Dianne Wiest (district attorney Nora Lewin), who left after two seasons, and a second female police officer, Milena Govick, who replaced Dennis Farina in season 16 (Stein, 2006). The mixed-gender ensemble cast that characterizes *Law and Order* thus reflects gains made by women in the workforce. The show is indicative of what Dow (1996) calls prime-time feminism, featuring mostly white, middle-class women and exploring workplace situations most likely to affect women (Lodz, 2006).

Law and Order can take credit for two other innovations in the police procedural. First, it added pretrial and trial scenes to the police investigation (Courrier & Green, 1999). The courtroom scenes shift the dramatic focus of the show from the point of arrest, where police officers would otherwise resolve plot tensions, to the point of legal judgment, where prosecutors win the convictions. In the early seasons of the show, two prominent actors, George Dzundza (detective Max Greevy) and Paul Sorvino (detective Phil Cerreta), left the show because prosecutors overshadowed detective roles (Courrier & Green, 1999). Moreover, courtroom scenes also dramatized aspects of criminal justice never seen on television: plea-bargaining sessions, lineups, grand jury activity, and psychiatric examinations, to mention just a few (see Escholtz, Mallard, & Flynn, 2004; Quinn, 2002). As a result, the *Law and Order* justice system has well-defined decision points, ranging from arrest to verdict, that reveal the processes that shape these judgments.

Second, the show's self-defined commitment to exploring fresh angles on the big issues is another innovation (Courrier & Green, 1999). Issues are handled differently depending on one of three types of episodes. Regular episodes are based on fictionalized crimes, and detectives, prosecutors, and defense attorneys may debate issues such as jury nullification or public hostility toward the police. "Ripped from the headlines" episodes are based on real-life crimes and allegedly give audiences the satisfaction of seeing how infamous cases (e.g., a closeted gay governor) would be handled in the criminal justice system. The third type, issue-oriented episodes, forsakes moral certainties and leaves the task of resolving issues to the audience (Courrier & Green, 1999). These episodes use ambiguity to enlist viewers in conversations about issues after turning off the television set (Courrier & Green, 1999). Because moral certainty is the basic rule of crime fiction, ambiguity is understood as innovation (Scraggs, 2005).

Mystery, Murderers, and Character Transformation

At the heart of every police procedural is a mystery. Audiences expect to be kept in the dark about which suspect committed the murder, and they expect to be surprised when the screenwriter exposes the killer at the end of the script (Scraggs, 2005). To achieve this effect, murderous characters have at least two personae: an inner malevolent core that accounts for the murder and a far less threatening outer facade that conceals his or her identity. The metaphor "a wolf in sheep's clothing" may help visualize the two-layer construction of murderous characters and may also help in seeing that disguised sheep are exposed quite dramatically as wolves.

Character transformations that unmask killers take place in two kinds of *Law and Order* scenes: plea-bargaining and cross-examination. Anyone familiar with the show should recognize scenes in which defendants and their families agree to consider a plea bargain. The prosecutor, Jack McCoy or his predecessor, Benjamin Stone, offers the defendant a consideration in exchange for a guilty plea. Considerations include a reduced charge, a concurrent sentence, or a reduction in counts. McCoy and Stone typically put a time limit on the offer, telling defendants that the present deal is the best one they can expect. In addition to plea negotiations, viewers should also be familiar with courtroom scenes in which prosecutors bully witnesses, turn alibi witnesses against defendants, produce last-minute evidence, and humiliate defendants foolish enough to take the stand to testify in their own defense.

In plea-bargaining and courtroom scenes, whether the defendant will be convicted or acquitted is at stake. The defendant's power and moral status are also in jeopardy, as suggested by George Gerbner's work on television villains (Gerbner, 2002, pp. 365–376). On the criterion of power, villains can be classified as "winners" or "losers." Winners are powerful figures who command their own destinies, whereas losers lack power and fail to achieve even modest goals. In being confronted by the prosecutor, a defendant may retain power or be reduced to the status of a loser. On the issue of moral standing, villains can be "good guys" or "bad guys." Good guys have ethical motives, which in the arena of murder may involve a just cause. Bad guys are driven to kill by venal or pathological motives. In facing the prosecutors, a good guy defendant risks being exposed as a bad guy. Consequently, prosecutors are in a position to transform murderous characters: They may confine defendants, destroy their power, and/or demean them.

As long as murderous characters are male, transformations take place in a straightforward manner. Masculine assumptions place men quite naturally in the public world of work, where police procedurals naturally unfold. Where women come into the picture, masculine assumptions about women complicate character transformations and require a deeper look at the meaning of gender. Here, the relevant conceptions include the so-called two-sphere argument, gender biases in legal decisions, and gendered concepts of power and morality.

Separate Spheres

"Separate spheres" is a phrase used to describe the assignment of women to the world of domesticity and men to the more powerful world of work. The concept is a poor description of gender inequality in the United States because the entrance of women into the labor market has blurred the once sharp line between the two spheres (Daly & Chesney-Lind, 1988). Ferree speaks of "the illusion of separate spheres" (Ferree, 1990). Television, for example, maintains the illusion by imposing gender restrictions on characters: Female characters are married, and unmarried men are free to go on adventures (Gerbner, 2002). If two spheres regulate the social construction of female killers, then the concept has value in determining how well television programming integrates women or feminist sensibilities. On the one hand, the assignment of women to home and family defines a masculine context for female killers, and domesticity reassures audiences about the traditional orderliness of the world (Taylor, 1989). On the other hand, the recognition that women work and raise families calls into question simplistic male versus female assignments, challenges the two-spheres illusion, and appeals to a different kind of audience (Dow, 1996).

Gender Biases

Insofar as police procedurals feature arrests, verdicts, and sanctions, they draw a line between acceptable and unacceptable behavior (Scaggs, 2005). The *Law and Order* formula, which has been criticized as repetitive and rigid, reassures its audience that murder is wrong and that the courts can be counted on to enforce laws against murder. Hence, killers are fated to be convicted, although in considering female killers, gender bias is an issue. Are female killers convicted more or less frequently than their male counterparts? In discussing gender biases, Belknap describes three hypotheses: the evil woman hypothesis, an equal treatment hypothesis, and the chivalry hypothesis (2001). If *Law and Order* officials perceive women as "evil" (that is, as having violated gender as well as legal norms), they may sanction them more severely than other women (Belknap, 2001). The equal treatment hypothesis, on the other hand, is about the absence of gender bias. The chivalry hypothesis predicts that officials would treat women more leniently than men (Belknap, 2001).

This study focuses on the middle stages of criminal justice processing, when prosecutors make decisions about whether to prosecute or dismiss charges, negotiate pleas, or go to trial. At these pretrial stages, due process standards do not apply, leaving more room for discretion and discrimination (Belknap, 2001). Research conducted in the 1980s, but not replicated since, produced contradictory results. In prosecutors' decisions to prosecute or dismiss charges, there is evidence of equal treatment and chivalry (see, e.g., Albonetti, 1886 and Ghali & Chesney-Lind, 1986 1986, as cited by Belknap, 2001). Chivalrous treatment, however, does not mean that all women have an advantage over men. The advantage goes to white women, with officials responding more severely to women of color, poor women, and younger rather than older women (Belknap, 2001, p. 135, see also Reiman, 2001). Because trials allow less room for discrimination, the conviction decisions are unaffected by gender bias (Belknap, 2001, p. 143).

Female Power and Morality

Because women are subject to male authority, typifying female killers as winners or losers presented some problems. First, in conceptualizing female power, one risks confounding power and essential qualities. The maternal role includes the nurturance of children, but it would be wrong to conclude that all women have nurturing qualities or that nurturance is the basis of female power. If nurturance is a myth, then its influence lies in the distinctive or unique qualities it appears to give to women. Men use these qualities to subordinate women (Van Wormer & Bartollas, 2007).

Second, winners and losers are not gender-neutral terms. A rigidly defined patriarchy might define all women as losers. A more traditionally masculine perspective might consider women who meet traditional role obligations (marriage and mothering) as winners, while those who fall short (unmarried or ineffectual mothers) might be losers. In challenging the view that winner status and masculine norms overlap, feminists would focus on the right to be judged by universal standards.

Common stereotypes about women's power also reflect masculine assumptions. Stereotypes about losers would include that women are "passive and weak" or "impressionable and in need of protection" (Raftner & Stanko, 1982). Such women are easily led astray by men and lack the necessary judgment to assume leadership roles. But active or strong women are stigmatized as overly aggressive, masculine, or lesbian (Raftner & Stanko, 1982). Not all stereotypes evoke weakness. The unchecked female rage embodied in Medea-like characters who take revenge on unfaithful husbands is a case in point (Jones, 2003). Alternatively, feminist media critics praise women for being tough, muscular, aggressive, and extremely violent (Innis, 2004).

Good guys and bad guys are also gendered categories. Male villains have character defects, according to Gerbner (2002), but popular culture tends to sexualize female motivation (Benedict, 1992). The sexualized distinction between "Madonna" and "whore" is central to masculine views about women. Women who meet male standards about premarital chastity and marital fidelity are rewarded and protected as "Madonnas"; women who violate these rules are isolated and demeaned as "whores." Sexual freedoms and modern lifestyles blur the distinction, but the illusion that sexual choices affect a woman's destiny persists. Feminists, however, are inclined to challenge the sexualized distinction. Men may be threatened by women, who act on their own desires and turn men into objects of desire or violence (Boyle, 2005, p. 108). Feminists are also likely to confront heterosexual standards, recognizing that human sexuality offers a broad range of gay, lesbian, bisexual, and transsexual options (Boyle, 2005).

In looking at the social construction of female killers on *Law and Order*, we focus on character transformations, meaning legal, power, and moral changes effected by prosecutors who confront female defendants in the course of plea bargains or in the context of the courtroom. Three basic questions guided the research described below: Are female killers located in the female world of domesticity or in the more powerful world of work? Do *Law and Order* justice officials treat female killers more or less harshly than men when it comes to plea-bargaining and courtroom decisions? What stigmatizing strategies are used to transform winners into losers and good gals into bad ones?

The Research

The study is based on a sample of 22 *Law and Order* episodes taped during a six-week period in the summer of 2001. As a convenience sample, it is free from obvious biases and reflects what an audience would have been exposed to during the period of data collection. It includes episodes from the first ten seasons that were written, directed, and produced by many different individuals. It includes a mix of ripped from the headline and issue oriented episodes, although regular fictionalized episodes predominate.

Research assistants taped and coded the sample, collecting demographic data on cast members. I reviewed the tapes first to summarize story lines and then to look more closely at the murderers, who were difficult to pin down: *Law and Order* suspects may be cleared, arrestees may be released, and guilty defendants may be acquitted. Murderers were therefore defined as suspects who had been convicted or pled guilty. Unindicted murderers were noted in a separate category. The definition yielded 31 murderers. As a group, murderers were white (90%), 35 years of age and older (97%), comprised slightly more men (58%) than women (43%), and were drawn equally from upper-, middle-, working-class, and poor backgrounds.

Coding focused on the context in which the killer encountered his or her victim: family versus work. In the case of career couples, the offender–victim relationship was taken into consideration: family, acquaintance, or stranger. In each episode, we selected a plea-bargaining or courtroom scene that captured the confrontation between defendants and prosecutors and then coded character transformations effected by the prosecutor. A defendant's legal status was determined by charging decisions, convictions, and acquittals. Murderers were either uncharged or pled guilty. If prosecutors took the case to trial, murderers were found guilty or acquitted. Hung juries were included among the acquittals. For moral and power status, we first coded the murderer's benign outer facade and then coded the malevolent inner core. For each murderer, we typed both personae and compared them to capture the direction of transformation. We defined winners as possessing charisma, a sense of destiny, or an ability to define and achieve goals. Losers were understood to stand in the background, express disgruntlement, or sabotage their own goals. We used motives to define moral status: Good persons had socially appropriate motives; bad persons had venal or pathological ones.

The findings are presented below and framed in a broader understanding of the dataset, including story lines, issues raised, and perspectives advanced by detectives, prosecutors, murderers, and defense attorneys.

Findings

Two-thirds of the *Law and Order* killers met their victims in the context of the family. Families were initially idealized as caring, children as well behaved, and households as orderly. Much to the show's credit, families included two-parent families, gay or lesbian parents, families with adopted children, single parents, and parents who had lost custody of their children. Murder took place in all types of families, from upper-class

WASP families to Hispanic families trapped in the barrio. The tensions that generated domestic murders exposed dysfunctions. Husbands took lovers, imposed cruelties, and risked family wealth. Wives exploited marriage as a source of income. Incest, prostitution, infidelity, abuse, and the deadening effects of poverty went a long way in eliminating first impressions that *Law and Order* families were ever-loving, orderly, or conventional.

Male and female killers were equally likely to meet their victims in the context of the family. However, whereas male killers were tied to work and family, female killers were disproportionately confined to the domestic sphere. In "Family Values," for example, a mother–daughter argument ended tragically after teenager Maggie Connor flaunted her affair with stepfather Steve Martel. In "True North," the murderess killed Mr. Harker's first wife in order to marry him and then killed Mr. Harker when he took steps to divorce her. The web of family can be tangled. The murder of a gay parent and abduction of his adopted child were traced back to the baby's mother and father in an episode that challenged traditional definitions of family. Moreover, a few killings tested the divide between family and work. In an episode entitled "Dissonance," the issues were marital, but the context was work. In it, the three members of a romantic triangle were professional musicians: the wife, the rival for the affections of her husband, and the husband. Only a few killings could be characterized as work related. For instance, a police patrol officer shot and killed her corrupt partner in self-defense, although the title "A Death in the Family" still blurs the work versus home distinction.

Conviction Rate and Gender Bias

Law and Order prosecutors won the vast majority of their cases against homicide defendants (77%) and thereby provided a measure of moral certainty that the police and the courts can be counted on to enforce the law. Female defendants were convicted by prosecutors with less success (69%) than their male counterparts (83%). The difference is not, however, a case of chivalry; rather, a higher conviction rate for men is related to the particular circumstances of plea-bargaining on *Law and Order*. The alibi witness is a key player in determining the outcome of plea bargaining sessions. Prosecutors win when they convince the alibi witness to testify against a defendant. Prosecutors were successful in convincing wives and mistresses to testify against male defendants but far less successful in getting male relatives to testify against female defendants. As a result, prosecutors were able to force more male defendants than female ones into accepting guilty pleas.

Wives or lovers take advantage of the deal offered by prosecutors to even the score against husbands who had ignored, mistreated, betrayed, or abused them. Such women initially appear as weak, shy, or passive characters, but they become empowered by the prosecutor's deal. In "Tabula Rasa," Eleanor Taska, an overly submissive wife, had to be convinced to testify against her obsessive and abusive husband, Nick Taska. On cross-examination, McCoy got Nick Taska to reveal his true feelings toward a wife who had sacrificed much to stay with him. Nick needed a woman—any woman—to mother his two daughters, the real obsession in his life. Humiliated, Eleanor agreed to testify, regaining her life by supplying the one piece of evidence that put her husband at the scene of the crime.

Winners and Losers

In almost half of the cases (46%), female killers were stripped of power by prosecutors. Most of the women, who seemed to have power, prestige, or position, were easily tripped up and exposed as losers. "Impressionable women in need of help" is a common stereotype (Raftner & Stanko, 1989). In *Law and Order*, the stereotype emphasizes the poor choices women make in selecting men. In an episode entitled "Venom," Joyce Pollack, an independent older woman who commanded vast wealth, was drawn into murder by her choice of a charming, much younger husband, who was also locked in an incestuous relationship with his mother, Liane Crosby. Note that Joyce Pollack entered the episode as a winner, in command of her own destiny, and that the prosecutor exposed her as a besotted woman, who lost everything in a romantic gamble. In an effort to free her husband from his mother's incestuous grip, Joyce conspired with her husband to kill his mother. The deal Jack McCoy offered Dennis Pollack tested the young husband's loyalties. If Pollack testified against his mother in a string of other murders, McCoy would not indict his wife Joyce. If Pollack refused, McCoy would indict his wife, who would pay dearly for her marriage to a younger man. Pollack refused McCoy's offer, leaving his wife to face certain conviction in the attempt on Liane Crosby's life.

Similar forces were at work in "Family Values," an episode in which Maggie Connor was both an angry daughter and the paramour of her mother's second husband, Steve Martel. During an argument with her mother, Maggie flaunted the affair with Martel, and when the battle turned physical, Maggie killed her mother. Maggie would have remained a hostile teenager except for Martel, who seduced her, fostered her romantic illusions, and thus set the murder in motion. Maggie was so smitten with Martel that she refused to implicate him as an accessory after the fact (he helped dispose of the body). At trial, however, McCoy exposed Martel's multiple affairs and got Maggie to testify against him. Doubly used, Maggie was not the well-heeled teen she first appeared to be.

In addition, "the killer as fraud" is a stereotype that exploits middle-class prejudices against upper-class and poor characters. The appearance of power and wealth (winner) turns out to be a cover for self-defeating manipulations associated with hardscrabble values and humble origins. In "True North," Mrs. Stephanie Harker first appeared as a soft-spoken, grieving widow who seemed a good fit for the elegant penthouse where she discussed the death of her late husband with detectives. By manner, appearance, and setting, the episode defined her as one of the privileged elite, but scriptwriters chipped away at the benign facade. Homicide detectives discovered that the young widow preferred parties, drugs, and lovers to the novels of Jane Austen. They traced her family to Niagara Falls, where she grew up as the daughter of a souvenir store owner who barely made a living. In the process, detectives also found an open hit-and-run case in which Mr. Harker's first wife had been run down by Stephanie Harker, his current wife. At trial, prosecutor McCoy cross-examined Stephanie Harker, provoking her to boast that she had outsmarted everyone and trapping her in a confession. She was not as smart as she believed.

Not all transformations followed the winner-to-loser model. A few killers started out as losers but revealed hidden resources in their confrontations with prosecutors. Selected female killers charted their own courses through life, family, and the criminal justice system. A self-effacing wife took control of her husband, and a troublesome older woman outmaneuvered the prosecutor, turning out to be an avenging angel.

The self-effacing wife who suffers in the shadow of an arrogant or overbearing husband is a staple character in many dramas and films. She is part martyr, having sacrificed her life for her husband's advancement, but she is also an icon of female subordination; in short, an angry woman with many reasons to want to even the score. "Dissonance" is an episode that began with the discovery of the body of a young, attractive violinist who played with the city orchestra. Always in the background, the self-effacing Mrs. Marian Reger went unnoticed. Detectives believed that her husband, Carl Reger, the orchestra's arrogant and dismissive conductor, killed the violinist as she tried to break off an affair with him. At trial, Mrs. Reger gave her husband an ironclad alibi and held firm even as her husband's defense attorney implicated her in an alternative theory of the crime, that Mrs. Reger may have killed her rival out of jealousy. Nonetheless, she refused to testify against her husband. In so doing, she managed to get her husband acquitted, avoided indictment herself, and reversed her marital fortunes. In the end, she held the reins of marital power.

The troublesome older woman is another stereotype frequently used to dismiss women. Such women complain about trivial matters, make threats against family and friends, and cause problems for those around them. They may be malicious or, as in the following example, they may be the instruments of revenge. The characterization of Mrs. Estelle Muller as a troublesome old woman requires some background because the plot in "Legacy" is unusually complicated. Mrs. Muller was first described by her daughter-in-law as disagreeable, meddlesome, and as inexplicably hostile to the daughter-in-law's new husband, Jim Sheppard. Mrs. Muller had taken things one step further in hiring a hit man to kill Jim Sheppard, and when questioned by detectives, she admitted the attempt on his life. In dealing with the prosecutor, however, she took command. Mrs. Muller believed that Jim Sheppard had killed her son in order to marry his widow. She would agree to plead guilty in the attempt on Sheppard's life provided the prosecutor promised to investigate her son's death. Set in motion by Mrs. Muller, the prosecutor made good on his promise and convicted Sheppard in the death of Mrs. Muller's son.

Humble circumstances, especially those of petty criminals, are rarely romanticized by *Law and Order* scriptwriters. In our sample, petty criminals and drug addicts are losers from the start, and their characterizations go downhill from there. Working with male partners, females appeared to have relatively more power than these male partners, whose senseless acts of violence defeated them both. In "Causa Mortis," for example,

Anna Galvez wanted a car to drive her mother to and from her nighttime job. Anna picked out a car, and Fernando Salva, her fiancé, carjacked the preselected model. In a senseless act of violence, Salva also killed the driver. Detectives tracked him down—the victim had made an audio recording of the deadly encounter. And ADA Jamie Ross, newly paired with Jack McCoy, pulled out all the stops to convict Salva on capital murder charges. Although Anna Galvez testified against Salva and avoided being charged herself, she and her mother were unaffected by events. They remained unrepentant and hostile to authorities.

Good Gals and Bad Ones

The *Law and Order* team typically exposed female killers as bad gals (62%), relying heavily on the sexualized distinction between whore and Madonna. In "Cradle to Grave," real estate developers Iris Coreman and Joseph Turner were convicted of negligent homicide in the death by exposure of a tenant's infant son in a building they hoped to convert to condos. The episode makes a strong case about the depravity of the Manhattan real estate market in the early 1990s (Courrier & Green, 1999). In making this point, however, there was no dramatic purpose in also ridiculing the much older Iris Coreman for her affair with the younger, handsome Joseph Turner. On a show where the average age of characters is around 35, it should come as no surprise that issues of sexuality and age would arise. On television, younger women have affairs; older women have sex at their peril.

The three murders committed by Mrs. Stephanie Harker in "True North" carried her from poverty to a Manhattan penthouse, but, when questioned by a detective, one of her friends described the incident that had fueled Harker's rage. As a pregnant teenager, Stephanie had expected to marry her wealthy boyfriend. He not only rejected her but tossed her aside as if she were disposable sexual trash. Although black widow murderess Liane Crosby was never charged, an incestuous relationship with her son, Dennis Pollack, plus a tendency to murder several husbands for profit, painted a picture of sexualized and lethal greed. In "Agony," one of the few double-plotted episodes in the series, the stigmatizing strategy turns on the portrait of an intensely jealous woman. One plot concerns a set of murders committed by a Ted Bundy–like serial killer, and the other focuses on a jealous girlfriend, Michelle Ashton. Michelle enlists her brother, Michael Ashton, in getting rid of Katherine Langston, the estranged wife of her wealthy boyfriend. Although horrific violence links the two plots, the point here is that a jealous woman directed her brother to inflict three days of sexual torture on Katherine Langston.

In sum, female killers on *Law and Order* operated in the domestic sphere, where they commanded the loyalty of relatives and held sway over families riddled with dysfunction. In the criminal justice system, a tendency for men to plead guilty when wives or lovers decided to testify against them explained why prosecutors convicted more men than women. Even so, most female killers were convicted. Powerful women were turned into pawns or exposed as frauds. Self-effacing wives, on the other hand, acquired power and in exceptional cases got away with murder. Sexual trash, sexual revenge, or jealousy were among the stereotypes instrumental in turning good gals into bad ones.

Discussion and Conclusion

By understanding the social construction of female killers, we aimed to shed light on how *Law and Order* integrated women as killers into its programming. On balance, female killers were more numerous than we expected, but masculine assumptions set the terms for constructing them as murderers. Two-thirds of the female murderers met their victims in the context of the family, suggesting that *Law and Order* draws from and reinforces the "illusion of two spheres" (Ferree, 1990). Women belonged in the family, where sexual trauma, dysfunctional relationships, or vengeance drove them to kill. Men, on the other hand, belonged in the more powerful world of work, where murder was the result of competition, greed, or depravity (Humphries, 2002). In imposing a sharp distinction between the two spheres, the picture is at odds with feminist sensibilities and reality, but even so, *Law and Order* did not ignore working women. We have noted episodes such as "Dissonance," which blurs the sharp line between the two spheres, and "Cradle to Grave," which located women in the world of work, although these are exceptions to the rule.

Three-quarters of the cases that *Law and Order* prosecutors processed resulted in convictions. In this way, *Law and Order*'s conviction rate exemplified the moral certainties of the police procedural. Prosecutors convicted women (69%) less often than men (83%). The difference is not a case of prosecutorial leniency toward women. Instead, the finding reflects the prosecutors' uncanny ability to get wives and lovers to testify against their husbands and paramours. The operative term would be female empowerment: Women agree to testify because they see a chance to even the score against abusive, arrogant, or indifferent males. However, there are other grounds on which to interpret the disparity in conviction rates as chivalry. In the *Law and Order* system of justice, privileged women fare better than poor women (Humphries, 2002). A few upper- and middle-class women avoided indictment, used the prosecutor to achieve their own goals, or were acquitted on the merits of their cases. Poor women were routinely convicted. A class-based chivalry explains these observations, as does the show's penchant for episodes that explore the difficulties prosecutors face in holding the rich accountable (Courrier & Green, 1999).

In the case of female killers, masculine assumptions characterized many but not all character transformations. In almost half the cases, female killers started out as winners but prosecutors soon exposed them as losers. The stereotypes used to effect these transformations reveal masculine assumptions about women. A weakness for unscrupulous men is the common element that explains Joyce Pollack's and Maggie Connor's involvement in murder. Both were impressionable women whose romantic longings led them to fall for the deceitful men who wrecked their lives. More victim than victimizer, these women were passive in comparison with the enraged Stephanie Harker, who first appeared as the grieving widow of a wealthy husband but was later exposed by prosecutors as a predator and fraud. In a small number of cases, female killers started out as losers but confrontations with prosecutors empowered them. Their control over family protected them from prosecution or the prosecutor unwittingly strengthened their hold over the family, putting them in a position to challenge male authority.

Female killers may start out as good gals, but screenwriters rely heavily on masculine assumptions about women's sexuality to define bad character. This entails efforts to sexualize motives and/or to paint murders as the work of disturbed or dysfunctional women. In the episode "Venom," Liane Crosby, the killer who came closest to stereotypes about evil women, relied on sexuality to lure men to their deaths and on sexual manipulation to hold her son in check. In the case of Iris Coreman (in the episode "Cradle to Grave"), screenwriters added sexualized details in an apparent effort to feminize a role that was indistinguishable from many male roles. Coreman was successful at her job, she was convicted on a negligent homicide charge, and she had not met the victim. The detail—an affair with her younger business partner—invoked gender–age rules about sexuality and made her the object of derision.

Overall, the social construction of female killers tends to show that *Law and Order*'s integration of violence and women is based on masculine assumptions. The construction is confined within the female world of domesticity. It is linked to a justice system that allows women, provoked by gender injustices, to convict their male partners and that shows leniency to privileged women but not poor ones. It is saturated with masculine stereotypes about helpless, manipulative, deceitful women and sexualized women motivated by incest, jealousy, and sexual revenge. How the masculine construction appeals to a female audience is perplexing, but the show's subtext about female empowerment may provide a partial answer. Alibi witnesses took advantage of the plea-bargaining deals to even the score against spouses and partners. A few female killers beat the odds and either avoided prosecution (Liane Crosby) or used the prosecutor for their own ends (Mrs. Muller).

Law and Order remains a creation of the 1990s, and though it accommodates feminist sensibilities, it draws heavily on masculine assumptions to construct and transform female killers. The mix has helped *Law and Order* fight off competition for viewers from other crime dramas, such as the short-lived *The Division*, a police procedural with an all-female ensemble cast. *Law and Order* has been less successful against forensic shows like *CSI*, where mastery over lab techniques puts men and women on a more equal footing. Cable networks have launched new procedurals with women in leading roles. How police procedurals like *The Closer* and *Saving Grace* will stack up against *Law and Order* may depend on how these newer versions of the police procedural integrate women and women's issues into their programming.

Albonetti, C. (1986). Criminality, prosecutorial screening, and uncertainty: Toward a theory of discretionary decision making in felony case processing. *Criminology, 24,* 623–645.

Belknap, J. (2001). *The invisible woman: Gender, crime, and justice.* Belmont, CA: Wadsworth/Thomas Learning.

Benedict, H. (1992). *Virgin or vamp: How the press covers sex crimes.* New York: Oxford University Press.

Boyle, K. (2005). *Media and violence: Gendering the debates.* London: Sage.

Courrier, K., & Green, S. (1999). *Law and Order: The unofficial companion.* Los Angeles: Renaissance Books.

Daly, K., & Chesney-Lind, M. (1988). Feminism and criminology. *Justice Quarterly, 5,* 479–538.

Dow, B. J. (1996). *Prime-time feminism: Television media cultures and the women's movement since 1970.* Philadelphia: University of Pennsylvania Press.

Escholtz, S., Mallard, M., & Flynn, S. (2004). Images of prime time justice: A content analysis of *NYPD Blue* and *Law & Order. Popular Culture, 10,* 161–180.

Ferree, M. M. (1990). Beyond separate spheres: Feminism and family research. *Journal of Marriage and the Family, 54 (4),* 866–884.

Gerbner, G. (2002). Casting and fate: Women and minorities on television, drama, game shows, and news. In M. Morgan (Ed.), *Against the mainstream: The selected works of George Gerbner* (pp. 365–376). New York: Peter Lang.

Ghali, M., & Chesney-Lind, M. (1986). Gender bias in the criminal justice system: An empirical investigation. *Sociology and Social Research, 70,* 164–171.

Humphries, D. (2002). Gender and diversity in *Law and Order.* Paper presented at the annual meeting of the American Society of Criminology.

Innis, S. A. (2004). Boxing gloves and bustiers: New images of tough women. In S. A. Innis (Ed.), *Action chicks: New images of tough women in popular culture* (pp. 1–17). New York: Palgrave McMillan.

Jones, J. (2003). *Media's daughter: Forming and performing the woman who kills.* Columbus: Ohio State University Press.

Klein, K. (1995). *The woman detective: Gender and crime* (2nd ed.). Urbana: University of Illinois Press.

Lotz, A. D. (2006). *Redesigning women: Television after the network era.* Urbana: University of Illinois Press.

Quinn, L. (2002). The politics of *Law and Order. Journal of American and Comparative Cultures, 25 (1, 2),* 130–133.

Raftner, N. H., & Stanko, E. A. (1982). Introduction. In N. H. Raftner & E. A. Stanko (Eds.), *Judge, lawyer, victim, justice* (pp. 1–28). Stoughton, MA: Northeastern University Press.

Reiman, J. (2001). *The rich get richer, the poor get prison.* Boston: Allyn and Bacon.

Scaggs, J. (2005). *Crime fiction.* London: Routledge.

Stein, J. (2006, July 16). This season, it's law & reorder. *New York Times,* Section 2, pp. 1, 30.

Strachan, A. (2006, November 25). Wolf's women: Strong, smart female characters key to *Law and Order*'s longevity, says creator. *Edmonton Journal* [on-line]. Retrieved December 1, 2006, from http://www.canada.com/Edmonontonjournal/news/culture/story.htm.

Taylor, E. (1989). *Prime time families: Television culture in postwar America*. Berkeley: University of California Press.

Van Wormer, K. S., & Bartollas, C. (2007). *Women and the criminal justice system*. Boston: Pearson.

CHAPTER 3

SCREENING STEREOTYPES
African American Women in Hollywood Films

Frankie Y. Bailey

In his study of white Hollywood and African American culture, Krin Gabbard observes: "At least since 1904, when the filmed version of *Uncle Tom's Cabin* became a great financial success . . . the best place to find out how things get constructed in American culture is a movie house" (2004, p. 8). Following Gabbard's advice, I set out to watch Hollywood films and to consider how they have been used to construct images of black women. Films are an important mechanism that perpetuates stereotypes, some of which, for example the "mammy" stereotype, originated in the era of slavery. The stereotypes themselves have worked to the detriment of black women. The careers of African American actresses have been artificially restricted to stereotypic roles. As professionals, African American women have been evaluated by white expectations about black women. As offenders or victims, black women have been demonized as "ghetto bitches" or "ho's." Black mothers have been blamed for failing to protect their children.

The results of my observations come closer to cultural criticism than to social science research because in this chapter I discuss films and their conventions, stereotypes and their development, career options open to black actresses, shifts in public life that reverberate in film, and newer trends such as color-blind casting. To do this, the chapter is organized into three sections. The first section deals with long-standing stereotypes (mammy, jezebel, and the tragic mulatto), which are discussed in relation to films from the 1930s to 1960s. Stereotypes of black women associated with several film genres from the 1970s to the present organize the discussion in the second section. In the final section, the discussion turns to the careers of African American actresses and the nature and scope of available roles.

Mammy, Tragic Mulatto, and Jezebel
Playing Mammy

In 1940, Hattie McDaniel became the first African American to win an Oscar for Best Supporting Actress, for her portrayal of Mammy, Scarlett O'Hara's servant in *Gone with the Wind* (1939). Butterfly McQueen had a standout role as Prissy, the flighty maid who provided comic relief during scenes of high melodrama. As black actresses, however, neither McDaniel nor McQueen were allowed to take part in the elaborate opening of the film in segregated Atlanta. Asked in an interview about the demeaning role she played, McDaniel quipped, "I'd rather make $700 a week playing a maid than earn 7 dollars a day being a maid" (Iverem, 2001). The choice would have been available to few: out of 2,909 Hollywood actresses in 1930 only 85 were African Americans (Bogle, 2005, p. 108).

In the 1930s and long after, black actresses looking for work had limited options. Some found work in "race films" such as those of legendary black filmmaker Oscar Micheaux, but when it came to mainstream Hollywood movies, African American actresses were relegated to stereotyped roles, usually as servants.[1] However, Bogle (1993) notes, black actresses created highly stylized servants, humanizing these roles and bringing their own unique stamps to the portrayal of domestics. Black maids often spoke their minds to their white masters or employers. They were the source of common sense and wisdom. They were also the trusted confidantes of white characters. Yet, as varied as their screen personae were—from Hattie McDaniel's sassy Mammy to Butterfly McQueen's flighty Prissy or Louise Beaver's sweet meekness in *Imitation of Life*—the roles conformed to what white moviegoers believed about black domestic servants. Louise Beavers, for example, who often lost weight during the stress of filming, "had to be padded to look more like a full-bosomed domestic who was capable of carrying the world on her shoulders" (Bogle, 1993, p. 63).

Even as African Americans began to make progress in their battle for civil rights after World War II, the black domestic in Hollywood films remained a stalwart character. In thoughtful films such as *To Kill a Mockingbird* (1962), the domestic existed in a world where there was some recognition of discrimination and bias. Black characters such as Calpurnia (Estelle Evans), the housekeeper in *To Kill a Mockingbird*, symbolized for a white audience the dignity and virtue of good black people, who were undeserving of the bigotry and violence directed toward them. Yet, when one of their own was put on trial for the rape of a white woman, it was this crisis in the African American community that provided the context for the noble and heroic actions of white attorney Atticus Finch (Gregory Peck). It is his struggle for justice, not theirs.

In addition to servant roles, roles based on mulatto and Jezebel stereotypes completed the narrow range of options offered to African American actresses. A film that incorporates the three roles is *Imitation of Life*, based on the novel by Fannie Hurst. The 1934 version of the movie starred Claudette Colbert as a white widow and mother, Louise Beavers as the African American woman who became her housekeeper and business partner, and Fredi Washington as the housekeeper's daughter. Beavers' character, Delilah Johnson, met Colbert's character, Bea Pullman, when Johnson came to the wrong address in response to an ad for a maid. Pullman could not afford a maid, but Johnson begged to stay, explaining that she needed a position where her child could live with her.

One story line in *Imitation of Life* traced the improving fortunes of Johnson and Pullman. When the two women met, the widowed Pullman had taken over her salesman husband's territory and was struggling to make a living. Then one morning Johnson served her pancakes for breakfast. The pancakes were made from a secret family recipe, and Johnson happily gave the secret to her employer, who opened a diner and then expanded into selling boxed pancake mix, with her maid's smiling face on the box. When Pullman offered Johnson a share of the profits, she assumed that Johnson would want a house of her own. Johnson's response defined the essence of the mammy stereotype. Johnson begged not to be sent away. She wanted to stay and go on serving "Miss Bea" and her daughter. In the 1959 version of the same film, a conversation between the servant (Juanita Moore) and her employer (Lana Turner) confronted the facade of the relationship. Turner revealed that her character knew nothing about the "off-duty" activities of the woman with whom she had lived intimately for at least a decade.

The second story line in *Imitation of Life* concerned the black servant's daughter. In the 1934 version, Johnson's daughter, Peola, was fair skinned, a tragic mulatto, who was "neither white nor black" (see Berzon, 1978). Peola was played by Fredi Washington, a black actress, but in the 1959 remake, the daughter, now called Sarah Jane, had a romantic life. The Hollywood Production Code, dating back to the 1930s, forbade "miscegenation," or interracial sexual encounters, in films (see Williams, 2001). Consequently, Sarah Jane had to be played by a white actress, and Susan Kohner took the role. Sarah Jane's love interest, a young white man, had believed she was white. When he heard rumors that Sarah Jane had a black mother—and was therefore black herself—he rejected her brutally. In the film's one violent scene, set to jazzy music, he knocked Sarah Jane to the ground, leaving her there, bruised and battered.

Sarah Jane ran away, hoping that, by putting distance between her mother and herself, she might yet pass as white. By the time her mother tracked her down for a last good-bye, Sarah Jane had found work as a chorus girl, a scantily clad figure who fit easily into a Jezebel stereotype. She cruelly rejected her long-suffering mother, who subsequently died from a "broken heart." Sarah Jane lived—contrary to the nineteenth-century motif of the "tragic mulatto" who dies—but she suffered, knowing that she was the cause of her mother's heartbreak and decline.

In the last decades of the twentieth century, African American domestics in Hollywood films continued to suffer with dignity even as they displayed extraordinary caring and concern for their white employers. Set in 1950s Los Angeles and loosely based on a true story, *Corrina, Corrina* (1994) cast Whoopi Goldberg as a college music major. Having been rejected in all of her efforts to find work in her field, she applied for a position as a nanny to the child of a widowed white ad executive. In real life, the African American woman who rescued the lost child depicted in the film was elderly; Corrina (Goldberg) was young enough to become not only a surrogate mother to the child but a G-rated romantic partner for the father. In her role as Corrina, Goldberg became the "magic Negro," another standard black character who provides selfless aid to troubled whites (Kempley, 2003). Magic Negro motifs are found in other Goldberg films, including *Sister Act* (1992), the hit movie in which Goldberg played a lounge singer who was on the lam from her mobster lover, hid out in a nunnery, and shaped up the church choir. Magical nurturing is overt in *Clara's Heart* (1988). In this film, Goldberg played Clara, a Jamaican woman who met a vacationing white family when they stayed at an island hotel where she worked as a maid. The mother hired Clara and brought her back with the family to the States, where in the midst of impending divorce, Clara cared for the American woman's son, becoming his confidante and his defender. *Clara's Heart* brought Clara's personal life to the screen. However, her care of the young boy extended into her off-duty hours, as he spent weekends at her Boston apartment and became a "cultural tourist" in her Jamaican community. In spite of the revelation of Clara's secret—how her own son had died—she remained steadfast in her loyalty to the American boy. A climatic breach in their relationship occurred when Clara refused to move with him to California. He lashed out in anger, using a racial slur, but when he returned to Boston to visit his father and sought her out to apologize, Clara forgave him.

From early Hollywood to the present, characterizations of mammy as a wise, caring, and loyal servant to whites have endured, providing work for black actresses in film and television. The first nationally broadcast weekly TV show to feature an African American in a leading role was *Beulah*, a radio hit that made the transition to television on ABC from 1950 to 1953. The show about a middle-age black domestic for a white family starred first Ethel Waters, then Hattie McDaniel, and finally Louise Beavers. In the 1980s, the black domestic reappeared when Broadway star Nell Carter played Nell Harper, the housekeeper for a widowed white police officer and his children in the TV sitcom *Gimme a Break!* (1981–1987). The critically acclaimed 1991–1993 PBS drama *I'll Fly Away* featured Lilly (Regina Taylor), a young black mother who kept house for a widowed district attorney and his son. As bell hooks (1992; 1995, p. 113) notes, because this drama was set in the South during the Civil Rights era, Lilly's situation did little to discomfort viewers. The slender, unmammy-like Lilly labored under the burden of centuries of preconceived notions about black women as servants, which may have spoken louder than her gentle narration about her growing sense of self.

The mythical image of mammy continues to affect perceptions of African American women even in nonservant roles (e.g., as teachers, nurses, or law enforcement officers). It is rare to see an important role in which an African American actress exercises authority, commands respect, and asserts herself with confidence. It is also difficult to avoid conclusions that an African American actress who shows caring behavior toward other characters—particularly if the black woman is middle-aged and buxom—is a *mammy* in the minds of viewers. This, one suspects, is also the case in real life.

Challenging Jezebel

Nominated for an Oscar for her performance in *Carmen Jones* (1954), Dorothy Dandridge was a black glamour queen. In the HBO biography about her life, Dandridge (played by Halle Berry) dangled her toes in the hotel swimming pool in defiance of a policy that barred African Americans from the guest facilities. The hotel management drained the pool rather than deal with Dandridge's gesture against Jim Crow practices.[2] Barred by race from roles considered suitable for Ava Gardner or Marilyn Monroe, Dandridge's breakout role came when she was cast as the "femme fatale" in *Carmen Jones* (1954), the film version of the all-black musical inspired by the opera *Carmen*.

Set in wartime America, *Carmen Jones* opens in a World War II munitions plant in the South where black women were employed making parachutes. Carmen, one of the parachute makers, flirted with a military police officer named Joe (Harry Belafonte), fought with another woman on the factory floor, and was arrested on sabotage charges. Joe's sergeant ordered him to transport Carmen to jail, forcing him to leave his visiting sweetheart behind. When Joe took custody of Carmen, she seduced him and then fled, leaving him to face a court martial, conviction, and a sentence to the stockade. Carmen tried to remain faithful while Joe served out his sentence. They were briefly reunited when Joe got out of prison, but a fight and manslaughter charges forced the couple to flee to the city. There Carmen took up with a prizefighter, betraying Joe again. This time, Joe killed her.

Carmen brought acclaim to Dorothy Dandridge. But at the pinnacle of her career, the Hollywood film industry had no other starring roles that might have showcased Dandridge's considerable talent. Racial mores and the Hollywood Production Code relegated other African American actresses to set pieces that the studio edited out when the film was shown in Southern theaters. Singer Lena Horne, who had acted in all-black films such as *Green Pastures*, often appeared in mainstream Hollywood films as a singer whose performance was a backdrop to the narrative. Performers such as Horne and pianist Hazel Wilson were allowed to be glamorous in this restricted context (see Bogle, 2005). Dandridge, however, was not suited for such cameo appearances or as an exotic performer in the style of Josephine Baker (who had left the United States for Paris). Nor did she fit into mainstream Hollywood roles as mammy or as Jezebel in the style of the mulatto mistress of a Northern senator in *The Birth of a Nation* (1915), the film prototype for future oversexed, treacherous black women. In *Carmen Jones*, Dandridge had projected both beauty and vulnerability. In this, her characterization was more complex than many of the roles that African American women would play in later Hollywood films.

A more sophisticated framework than Hollywood's might have accommodated Dandridge, but Hollywood has found it particularly difficult to deal with black female sexuality. With some creative exceptions,[3] the film industry has tended to rely on rigid distinctions between good (asexual) and bad (sexual) women, often contrasting the two within a single film. In *New Jack City* (1991), a film directed by African American Mario Van Peebles, the good Selina (Michael Michele)[4] was an upper-class woman who fell for Nino (Wesley Snipes), a drug kingpin from "the hood." Selina stood in stark contrast to her rival, bad Uniqua, a seductive black woman played by Tracy Camilla Johns. Nino soon tired of good Selina, attracted by the more sexually demonstrative Uniqua, with whom his best friend and partner was romantically involved. In a scene that defined "bad girl," Uniqua shed her skirt and danced in her blouse and panties on a table top as her lover and Nino watched. The performance was pure Jezebel. As the object of desire, Uniqua literally offered herself up to the male gaze. As the model of treachery, she came between two friends and her betrayal triggered her former lover's spiral into drug addiction. In the final confrontation between Nino and his partner, however, it was clear that the two men were more concerned about their broken bond than with the seductive Uniqua.

As long as the film industry makes rigid moral distinctions between good and bad, it will continue to equate the sexuality of black females with the bad side of what it means to be a woman. This not only stifles artistic expression, but stereotypes of oversexed black women spill over, affecting public perceptions about the sexual availability of African American women as they go about daily life. One does not see roles in which African American actresses both assert their sexuality and possess goodness. Instead, black actresses who take on sexualized roles are viewed as morally compromised, a Jezebel in the minds of filmgoers and perhaps the general public as well.

Ineffectual Mothers, Action Heroes, and Tough Gals
Ineffectual Mothers

In popular culture, the 1990s marked the appearance of a new generation of urban crime films that debuted with *Boys N the Hood* (1991). The genre focused on young black men in coming-of-age narratives. Other films reinvigorated the gangster movie with black actors, as in *New Jack City* (1991) and *Sugar Hill* (1994). Denzin (2002, p. 113) notes that although these films offer criticism of the social structures that create violent ghettos, they present "negative images of welfare mothers and violent gang members . . . [and] also reproduce longstanding conservative criticism of the Black family: namely the inability of Black mothers to raise Black sons who do not become infected with the pathologies of the hood." The female roles created by these films recalled images of the black matriarch, the single mother and head of household on whom the 1965 Moynihan Report had placed so much blame for the "dysfunctions" of the black family.

Boyz N the Hood, directed by John Singleton, a young African American filmmaker, won critical praise and has been used for classroom teaching for its positive portrayal of the father in the rearing of his son. However, from the vantage point of black women, there is reason for criticism. Jones (1996, p. 45) observes that the film "engages in the constant, hostile objectification of women through the standard bitch/ho device." There are no positive images of mothers. Reva (Angela Basset) is the mother of Tre, the young and rebellious protagonist whose life is detailed in the film. Reva turned Tre over to his father and seemed to privilege career goals over her commitment to motherhood. Brenda (Tyral Ferrell), the mother of "Doughboy" and Ricky, the two boys who lived across the street from Tre and his father, Furious, favored her handsome and athletic son, Ricky (Morris Chestnut), over his half-brother, Doughboy (Ice Cube), who she verbally berated and abused. When Ricky was killed in a drive-by shooting, Brenda was understandably grief-stricken, but she again turned on the other son, hitting him and blaming him for his brother's death. A drug-addicted third mother had neglected her child, who was rescued and returned by Tre. Tre then ordered her to keep her child out of the street. Moral superiority is an attitude that Tre shared with his father, who was amused by neighbor Brenda's interest in him. Even Tre's good girl girlfriend, Brandi (Nia Long), had no visible mother, although the film suggests that her parents were present in her life because she was shown at home doing homework. She told Tre that she did not want to have sex and that she wanted to go to college. But when he came to her, angry enough to weep after being harassed by an African American police officer, Brandi responded to his need for her. Both Tre and Brandi escaped from the violence of South Central Los Angeles. We learn at the end of the film that the two went south to Atlanta to attend college.

Unlike the coming-of-age narrative of *Boyz N the Hood*, *Sugar Hill* tells the story of two brothers who were drug kingpins in Harlem. The angst-stricken Roemello (Wesley Snipes) wanted to get out of the business, whereas his brother, Raynathan (Michael Wright), wanted to work out a better deal with the Italian mobsters. Here, too, the mothers fell short. The addicted mother of Roemello and Raynathan overdosed in front of them in the flashback scene that opened the film. The striking element of this scene was that the death occurred in a well-kept apartment. The boys were dressed in white shirts and bowties as if for Sunday morning church. The mother was in her slip about to dress, but first she had her oldest son help her to shoot up. She fell from her chair and died in convulsions.

Later, the audience learns that it had been the boys' father who had gotten their mother hooked on drugs and had continued to supply her. The father had worked as a money collector for the local Italian mafioso until he was caught stealing and was brutally beaten. Now, he was a shambling old man to whom Roemello, the sensitive one, was still devoted. Roemello's sensitivity led him to fall hard for Melissa (Theresa Randle), a good girl he had met in a club. Although this young woman was middle class and had a mother present, her mother (Leslie Uggams) was rigid and harsh, which drove the daughter into rebellion. After he was shot by his brother, Roemello escaped with Melissa to the peace of the South. In the final scene, Roemello, confined to a wheelchair, sits on a terrace by the water playing with his son. Melissa, presumably now his wife, looks on with a loving expression on her face.

The helplessness of mothers in the face of violence and the toll it can take on their lives—particularly when male-initiated—was addressed in *Clockers* (1995), directed by Spike Lee, an African American filmmaker. In this film, the mother (Regina Taylor) was caring and a law-abiding citizen. She called on an African American male police officer who lived in her apartment complex to help her when her young son started to spend time with Strike (Mekhi Phifer), the drug-dealing young protagonist of the film. Feisty and assertive, she scolded the young men who sat out in the courtyard of the project waiting to make drug deals. Yet, in spite of her best efforts, her son ended up shooting a would-be hit man with a gun he had stolen from Strike. He was saved by the African American police officer, who explained to the white male detective (Harvey Keitel) that the boy was a "good kid." The white detective walked the boy through his statement to make sure that it met the requirements for self-defense. In the final scene, the boy's mother makes an attempt to connect with her son as he plays with the railroad set left by Strike, who had boarded a real train out of town. The mother asks, "You know I love you, right?" The son replies, "Yes, mama." But the audience should have doubts that motherly love is sufficient to ensure the boy's survival in such a violent environment. They have seen that Strike's mother, another good woman, has not been able to protect her two sons.

Female Action Heroes

The "tough gal" roles that opened up for African American actresses in the 1990s have unexpectedly complex social and political roots. Expanded opportunities for African American women in the film industry would have seemed to follow naturally from earlier gains (e.g., civil rights), but postwar changes took urban crime films in another direction. Films with African American protagonists such as *Nothing but a Man* (1964), *Sounder* (1972), and *The Learning Tree* (1969) respectively offered thoughtful examinations of blue-collar manhood, sharecropper families, and a young boy's coming of age in a Southern town. Such films may have reflected the post–World War II acceleration of black demands for democracy and justice and the gains won with *Brown v. Board of Education* (1955), boycotts, and sit-ins for the end of de facto discrimination in public accommodations. Films that would eventually yield new roles for African American actresses, however, had their roots in the urban riots of the 1960s, which marked a shift in public focus from white crime to black urban crime (Barlow, 1998). "Blaxploitation films," "produced and marketed by white Americans" (Leitch, 2002, p. 42; see also Massood, 2003, pp. 81–84) and aimed at black urban audiences, captured aspects of black urban inner city culture. In films like *Shaft* (1971) and *Superfly* (1972), African

American male protagonists vanquished corrupt white cops, mobsters, or racists. On occasion, African American women played significant roles in these films.

Two such actresses, Pam Grier and Tamara Dobson, emerged in urban crime films as "action heroines" who emulated their male counterparts in their kick-ass, take-no-prisoners style. This was new territory, as few women of any race or ethnic background had been cast in such roles. Grier, who would have a long and colorful career, gained fame—and the adoration of director Quentin Tarantino and countless other men and boys—as the "queen of the blaxploitation film." Early in her career, she was a B-movie star in women-behind-bars prison films such as *The Big Bird Cage* (1972) and *Black Mama, White Mama* (1973). She reemerged in the 1990s in a starring role in an A-level movie, *Jackie Brown* (1997), but in the 1960s and 1970s, the talent for which she was most admired was her ability to project her sexuality. In *Coffy* (1973) and *Foxy Brown* (1974), two of her best-known films, Grier had scenes in which she appeared with breasts heaving or bared. She was sexually abused and assaulted to such an extent that some critics asserted that her films bordered on soft-core pornography.

As an action heroine, however, Grier's characters were triumphant. As a vigilante in *Coffy*, she targeted the drug dealers she blamed for her sister's overdose. In *Foxy Brown*, she avenged the murder of her lover, an undercover law enforcement agent: She had the white male villain castrated and delivered his genitals in a pickle jar to his white female lover and partner in crime. Whereas Grier played women who sought justice outside the system, Tamara Dobson, who played government agent Cleo Jones, fought drug traffickers and criminals and won from within the system. In *Cleopatra Jones* (1973), Jones returned to her old neighborhood to help a friend and former lover fight the drug problem that threatened the community. The white villain Cleo Jones battled in this film was played by Shelley Winters; in the sequel, *Cleopatra Jones and the Casino of Gold* (1975), Cleo's antagonist was once again a white female. In the latter film, Cleo flew to Hong Kong to find two male African American agents who had disappeared during an undercover drug operation. Cleo fights the Dragon Queen (Stella Stevens) and succeeds in freeing the undercover agents. At 6′2″, former model Dobson was a dominating presence on the screen and brought style to her films. With sweeping full-length coats, wide hats, and striking makeup, Dobson's "foxy lady "character captured urban culture almost to the point of parody. Even though the Cleopatra Jones films lacked the spectacular special effects of the James Bond films, the character of Cleo Jones embodied the sophistication of a Bond-like agent. She drove a sports car, arrived by helicopter to the salutes of men in uniform, and strolled confidently through Hong Kong streets.

Although Grier and Dobson were both groundbreaking female action heroines, Bogle (1993) argues, with some justification, that the roles were also bizarre caricatures that combined Jezebel and mammy stereotypes. He writes, "Each was a high-flung male fantasy . . . as ready and anxious for sex and mayhem as any man." But, at the same time, like the older mammies, they represented "Woman as Protector, Nurturer, Communal Mother Surrogate" (Bogle, 1993, p. 251).

Tough Gals

In the 1980s and 1990s, urban crime films like *48 Hours* (1982), *Another 48 Hours* (1990), and the *Lethal Weapon* series (1987, 1989, 1992, and 1998) featured African American actors as sidekicks or in partnership with white actors. Some urban crime films also cast women in tough gal roles. In *New Jack City*, Keisha (Vanessa A. Williams) was a female hoodlum who was every bit as violent as the men in her gang. She carried out an assassination, killing a rival drug dealer. As the dealer walked up to the car in which her male associates sat, she walked up behind him, put the gun to his head, and blew out his brains. In the car, one of her male associates laughed and offered his approval: "That's the way to do it." Keisha's own death was no less dramatic. Standing on the steps of a church, she fired away at the rival gangsters who had disrupted a wedding with a drive-by attempt on her boss's life until she was killed in a hail of gunfire. Jones describes Keisha as a "'bitch' . . . elevated to the status of psychopathic murderer," which she notes "hardly seems an achievement" (Jones, 1996, p. 43).

That tough gals die is a convention also seen in *Set It Off* (1996), the tale of four inner city women who turn to bank robbery to secure their futures. The four were childhood friends, each of whom had suffered injustice. Frankie (Vivica A. Fox) was dismissed as a teller in a bank after a man she knew held up the bank and she failed to immediately push the alarm. "Stony" (Jada Pickett Smith), who sold her body to an older suitor to help pay her brother's college tuition, was embittered when the police killed him by mistake. The child of the third woman, T. T. (Kimberly Elise), had been taken away by child protective services. T. T. had brought the toddler to her building maintenance job, where he drank from a bottle of cleaning fluid. Last, Cleo (Queen Latifah) was a lesbian who was into guns and cars and believed that the four of them could pull off a bank robbery. *Set It Off* is in the Hollywood tradition of caper films, in which the audience is encouraged to identify with the bank robbers as good bad guys [5] and urged to hold society responsible for the injustices done to them. In this narrative, the four women's troubles are easily attributed to the effects of institutionalized racism.

Even though films in the 1990s offered new roles for black actresses, characterizations of African American women as ineffectual mothers, caricatured action heroines, and lethal criminals were a mixed blessing. Although such films had commercial value as entertainment, they oversimplified difficult problems such as the violent circumstances that African American families face in raising children. Women in these films were held accountable for the problems in their sons' lives, but they were also portrayed as helpless. No one listened to the mothers when the decisions that mattered were made. Although roles as action heroines and lethal criminals provided black actresses with a chance to exercise authority and to confidently assert themselves in the world, such figures wove fantasy solutions to the injustices of crime and violence.

Contemporary African American Stars and Color-Blind Casting
Whoopi Goldberg and Restricted Roles

Whoopi Goldberg has challenged many of the restrictions imposed on African American actresses in Hollywood, but even a star of her stature often has been limited to stereotypical roles. One exception is her role as Celie in the 1984 film *The Color Purple*, which also established her reputation as an actress whose range went beyond comedy. Based on the novel by African American author Alice Walker and directed by white director Steven Spielberg, those involved in the film's production were accused of "bashing" black males. True, African American women in the film were engaged in an ongoing state of conflict with African American men, who were depicted as selfish, brutal, violent, and domineering, but the film also released black actresses from the strictures of Hollywood stereotypes to play a set of spirited, self-assertive, and fully drawn black women.

Set in 1910–1940 rural Georgia, *The Color Purple* is about Celie (Whoopi Goldberg), a young black girl who was raped and impregnated by her stepfather and gave birth to his two children. When her mother died, she was given in marriage to "Mister" (Danny Glover), a neighbor in need of a mother for his children. Celie suffered great loss: Mister put Celie's sister out of the house after she refused his advances. Her children were also taken away from her. Cowed by her husband and lacking in self-esteem, Celie observed the feisty Sofia (Oprah Winfrey), who had married Mister's son. When asked, she advised Sofia's husband to beat her. Befriended by Shug, the blues singer Mister worshipped, Celia began to take her first awkward steps toward personhood and eventual escape from her oppressive marriage. In contrast, Sofia slapped a wealthy white woman who wanted her to work as a domestic, and as a consequence she was beaten, arrested, convicted, and sent to prison. On her return, the woman responsible for her imprisonment forced Sofia to work for her as a domestic.

Other roles offered to Whoopi Goldberg were far more restrictive than that of Celie had been. In *Fatal Beauty* (1987), Goldberg played detective Rita Rizzoli, who explained that she became a cop to save children. As a teenage mother and a drug addict, she had neglected her baby, who died after eating from her drug stash. So now she was on a mission to save other people's children, much as Goldberg had done in *Clara's Heart* and *Corrina, Corrina*. In *Fatal Beauty*, that mission involved disrupting an upper-class pool party to confront the white mother who was responsible for the drugs that had killed teenage partygoers. As the unruly black character who disrupted an elite social gathering, Rizzoli required restraint and rescue (see Entman & Rojecki, 2000) by the white male lead in the film. Reflecting the prevailing Hollywood images of female police officers, Goldberg's detective Rizzoli also was the target of male detectives who taunted and teased her, challenging her skills as a detective (see Hale, 1998). Even though her character held her own, Rizzoli's race was an inescapable, though never mentioned, subtext to her contentious exchanges with her colleagues. Rizzoli's Italian surname provided the basis for a flirtatious come-on by Mike Marshak (Sam Elliott), the white bodyguard of the drug dealer she was trying to put in prison. According to Hale (1998), in film conventions of the 1980s, the female police officer was often aided by a male civilian, who then became her love interest. Marshak, who had been ordered to kill Rizzoli, switched sides and saved her when she was about to be shot. He was wounded himself, and when Rizzoli returned to him after her shootout with the bad guys, she assured him that she would be waiting for him when he got out of prison. However, as Bogle (1993) observes, it was race that shaped the narrative, to the extent that a bedroom scene between Marshak and Rizzoli was edited out of the film after preview audiences on the West Coast reacted negatively to the encounter.[6]

Even in *Ghost*, the film that earned her the 1991 Oscar for Best Supporting Actress, Whoopi Goldberg played a magical, nurturing medium, Oda Mae Brown. As Sterritt (1990) observes, the treatment of Oda Mae as a character ranged from caricature to servant for Sam, a murdered white stockbroker. Oda Mae was able to see and hear Sam (Patrick Swayze), and she gave in to Sam's requests to convey his warnings and instructions to Molly (Demi Moore), the lover Sam wanted to protect. The connection between Oda Mae and Sam took physical form in the last scene, when Sam's spirit entered Oda Mae's body for one last embrace with Molly, his lover. This is as close to a love scene as Goldberg has gotten. As for caricature, it is difficult to take the role of a medium seriously; its magic and servitude to ghosts come too close to stereotypes of black servants. To Goldberg's credit, she did not play it straight; rather, she exploited the stereotype's comic potential, rarely missing an opportunity to parody magic, trances, séances, and people on the "other side" with unexpected characters.

Halle Berry and the Careers of Black Actresses

The progress made with regard to film images of African American women has been mixed (Carter, 2003; Davis, 2003). Halle Berry broke significant racial barriers by becoming the first African American actress to win an Oscar for Best Actress for *Monster's Ball* (2001), and by playing an interracial sex scene in a major motion picture. The sex scene stirred controversy or raised questions about Berry's character, Leticia: Was she a complex and troubled woman adeptly played by Berry? Or did Leticia simply epitomize racial stereotypes of black women? As the wife of a prisoner on death row, Leticia unwittingly became involved with the corrections officer, Hank (Billy Bob Thorton), who had carried out the execution. She was poor and uneducated. She was a bad mother: She drank and was both psychologically and physically abusive to her overweight son, who was killed by a hit-and-run driver as the two walked along the road in the rain. It was Hank who had stopped to help her, and later the grieving and drunken Leticia begged Hank to make love to her so that she would "feel good." Both characters were needy, in search of human comfort. Hank himself was a bad father. His son had committed suicide after a bitter exchange between the two of them. Hank's own father was a racist, but Hank and Leticia found comfort in each other. The deeper emotional context of the film and of Leticia's character no doubt fueled Berry's award-winning performance. But, stripped of emotion, one might see in Leticia's actions an oversexed black woman who seduced a white man, seeking her own pleasure rather than responding with true grief to her son's death.

Halle Berry's post-Oscar career has depended on the availability of suitable roles. Cast as a "Bond girl," Jinx, in *Die Another Day* (2002), Berry played an espionage agent, the American co-partner to James Bond and his love interest. As a Bond girl, she followed a career path forged by other African American actresses[7] who benefited from "color-blind casting" (that is, when race or ethnic background are not considerations in casting actors). Berry's next project, the psychological thriller *Gothikica* (2003), was not a critical or commercial success, nor was *Cat Woman* (2004) (Longino, 2004), although she broke new ground in both films.[8] Berry's decline might be attributed to the "Oscar curse" that has befallen other award-winning actresses. The question most debated is whether Berry's award, a landmark for African American actresses, represents a true breakthrough. Will Hollywood offer more black actresses more work? Will color-blind casting open up new roles for African American actresses?

Even before Berry's Oscar, independent filmmakers had begun to create new and better roles for black actresses. Pam Grier, formerly the queen of blaxploitation films, made a much heralded comeback in a part crafted for her by director Quentin Tarantino. In *Jackie Brown* (1997), Grier's role recalled *Foxy Brown* and the movies that made her famous, but the role was anything but action heroine. As Jackie Brown, Grier played a down-on-her-luck flight attendant who pulled off one scam against an arms dealer (Samuel L. Jackson) for whom she moved drugs and another against the feds who wanted to use her in a sting to trap him. Aided by a white bail bondsman (Robert Forster) who fell for her, Grier got the money, set up the arms dealer to be killed by the feds, and left town to the tune of music from the 1970s. Less triumph than simple survival, her departure signaled the end to a stunning performance. In the aftermath of *Jackie Brown*, Grier has been visible in supporting roles such as the lesbian commander of a space patrol in *Red Planet* (2000), which raises questions about Hollywood's inattention to actresses of Grier's caliber.

Angela Bassett, another African American actress, achieved success in *Waiting to Exhale*, in which her character sets her adulterous husband's possessions on fire, and in *How Stella Got Her Groove Back*, in which her character found love on a Jamaican vacation. In contrast to these "chick flicks," Bassett took a supporting role as Lornette Mason in the science-fiction movie *Strange Days* (1995). Allying with Lenny Nero (Ralph Fiennes), her best friend and a seedy, down-on-his-luck dealer in virtual reality, the two battle the bad guys. What makes the film noteworthy is that: Bassett's "hard body" tough gal persona matched the demands of the Mason role. The film also featured a bitter-sweet love story between the two. Disillusioned by another woman, Nero acknowledged and apparently returned Mason's feelings for him in the film's final scene.

Arguably, Bassett's role in *Strange Days* is another example of color-blind casting. However, one of the issues raised by such casting is the extent to which African American women are stripped of ethnicity. This is less a question with Bassett, who with braids and style always seems to convey her cultural roots. But when Vanessa L. Williams played Lee Cullen opposite Arnold Schwarzenegger's U.S. Marshall John Kruger in *Eraser* (1996), the only reference to race was oblique. It did not help that the first character killed was an African American: He was a disposable extra brought in to heighten the level of danger and stress the heroism of Kruger's rescue of Williams. The audience learned little about Cullen's background: Her former lover was black and she had a white female friend, a reporter who was killed. The audience knew even less about Marshall Kruger, who seemed to live only for his work. But Williams's identity as a woman of color might well have been an issue for audience members familiar with action movies that place women in jeopardy. After the climatic struggle to defeat his corrupt boss (James Caan), Kruger watches as the boss was taken to an ambulance. Cullen called to Kruger, ran toward him as the music soared and signaled romance. They embraced. They pulled apart and gazed into each other's eyes—and embraced again. What happened to the kiss?

Is the audience to assume that Kruger did not kiss Cullen because he was a lone wolf who cared for his charges but did not allow himself to become emotionally or physically involved with them? Or should we interpret the absence of a kiss as the rejection of romance between a white hero and a black heroine? And what does it mean in the final scene when, after faking their deaths, the two of them drive off together? The ambiguity might well have been there even if the heroine had been white. It may even be the case that Schwarzenegger is a poor romantic lead, despite his leading role in *True Lies* (1994). But the fact of Williams's ethnicity—which goes without comment in the plot—is visible to the audience and therefore is an issue that complicates the reading of the narrative.

Two British actresses, Thandie Newton and Naomi Harris, are part of a younger generation of black women with experience in color-blind casting in films. Newton[9] was cast opposite Tom Cruise in the action film *Mission: Impossible 2* (2000), but the color of her skin was less important than the fact that the two stars looked beautiful together. Newton played Nyah Nordoff-Hall, a cat burglar, recruited for the *Mission Impossible* team less for her skills than for a prior relationship with the villain Ethan Hunt (Tom Cruise) had been assigned to stop. The villain planned to unleash a deadly virus and then extort money for the vaccine. To stop him, Hunt placed Nordoff-Hall, with whom he was becoming romantically involved, in harm's way, a plot line that echoed that in the Alfred Hitchcock film *Notorious* (1946). Just as the agent played by Cary Grant forced Ingrid Bergman's character to spy on a group of Nazis and to sleep with their leader, Hunt called on Nordoff-Hall to spy on and to sleep with this villain. In both films, the heroine's sacrifices served to heighten the romantic tension. Grant saved Bergman from death by poison at the hands of Nazis. Nordoff-Hall risked death, too. She had infected herself with the virus in order to prevent the villain from getting his hands on the only vial. The clock ticked as Hunt, in nonstop, over-the-top action, rescued her before she killed herself to avoid being used to infect the populace. As in *Notorious*, the villain was defeated, and the lovers were united. Hunt negotiated to have Nordoff-Hunt's criminal record expunged before the two of them went off together to "get lost."

The only point about which critics disagreed was the amount of on-screen sexual energy between the two.

In the doomsday film *28 Days Later* (2002), British actress Naomi Harris established herself as an action heroine. On the surface, the casting in this film is indeed color-blind. There were no references to race in character development or in the background story. The fact that Harris is black was not relevant to the plot. In the context of a terrible epidemic, the pharmacist played by Harris had hardened herself in order to survive the death around her. She did not hesitate to kill those infected because killing them was the only way to stay alive. In short, the role as she played it embodied the image of a tough gal. As in the Angela Bassett film *Strange Days*, the toughness of character and the ability to fight seemed to blend the subgenre of hard-bodied women and the strength of black women. The role Harris played involved something more. When the father of the young girl that Harris and the male lead, Cillian Murphy, were traveling with was killed by a soldier because he had become infected, Harris became the girl's protector. Even though the protector role can be played by actresses from any background, when a black actress is cast as protector, there are unavoidable reflections on the black woman as nurturer, a latter-day version of the mammy stereotype.

Other roles such as the one Vivica A. Fox played in Quentin Tarantino's *Kill Bill: Volume 2* (2004) have provided African American actresses with an opportunity to play other atypical characters. In this film, "the bride" (Uma Thurman) survived a wedding party massacre and tracked down the women, her former comrades, who had carried it out. When the bride found the character played by Fox, she had become a suburban housewife and mother, married to a physician. But apparently the transition from assassin to an upper-middle-class lifestyle and soccer mom conformity had not affected her ghetto-girl accent—or maybe she just reverted to a "home girl" when talking with someone who knew her past. The matter of Fox's accent in this film speaks to (no pun intended) the issue of color-blind casting in which the African American actresses (e.g., Vanessa A. Williams and Thandie Newton) have no ethnic markers other than skin color. Notably, Fox does not "sound white"; hence, any interpretation of her profanity is complicated by the fact that her "black" accent provokes stereotypes that the use of profanity by white actresses in this film would not (see Entman & Rojecki, 2000, on profanity as a racial guise). Perhaps the audience assumed that Fox's character was intelligent enough to have learned to act and sound middle class (read white). When she was with the suburban soccer moms (as was suggested in her conversation with her daughter), she might have engaged in the type of real-life language shifts that African Americans sometimes engage in to diminish differences between themselves and whites with whom they are interacting. At the same time, the impending and violent confrontation between Fox and Thurman may have added another layer of racial stereotyping to the film. In a scene that had Fox's character offer coffee to and talk about honor with Thurman's character, Fox went for her gun, a clear act of treachery. Is this because Fox's character was an assassin, a killer, and this was how she had been trained to survive? Or, does the fact that Fox is black and that her scripted actions were treacherous complicate audience interpretation and reaction? Moreover, why is Fox the first to die? Is *Kill Bill: Volume 2* a "slasher" movie in which black characters are killed first?

But, on the other hand, African American characters who are good women may be prone to victimization. In *Eraser* (1996), Vanessa L. Williams played Dr. Lee Cullen, a defense contractor employee who found herself in jeopardy after blowing the whistle on a criminal conspiracy within her company to sell super weapons to foreign buyers. In *Hoodlum* (1997), Williams was the good woman who fell for a black gangster, Bumpy Johnson, who seduced her. That Vanessa L. Williams is typecast as a well-educated middle-class woman is in keeping with her real-life persona. However, typecasting also raises an interesting issue about light-skinned African American women with "white" features. Are they stereotyped as good women who are more ladylike than their darker sisters? The dark-skinned Angela Bassett played a well-to-do, well-educated woman in *Waiting to Exhale* (1995). When she set her ex-husband's car on fire in her driveway, a white male firefighter berated her, telling her she had crossed a line of what was acceptable in her upper-class neighborhood. Her response to her husband's deception and desertion for his white lover was not unrealistic, but clearly she appeared to the firefighter as an evil-tempered, destructive black woman. Would this exchange have been as believable had Vanessa L. Williams played the role?

The careers of contemporary African American actresses illustrate the ambiguities and uncertainties of stardom. On the one hand, major stars like Whoopi Goldberg, who have worked consistently in Hollywood films, are still stuck in roles dictated by racial stereotypes. On the other hand, the difficulties of younger stars like Halle Berry may reflect the career uncertainties that color-blind casting may alleviate, perhaps without sacrificing ethnicity.

Conclusion

As a cultural critique, this chapter has demonstrated the persistence of older stereotypes and the negativity of new images in selected films, and it went on to address some of the issues associated with the potential expansion of film roles for African American actresses. Others have noted, and this chapter concurs, that the progress made with regard to film images of African American women has been mixed (see Carter, 2003; Davis, 2003).

Mammy roles offered film work to and critical acclaim for African American actresses such as Hattie McDaniel. For Dorothy Dandridge, poised to become a significant presence but denied star roles, the limited job options that servant and siren roles entailed signaled the end of the road. And yet, mammy and Jezebel stereotypes lived on, their commercial value affirmed in films that featured black domestic servants, treacherous black femmes fatales, or sexually aggressive but nurturing black female action heroines.

One film that stands out for its portrayal of African American women as spirited and assertive in their response to injustices and violence is the 1984 film *The Color Purple*. Criticism that it characterized African American men as abusive and violent has to be weighed against images of women in urban crime films of the 1980s and 1990s. The critique of ghetto violence as generated by social structures raised the level of discussion about urban crime, but films like *Boyz N the Hood* and *Sugar Hill* also tended to objectify women as selfish, ineffectual, or as drug-addicted mothers who were powerless to protect their sons from the violence of the streets. *New Jack City* and *Set It Off* offered portraits of African American women as assertive, exercising authority, but also as psychopathic murderers or self-destructive bank robbers.

Color-blind casting has opened up new kinds of roles for African American actresses, but these options are complex and equivocal. Color-blind casting opened up a post-Oscar career path for superstar Halle

Berry as a Bond girl. It also enabled Pam Grier to restore her career as a film star by taking the lead role in *Jackie Brown*. But color-blind casting, as I have argued, also raises some difficult, albeit intriguing, issues. Do color-blind roles strip African American actresses of their ethnic identity? For actresses with obvious ethnic markers, color-blind casting may be problematic. The markers are there for audiences to read. Where markers are missing or where skin color alone conveys an actress's ethnicity, it is difficult, as I have suggested, for audiences to interpret such things as status, romance, or even treachery.

NOTES

1. One of the earliest and most compelling images of mammy can be found in D. W. Griffith's epic *The Birth of a Nation* (1915). The film cast only one black actress, Madame Sulk-Te-Wan, who played several roles. The role of mammy, that spirited defender of her white Southern family, was played by a white actress in "blackface," ensuring that the characterization met white expectations.

2. This account is based on a pivotal scene in *Introducing Dorothy Dandridge*, the film biography of her life. Dandridge was one of the most beautiful and glamorous actresses of the 1940s and 1950s. A contemporary of Ava Gardner and Marilyn Monroe, Dandridge was originally marketed as a glamour queen, but as an African American actress, she was barred from the roles in which Gardner and Monroe were cast (Rippy, 2001, pp. 178–211).

3. In her discussion of the selling of black female sexuality as a cultural commodity, bell hooks (1992, p. 68) offers this observation about a role played by singer/actress Tina Turner: "Playing the role of Aunty Entity in the film *Mad Max: Beyond Thunderdome*, released in 1985, Turner's character evokes two racist, sexist stereotypes, that of the 'Black mammy' turned power hungry and the sexual savage who uses her body to seduce and conquer men." Aunty Entity demonstrates the inventiveness of an industry that has historically tended toward rigid gender categorizations of white women as "good women."

4. Michael Michele, who played Selina in *New Jack City* (1991), later played Dr. Cleo Finch in the popular NBC medical show *ER*.

5. The film also reflects the feminization of the subgenre seen in other films, such as *Bound* (1996), which features two white females—an ex-con and a mobster's mistress—who become lovers, kill the abusive mobster, and escape with the mob's money.

6. Although cast as the female lead in both *Fatal Beauty* and *Jumpin' Jack Flash* (1987), in which she plays a computer programmer who aids a British spy, Goldberg is rendered "asexual" (Bogle, 2005, p. 298).

7. Gloria Hendry had a prominent role in *Live and Let Die* (1973), which included a

sexual encounter with James Bond (Roger Moore). In *A View to a Kill* (1985), Grace Jones gave a memorable performance as the sexually aggressive May Day, who also had a bedroom scene with Bond (Roger Moore). In it, her villainous lover nodded his approval, encouraging her to use her sexuality to further his aims, as she went into Bond's room.

8. Although black actress/singer Eartha Kitt was among those to portray Cat Woman on the *Batman* television show, Berry (who has also portrayed the mutant comic book heroine Storm in *X-Men*) was the first actress of any color to portray the character in a film.

9. Thandie Newton appeared on U.S. television as the Ugandan–British love interest of Dr. John Carter on *ER*.

REFERENCES

Barlow, M. H. (1998). Race and the problem of crime in 'Time' and 'Newsweek' cover stories, 1946 to 1995. *Social Justice, 25,* 149–184.

Berzon, J. R. (1978). *Neither white nor black: The mulatto character in American fiction.* New York: New York University Press.

Bogle, D. (1993 [1973]). *Toms, coons, mulattoes, mammies, and bucks: An interpretative history of blacks in American films.* New York: Continuum.

———. (2005). *Bright boulevards, bold dreams: The story of black Hollywood.* New York: One World.

Carter, K. (2003, March 19). Berry widens window for black actresses. *USA Today,* Life, p. 1D. Retrieved February 19, 2005, from Lexis-Nexis academic database.

Davis, K. (2003, March). After Halle's Oscar: Why black actresses still can't get any respect in Hollywood. *Ebony,* Entertainment, p. 38. Retrieved February 19, 2005, from Lexis-Nexis academic database.

Denzin, N. K. (2002). *Reading race: Hollywood and the cinema of racial violence.* Thousand Oaks, CA: Sage.

Entman, R. M., & Rojecki, A. (2000). *The black image in the white mind: Media and race in America.* Chicago: University of Chicago Press.

Gabbard, K. (2004). *Black magic: White Hollywood and African American culture.* New Brunswick, NJ: Rutgers University Press.

Hale, D. (1998). Keeping women in their place: An analysis of policewomen in videos, 1972–1996. In F. Bailey & D. Hale (Eds.), *Popular culture, crime and justice* (pp. 159–179). Belmont, CA: West/Wadsworth.

hooks, b. (1992). *Black looks: Race and representation.* Cambridge: South End Press.

———. (1995). *Killing rage: Ending racism.* New York: Henry Holt.

Iverem, E. (2001, September 10). What we don't know about Mammy. Retrieved May 29, 2005, from http://www.seeingblack.com/x091001/hattie.shtml.

Jones, J. (1996). The new ghetto aesthetic. In V. T. Berry and C. L. Manning-Miller

(Eds.), *Mediated messages and African American culture* (pp. 40–51). Thousand Oaks, CA: Sage.

Kempley, R. (2003, June 7). Too too divine; movies' 'magic Negro' saves the day, but at the cost of his soul. *Washington Post*, Style, p. C-1. Retrieved May 31, 2005, from Lexis-Nexis academic database.

Leitch, T. (2002). *Crime films*. New York: Cambridge University Press.

Longino, B. (2004, July 23). Hissss—this kitty's a dog. *Atlanta Journal-Constitution*, Movies & More, p. 1C. Retrieved February 22, 2005, from Lexis-Nexis academic database.

Massood, P. J. (2003). *Black city cinema: African American experiences in film*. Philadelphia: Temple University Press.

Rippy, M. H. (2001). Comedy, tragedy, desire: Female sexuality and blackness in the iconography of Dorothy Dandridge. In D. Bernadi (Ed.), *Classic Hollywood: Classic whiteness* (pp. 178–211). Minneapolis: University of Minnesota Press.

Sterritt, D. (1990, August 22). 'Ghost' provides a second-rate showcase for a first-rate talent: Whoopi Goldberg. *Christian Science Monitor*, The Arts, p. 11. Retrieved February 22, 2005, from Lexis-Nexis academic database.

Williams, L. (2001). *Playing the race card: Melodramas of black and white from Uncle Tom to O. J. Simpson*. Princeton, NJ: Princeton University Press.

CHAPTER 4

WHAT ABOUT WOMEN?

*The Representation of Women in Media,
Crime, and Violence Textbooks*

Zoann K. Snyder

Police once ignored domestic violence, refusing to answer calls for service that entailed altercations between intimates. Domestic violence is now, however, regarded as a public health problem of sufficient magnitude to justify federal legislation (see Tjaden & Thoennes, 2000, p. 4). Much credit goes to various groups that made up the women's movement and were instrumental in publicizing violence against women and prodding legislative bodies to act. Efforts culminated in the Violence Against Women Act of 1994 and its 2000 revision that stimulated research and funded interventions (P. L. 103-322; P. L. 106-386).[1] Violence against women is "classified as a major public health and criminal justice concern in the United States" (Tjaden & Thoennes, 2000, p. 4).[2] When policy shifts so dramatically, one also expects the public to recognize emerging definitions of domestic violence. Feminist definitions attribute violence against women to the subordination of women within patriarchy and press for social changes that equalize gender inequities. Public health, on the other hand, seeks to reduce risk factors, build up resiliency among victims, and thereby reduce the incidence of intimate violence. Both represent an astounding shift from prior tendencies to blame victims and avoid the broader subject of male violence, but one can ask whether these shifts are widely recognized or whether they are confined to smaller circles of domestic violence experts.

On the one hand, research has shown very little movement in the public perception of domestic violence over the last several decades (see Kozol, 1995; Tierney, 1982). The stability of perceptions makes some sense in light of findings that the media tend to underrepresent or marginalize women while ignoring the social context in which men offend against women (Carll, 2003; Kasinsky, 1998; Katz & White, 1993; McDonald,

1999). "Mainstream" as opposed to "specialty" textbooks tend to over-look women in their discussions of violence or relegate gender issues to a chapter or two (Baro & Eigenberg, 1993; Lomire, 1992; Lowe & Sher-rard, 1999; Wright, 1987, 1990, 1994, 1995).

On the other hand, there are reasons to expect that emerging defini-tions will reach a wider audience. Feminist scholarship has increased, rais-ing the profile of women in all areas of criminology. A leading feminist text is predicated on making visible the "invisible woman" (Belknap, 2001). Special issue monographs have served to make women a more cen-tral part of criminology (Enos, 2001; Humphries, 1999; O'Brien, 2001; Owen, 1998). Other feminist contributions place violence in the context of patriarchy and conceptualize media representations as reinforcing sex-ist patterns of domination (Chesney-Lind & Pasko, 2004; Miller, 1998; Pollock, 1999; Price & Sokoloff, 2004).

The present study, like others, looks at textbooks to determine whether and to what extent they reflect emerging definitions of domestic violence. Textbooks are established indicators of shifting trends. The textbook in-dustry is sensitive to teacher demands for new policy, new problems, and feminist-, gender-, or diversity-based materials, but some areas, as I re-cently learned, have a more limited selection of texts than others do. The mainstream text I selected for a Media and Crime course covered media representations of crime, but its discussion of women and offenses against women was less than ideal. Much to their credit, my students noticed and asked, "What about women?" My efforts in "adding" women had not com-pensated for the omission because the subject matter—violence against women—required a deeper integration of media analysis and feminist theory than the text provided. The incident prompted me to take a hard look at textbooks; it also explains the focus in this study on texts appro-priate to courses on media and crime.

Methods

My research is designed as a cross-sectional, exploratory inquiry and is based on a sample of academic books about the media and crime or vio-lence. The decision to look at media texts was prompted by questions from students, and it gives the study a unique focus. Media texts typically address representations of the perpetrators, witnesses, and victims of crime or violence as well as the officials who deal with these crimes. All things being equal, we would expect representations to include women and crimes or violence affecting women. Consequently, the investigation is guided by three questions. First, to what extent are women and women's issues represented in media texts that address violence against women? Second, are women or women's issues a central or marginal focus in those texts? Lastly, do the texts discuss violence against women as a social problem or do they reduce it to a set of individual troubles?

Representation, marginalization versus centralization, and the level of explanation are concepts central to questions posed by the study. "Representation" refers to the degree to which academic texts draw attention to female victims of crime, rape or sexed crimes, sex, gender, domestic violence, and battered women. The more attention or space devoted to women or women's issues, the greater the representation and the more a text approximates feminist ideals of centralizing women. Representation is measured in two ways. First, the percentage of titles or subtitles that refer to women or women's issues provides the basic measure. A second measure is based on the percentage of a text's pages that mention women or women's issues. It may overrepresent women and women's issues in a given text. Grouped intervals are broad (1%–20% of the text), and I have not distinguished between single and multiple references, although references tended to cluster at the low end of the intervals.

Although a text's title or subtitle may refer to women's issues (female victims of crime, rape or sexed crimes, sex, gender, domestic violence, and battered women), the number of chapters related to women in a text is the basis for measuring "centralization" and "marginalization." How many texts lack chapters related to women or women's issues? How many texts, for example, contain from four to six chapters related to women's issues? The more chapters devoted to these issues, the higher the profile for women and the closer the text is to feminist research goals. In addition, I make a global assessment of the relationship between women's issues and textbooks. Based on my judgment, I determined for each text whether women were marginal to a more central idea or whether women's issues were the text's central focus.

Finally, I evaluate the "level of explanation" in each text, determining whether it treated violence against women as a "social problem," whether it treated those problems as "personal troubles," or whether it addressed women in other contexts (see Mills, 1959). By using the search terms "social problems" or "structural analysis," I seek in the texts the sort of causal connections that go beyond individual responsibility and that may sustain social action. Personal issues, on the other hand, may require individuals to solve problems, but those problems typically require personal solutions, not social action. "Other contexts" serves as a residual category.

When complex judgments are required of coders, a single-coder design, such as I used in this study, is subject to potential bias. Global judgments about marginality, however, are easily compared with quantitative estimates to establish the direction of findings. Most sociologists are well equipped to distinguish between impersonal forces that shape reality and troubles that befall individuals. In reviewing media texts, one is confronted with an unusual juxtaposition of problems and troubles. Characteristically, media scholars, who use a sociological perspective, work to expose misrepresentation, distortion, and bias, although not all scholars are as ready to identify larger purposes such as the role of misplaced ideas in perpetuating beliefs that justify inequality. Hence, in this study, we are led to expect gradations in the level of explanation, ranging from the identification of distortion to the broader social control functions of ideas.

The sample was selected in a two-step process. The first step estimated the population of relevant texts. Using "media and violence" and "media and crime" as search terms, I searched Bowker's *Books in Print* and other on-line sources. A review of library stacks and databases yielded 140 titles. Within these, I identified 26 titles and subtitles that referred to women or women's issues (i.e., female victims of crime, rape or sexed crimes, sex, gender, domestic violence, and battered women). In the second step, I selected a purposive sample of 21 texts from the longer list of 140 titles. I wanted to include mainstream and female-oriented texts, but I excluded texts about female offenders in order to concentrate on violence against women.[3] I also wanted to include a variety of media outlets, so the sample includes texts that address entertainment (seven), news (ten), or a blend of news and entertainment (four). In addition, I wanted to look at texts published over a reasonable time span. Half the texts in the sample were published in the 1990s, the other half after 2000. The sample also includes an equal mix of authored monographs and edited collections. Women represent one-third of the authors or editors. The titles that make up the sample are marked with an asterisk in the list of references.

The data analysis focuses on the 21 texts and relies on descriptive statistics, primarily relative frequency distributions, to characterize the content of textbooks. It begins with the question of representation and presents findings based on textbook titles and subtitles. The analysis then moves on to consider marginality and centrality: how many textbooks lack chapters that refer to women or women's issues. Included in this section is a discussion of material taken from texts that marginalize and centralize women's issues. The final part of the analysis concerns the level of explanation (i.e., whether texts treat women's issues as problems or personal troubles). Again, examples drawn from texts detail the meanings of a social problem explanation.

Findings
Representation and Women's Issues

In Table 4.1, one finds frequencies for mainstream and female-oriented texts. Of the 134 titles, over 80% fall into the mainstream category, whereas less than one-fifth of the titles or subtitles refer to female victims of crime (i.e., rape or sexed crimes, sex, gender, domestic violence, or battered women). Underrepresentation is more pronounced among "media and crime" titles than among "media and violence" titles. The same pattern of findings is discernible in the purposive sample of 21 titles that were examined in this study.

Table 4.2 shows that in over half (61%) of the 21 textbooks, references to women are limited to no more than 20% of the pages. In only 3 out of

TABLE 4.1

Mainstream and Female-Oriented Texts by Search Terms, N = 134

| | SEARCH TERMS | | | | | |
| | Media & Crime | | Media & Violence | | Totals | |
Texts	*N*	%	*N*	%	*N*	%
Mainstream	57	90	53	75	110	82
Women's issues	6	10	18	25	24	18
Total texts	63	100	71	100	134	100

Sources: Compiled from Bowwker's *Books in Print*, on-line searches, University of Delaware Library, and personal collection.

TABLE 4.2

Space Allocated to Women's Issues in Sampled Texts, N = *21*

Space Allocated to Women's Issues	SAMPLED TEXTS		
	N	%	Cumul. %
0	1		4
1%–20%	12	57	61
21%–40%	4		81
41%–60%	1		86
61%–80%	0		86
81%–100%	3		100
Total texts	21	100	

21 texts are references to women or women's issues cited on 80% or more of the pages.

Marginal versus Central Status of Women's Issues

Tables 4.3 and 4.4 demonstrate that textbooks also tend to marginalize women's issues. Data reported in Table 4.3 indicate that 43% of the texts lack chapter references to women and 33% of the texts fall into the interval in which references are limited to one to three chapters.

Table 4.4 provides a global assessment of whether chapters marginalize or centralize women's issues. Women's references are central in 64% of the chapters and marginal in 36% of them.

Chapters that marginalize women's issues tend to focus on topics that engage women while attending to other concerns. Mothers Against Drunk Driving (MADD), for instance, addresses women insofar as their efforts result in the construction of drunk driving as a social problem (Reinarman, 1998). Sparks (2002), who is concerned with the effects of pornography—a topic that many believe affects women directly—mentions that women are featured in such films but does not go beyond observing stereotypes.

In contrast, texts that centralize women or women's issues[4] do so by placing women at the center of inquiry. They tend to challenge gender and other stereotypes that shape perceptions of crime and violence. Young (1998) finds a disturbing tendency in popular films to blur the dis-

TABLE 4.3

Chapters about Women's Issues in Sampled Texts,
N = *21*

	SAMPLED TEXTS	
Number of Chapters	*N*	%
0	9	43
1–3	7	33
4–6	3	
7–10	2	
Total texts	21	100

Note: All the chapters were devoted to women or women's issues in three of the texts: one text having six chapters, one having eight chapters, and one having nine chapters.

tinction between rape and seduction. The resulting ambiguity serves to perpetuate rape myths ("she wanted it") and to normalize such violence (Young, 1998). Carmody (1998) exposes the misrepresentations conveyed by television's reality crime shows. Such shows tend to concentrate on stranger attacks, heighten fears about unlikely attacks, and downplay the common risks of violence against women by male intimates, friends, and family members. Like Carmody (1998), Dobash, Schlesinger, Dobash, and Weaver (1998) find that reality crime shows emphasize female victimization and that they attribute responsibility for injury to the victim, not the male perpetrator. Elder (1998, p. 8) discusses sexed and

TABLE 4.4

Centrality of Women's Issues to Chapters, N = 22

	CHAPTERS	
Presentation	*N*	%
Marginal	8	36[a]
Central	14	64
Total chapters	22	100

[a] Chapters that marginalized women's issues were written by male authors.

racialized stereotypes. Whereas the media may demean victims who are white and women, they disregard women of color, especially when their victimization conforms to stereotypes about race and violence. If men of color are believed to be violent, then women who are involved with them are perceived as understanding the risk and as bearing some responsibility for injuries (Elder, 1998). Likewise, Grimwade (1998) exposes media stereotypes that devalue women who suffer from HIV/AIDS, that hold them responsible for the infections, and that ignore women's needs for greater access to affordable birth control, health care, and HIV/AIDS education.

In addition to challenging stereotypes, chapters that centralize women are attuned to less obvious features of the way violence against women is represented. For example, De Beer and Ross (2001) point to tensions between two kinds of South African media accounts. On the one hand, some accounts report the magnitude of the problem of violence against women. On the other, media accounts give their male attackers equal or greater space to tell "their" side of the story, thereby silencing women. De Beer and Ross (2001) note that even with greater efforts to increase the news coverage of violence against women, most crimes are ignored by the press or are sensationalized to such an extent as to call into question whether the victim or the offender was responsible for the attack. Others, such as Wykes (2001), focus on taken-for-granted assumptions about masculinity, patriarchy, and attributions for violence, noting that women are especially vulnerable to media attacks when they can be characterized as acting outside of traditional women's roles or following feminist values. In these cases, the media appear to excuse male violence, reinforcing male domination, according to Wykes (2001).

Language choices are a matter of importance in chapters that centralize women and women's issues (see Howe, 1998a, 1998b; Mead, 1998). Howe (1998a) draws attention to media terms such as "human problem" or "domestic" and "family" violence, all of which neutralize male responsibility for violent attacks on intimates (Howe, pp. 30, 37). Howe (1998b) also introduces the term "sexed crimes" to make the point that men's violence against women is not about sexuality (sex crimes); rather, she argues that it is about male power and domination expressed violently against women (e.g., domestic assault, sexual harassment, rape, and sexual assault). In an insightful analysis of a sexual harassment case, Mead (1998) exposes the power of language to neutralize male aggression. What started out as a sexual harassment charge filed by two college students against an administrator ended with an apology and resignation, prompting the headline "Uni-sex case apology." The language (uni-sex) neutralized the administrator's responsibility, but a subsequent book reversed attributions of responsibility (Mead, 1998, p. 77). In it, "indecent assault" replaced sexual harassment, and it blamed "young feminists" for having caused the administrator to lose the job (Mead, 1998, p. 78).

Level of Analysis and Women's Issues

Table 4.5 provides an answer for the last research question: Is violence against women presented as a social problem or as an individual trouble in the texts sampled? In 64% of the texts, a social problems approach is taken. The antithesis to a social problems approach is not, however, individual troubles. None of the texts could be described as individualizing problems of violence against women. Instead, Table 4.5 indicates that "other context" serves as an alternative to a social problems approach in 36% of the texts. For example, Sharrett (1999), who focuses on violence in popular films, discusses female roles but concentrates on male violence, a context identified as "other." (See "Gender Violence and Male Madness" in Sharrett, 1999.) In a number of action films (*Natural Born Killers, Raging Bull, Rambo*, and *Braveheart*), contributors to Sharrett's collection address females as secondary objects dominated by leading male actors playing strong and violent characters (Caputi, 1999; Gallagher, 1999; Luhr, 1999; Tomasulo, 1999).

TABLE 4.5

Presentation of Women's Issues in Chapters,
N = 22

Presentation	CHAPTERS	
	N	%
Social problems	14	64
Individual troubles	0	
Other	8	36
Total chapters	22	100

social problems approach identified media deficien-
ns of violence. Chapters in McCormick's edited vol-
s how media accounts largely fail to recognize male vi-
omen as a "social problem." Similarly, Fraser (1995)
media, which underreport rape, nonetheless perpetuate
cluding victim blaming and denial of offender responsibil-
it,   s" are represented as deviant, whereas the men who solicit
them are resented as normal, according to Derrick's work on the news
(1995). Finally, Forsyth-Smith (1995) attributes the tendency to underreport female victimization to sensationalism. Although these chapters
point to distortions in media coverage, they stop short of connecting gender bias to larger ideological functions.

Meyers (1997), who interviewed reporters about the stories they write,
makes a comprehensive case that media constructions of violence against
women reinforce a wide array of ideologies. First, they embody the kinds
of individualistic ideologies that preclude action. Meyers distinguishes
between "survivors" and "victims" and demonstrates that the media place
survivors in the role of "victim," a diminished status with limited, individualized solutions: leaving bad relationships and making use of shelters
and counseling facilities. Second, media constructions leave unchal-
lenged misogyny or the patriarchal ideas (such as victim blaming) that
justify violence against women while also misdirecting attention to unusually violent or otherwise sensational crime. Third, they omit problems
of inequality, ignoring the enduring and powerful subordinating effects
of race (nonwhite) and class (nonaffluent) in addition to those of gender
(women) in violent exchanges with members of the dominant group.

Like Meyers (1997), Berns concentrates on ideology, even though her
findings are limited to a critique of the "individual frame of responsibility" that permeates articles about domestic violence found in many
women's magazines (Berns, 2004, pp. 57–58). Female victims are ap-
plauded by magazine writers for their individual efforts to leave abusive
relationships, but the men who abuse and the larger social problem of violence are not addressed. In an attempt to test an individualistic grain,
Cuklanz (2000) tracked the impact of the feminist movement on the entertainment industry's penchant for stories with a personal appeal. She
noted a shift from stranger to acquaintance rape in television programs
aired from 1976 to 1990 (Cuklanz, 2000, p. 154) but concluded that the

programming individualized rape incidents and made rape victims secondary to heroic male professionals who rescue women and fight injustice.

To sum up, academic texts reviewed for this study underrepresent female-oriented issues such as female victims of crime, rape or sexed crimes, sex, gender, domestic violence, or battered women. Underrepresentation is more characteristic of "media and crime" texts than "media and violence" texts. In addition, texts tended to marginalize women and women's issues: Over a third of the texts (43%) lacked chapters that addressed women's issues at all, and another third (33%) addressed women's issues in just a few chapters. And yet, a surprisingly high percentage of texts centralized women's issues, challenging gender stereotypes and their consequences, exposing media emphases and omissions, and drawing attention to the reality-altering consequences of language choice. In addition, texts tended to frame the issues related to women as social problems, ranging from media deficiencies to comprehensive analysis of multiple systems of domination.

Discussion and Conclusion

The underrepresentation and marginalization of women by academic texts is surprising because media studies, which are typically attuned to identifying frameworks, were expected to emphasize gender and its distortions in the examination of crime and violence. Indeed, in constructing the sample, I exploited gendered terms to identify female-oriented texts, although I doubt whether I fully realized the invisible way in which gender privileged "mainstream" titles, that is, how much they reflected a system of male domination. As Lucal (1996) suggests regarding race, representatives of the dominant culture (e.g., whites) are viewed as the norm, thereby rendering invisible the privilege attached to being a member of the dominant culture. If white is the norm, then "race" refers to being nonwhite. Likewise, if male is the norm, then "sex and gender" refer to being a woman. Mainstream texts are the norm, the absence of male designators being a sign of privilege: They have general utility, report core research, and are academic. Female-oriented texts represent deviations from the norm, the visibility of the designators being a sign of deviation. These texts are vulnerable to criticism as too specialized for general use, as covering peripheral issues, or as ideological. That the production of knowledge is gendered should make us pause in the face of persistent findings that women's issues are underrepresented and marginalized in the textbooks adopted by instructors and intended for college students (see Baro & Eigenberg, 1993; Lomire, 1992; Low & Sherrard, 1999; Wright, 1987, 1990, 1994, 1995).

The lack of change in textbook conceptions of domestic violence is usefully placed in the context of public perceptions and social problems.[5] A "personal issue" becomes a "social problem" when it affects a large number of people, when it threatens cherished values, and when it requires an institutional response, according to C. Wright Mills (1959). The transition between the two is a matter of social construction: Blumer reminds us that, "Social problems are fundamentally products of a process of collective definition instead of existing independently as a set of objective social arrangements with an intrinsic makeup" (Blumer, 1971, p. 298). The transition between the two is political: Spector and Kitsuse suggest that social problems result from "the activities of groups making assertions of grievances and claims to organizations, agencies, and institutions about some putative conditions" (Spector & Kitsuse, 1973, p. 146). The success of such collective efforts, however, is an empirical question. Tierney's (1982) account of the battered women's movement and Kozol's (1995) discussion of political conservatism shed light on why a problem may engage the public without effecting enduring change.

In the battered women's movement, established feminist groups and activists formed networks to provide services for battered women (Tierney, 1982). In the process, they became seasoned leaders who helped coordinate activities within and among an expanding number of groups. Attracted by activities of the movement—some of which had entertainment value—the media aided the movement's drive for resources, introduced a "new" social problem, and helped solidify support for social change (Tierney, 1982, pp. 213–214). The movement developed shelters and intervention programs, opting for a service model in which responsibility for accessing services shifted to the individual victim of male violence. C. Wright Mills's (1959, p. 130) observation about causation is prescient. He writes that social problems must "open up for inquiry the causal connections between *milieus* and social structure." Without an understanding of causal connections linking the plight of women who are battered to the impersonal forces that encourage battering, the public falls back on individualistic explanations that blame women for male aggression. Feminism might have provided the conceptual link between battered victims and patriarchal structures except for the rise of cultural conservatism. Since the 1980s, cultural conservatives have succeeded in defining feminism as a significant threat to domesticity, according to Kozol's (1995) survey of film and television portrayals of domestic violence. Hence a broader analysis of domestic violence fell victim to a popular narrative in which feminists threaten the autonomy of the family by inviting government intrusion and by supporting equal rights in the workplace, reproductive rights, and rights for gays and lesbians (Kozol, 1995).

The absence of significant change in public perceptions about battering thus reflects the persistence of individualistic modes of thought and the continuing sway of cultural conservatism. In this light, my last finding—that media textbooks surveyed adopt a social problems approach to domestic violence—requires explanation. Social scientists are trained to relate a collection of troubles to larger social problems, but qualitative results from this study should make clear that not all social problems are conceived in the same manner. Differences in conceptualization may be related to the gender of the author or editor, although this is a suggestive observation rather than a finding. Males authored or edited six of the seven texts that treated women in a context labeled "other" (e.g., women, as in Mothers Against Drunk Driving, were incidental to the violence, or rape and sexual assault were treated in the same vein as armed robbery or homicide). Women, and men working with women, are responsible for the treatment of domestic violence as a gendered social problem. Why does the task of answering these questions continue to fall to women? C. Wright Mills (1959) points to the importance of values and power in understanding threatening ideas. Calls for the return to traditional family values by right-leaning politicians are predicated on perceived threats. When activated by fears about abortion or government intrusion, the base responds by protecting conservative elites, who have controlled the White House, the U.S. Congress, and the Supreme Court of the United States for much of the last decade. Efforts to define family or to identify other values that would protect women against male violence are ignored or denigrated, and rarely do they coalesce enough to alter the terms of debate, stem the backlash, or encourage the recognition of emerging gendered definitions of violence against women.

Rather than retreat into sullen silence, the challenge of researchers and academics is twofold. College and university teachers, who have the opportunity to engage students, have to bring critical and feminist dialogue into the classroom, and perhaps this study will aid in identifying those sources that challenge male violence against women. Second, there is an immediate need for research and cultural criticism of the conservative culture that silently and not so silently acquiesces to male violence against women. Critical research is crucial in generating alternative accounts for why male violence against women occurs and how it can be changed. In the best of all worlds, this inquiry will be addressed by both female and male researchers in an attempt to increase knowledge, raise awareness, and initiate change aimed at ending violence against women. Until then, I expect that women will have to shoulder most of the burden of keeping the issue of violence against women in the public eye. It is time again to make the personal political and to remove the protection of privacy from male violence.

NOTES

1. Title IV of the Violent Crime Control and Law Enforcement Act of 1994 (P. L. 103-322).
2. The National Violence Against Women Survey was a joint endeavor of the National Institute of Justice and the Centers for Disease Control and Prevention. The survey was administered between November 1995 and May 1996 (Tjaden & Thoennes, 2000).
3. It is important to note, however, that many female offenders are themselves survivors of male violence. Greenfeld and Snell (1999) report that nearly 60% of incarcerated women experienced physical or sexual abuse in the past. Although the impact of male violence against women is a significant consequence of the larger social problem, I chose to keep to the immediate textual depiction of male violence against women for my research.
4. Because a subcategory of chapters are only indirectly related to violence, I have limited the discussion of Bailey, Pollock, and Schroeder (1998), who deal with female attorneys, and Hale (1998), who addresses female police officers. Bailey, Pollock, and Schroeder (1998) find that female attorneys are presented as professionals who may be conflicted about men but assume traditional feminine roles. Conversely, women who compete with male attorneys are portrayed as unfeminine, aggressive, or obsessed with a case. Hale (1998) found that female police officers were portrayed in traditional caring, nurturing roles or as conflicted about sexual attraction and/or sexual relationships with male colleagues. Women who played stronger characters were "kept in their place by either injury or romantic involvement" (Hale, 1998, p. 175).

5. Although I have not mapped out the history of rape as a social problem, the feminist movement in support of rape law reform and consciousness raising encountered a similar period of media attention and then a period of disinterest or disregard for women who had survived being raped (see Caringella-MacDonald, 1998; Rose, 1977).

REFERENCES

Note: Titles that make up the sample are marked with an asterisk in the reference list.

*Althiede, D. L. (2002). *Creating fear: News and the construction of crisis*. New York: Aldine de Gruyter.

*Bailey, F. Y., & Hale, D. (Eds.). (1998). *Popular culture, crime and justice*. Belmont, CA: West/Wadsworth.

Bailey, F. Y., Pollock, J. M., & Schroeder, S. (1998). The best defense: Images of female attorneys in popular films. In F. Y. Bailey & D. Hale (Eds.), *Popular culture, crime and justice* (pp. 180–195). Belmont, CA: West/Wadsworth.

*Barak, G. (Ed.) (1994). *Media, process, and the social construction of crime: Studies in newsmaking criminology*. New York: Garland.

*Barker, M., & Petley, J. (Eds.). (2001). *Ill effects: The media/violence debate*. London: Routledge.

Baro, A., & Eigenberg, H. (1993). Images of gender: A content analysis of photographs in introductory criminology and criminal justice textbooks. *Women and Criminal Justice, 51*, 3–35.

Belknap, J. (2001). *The invisible woman: Gender, crime, and justice* (2nd ed.). Belmont, CA: Wadsworth/Thompson Learning.

*Berns, N. (2004). *Framing the victim: Domestic violence, media, and social problems*. Hawthorne, NY: Aldine de Gruyter.

Blumer, H. (1971). Social problems as collective behavior. *Social Problems, 18*, 298–306.

*Brown, S. (2003). *Crime and law in media culture*. Buckingham: Open University Press.

Caputi, J. (1999). Small ceremonies: Ritual in Forrest Gump, Natural Born Killers, Seven and Follow Me Home. In C. Sharrett (Ed.), *Mythologies of violence in postmodern media* (pp. 147–174). Detroit: Wayne State University Press.

Caringella-MacDonald, S. (1998). The relative visibility of rape cases in national popular magazines. *Violence Against Women, 4*, 62–80.

Carll, E. K. (2003). News portrayal of violence and women: Implications for public policy. *American Behavioral Scientist, 46*, 1601–1610.

Carmody, D. C. (1998). Mixed messages: Images of domestic violence on "reality" television. In M. Fishman and G. Cavender (Eds.), *Entertaining crime: Television reality programs* (pp. 159–174). New York: Aldine de Gruyter.

*Chermak, S. M. (1995). *Victims in the news: Crime and the American news media*. Boulder, CO: Westview Press.

Chesney-Lind, M., & Pasko, L. (2004). *The female offender: Girls, women and crime* (2nd ed.). Thousand Oaks, CA: Sage.

*Cote, W., & Simpson, R. (Eds.). (2000). *Covering violence: A guide to ethical reporting about victims and trauma.* New York: Columbia University Press.

*Cuklanz, L. M. (2000). *Rape on prime time: Television, masculinity, and sexual violence.* Philadelphia: University of Pennsylvania Press.

De Beer, A. S., & Ross, K. (2001). Women, media, and violence in the new South Africa: Disciplining the mind (the body is irrelevant). In Y. Kamalipour & K. R. Rampal (Eds.), *Media, sex, violence, and drugs in the global village* (pp. 167–199). Lanham, MD: Rowman and Littlefield.

Derrick, A. (1995). Women who work as prostitutes: The sex trade and trading in labels. In C. McCormick (Ed.), *Constructing danger: The mis/representation of crime in the news* (pp. 36–55). Halifax: Fernwood.

Dobash, R. E., Schlesinger, P., Dobash, R., & Weaver, C. K. (1998). *Crimewatch UK*: Women's interpretations of televised violence. In M. Fishman & G. Cavender (Eds.), *Entertaining crime: Television reality programs* (pp. 37–58). New York: Aldine de Gruyter.

Elder, C. (1998). Racialising reports of men's violence against women in print media. In A. Howe (Ed.), *Sexed crime in the news* (pp. 12–28). Sydney: Federation Press.

Enos, S. (2001). *Mothering from the inside: Parenting in a women's prison.* Albany: State University of New York Press.

*Fishman, M., & Cavender, G. (Eds.). (1998). *Entertaining crime: Television reality programs.* New York: Aldine de Gruyter.

Forsyth-Smith, D. (1995). Domestic terrorism: The news as an incomplete record of violence against women. In C. McCormick (Ed.), *Constructing danger: The mis/representation of crime in the news* (pp. 56–73). Halifax: Fernwood.

Fraser, S. (1995). A string of stranger sexual assaults: The construction of an orthodox account of rape. In C. McCormick (Ed.), *Constructing danger: The mis/representation of crime in the news* (pp.16–35). Halifax: Fernwood.

Gallagher, M. (1999). I married Rambo: Spectacle and melodrama in the Hollywood action film. In C. Sharrett (Ed.), *Mythologies of violence in postmodern media* (pp. 199–225). Detroit: Wayne State University Press.

Greenfeld, L. A., & Snell, T. L. (1999). *Women offenders.* Washington, DC: Bureau of Justice Statistics, Department of Justice.

Grimwade, C. (1998). Reckless sex: The discursive containment of gender, sexuality and HIV/AIDS. In A. Howe (Ed.), *Sexed crime in the news* (pp. 56–76). Sydney: Federation Press.

Hale, D. (1998). Keeping women in their place: An analysis of policewomen in videos, 1972–1996. In F. Y. Bailey & D. Hale (Eds.), *Popular culture, crime and justice* (pp. 159–179). Belmont, CA: West/Wadsworth.

Howe, A. (1998a). Notes from a 'war' zone: Reporting domestic/family/home/epidemic (men's) violence. In A. Howe (Ed.), *Sexed crime in the news* (pp. 29–55). Sydney: Federation Press.

*————. (Ed.) (1998b). *Sexed crime in the news.* Sydney: Federation Press.

Humphries, D. (1999). *Crack mothers: Pregnancy, drugs, and the media.* Columbus: Ohio State University Press.

*Kamalipour, Y. R., & Rampal, K. R. (Eds.). (2001). *Media, sex, violence, and drugs in the global village.* Lanham, MD: Rowman and Littlefield.

Kasinsky, R. G. (1998). Tailhook and the construction of sexual harassment in the media: "Rowdy Navy boys" and women who made a difference. *Violence Against Women, 4,* 81–99.

Katz, J. E., & White, G. F. (1993). Engaging the media: A case study of the politics of crime and the media. *Social Justice, 20,* 57–68.

*Koopsman, A. (Ed.). (2003). *Crime and criminals: Examining pop culture.* San Diego, CA: Greenhaven Press.

Kozol, W. (1995). Fracturing domesticity: Media, nationalism, and the question of feminist influence. *Signs, 20,* 646–667.

Lomire, P. A. W. (1992). Women and crime in criminology textbooks. *The Great Plains Sociologist, 5,* 78–90.

Low, J., & Sherrard, P. (1999). Portrayal of women in sexuality and marriage and family textbooks: A content analysis of photographs from the 1970s to the 1990s. *Sex Roles: A Journal of Research, 40,* 309–318.

Lucal, B. (1996). Oppression and privilege: Toward a relational conceptualization of race. *Teaching Sociology, 24,* 245–255.

Luhr, W. (1999). Mutilating Mel: Martyrdom and masculinity in *Braveheart.* In C. Sharrett (Ed.), *Mythologies of violence in postmodern media* (pp. 227–246). Detroit: Wayne State University Press.

*McCormick, C. (Ed.). (1995). *Constructing danger: The mis/representation of crime in the news.* Halifax: Fernwood.

McDonald, M. G. (1999). Unnecessary roughness: Gender and racial profiles in domestic violence media events. *Sociology of Sport Journal, 16,* 111–133.

Mead, J. (1998). The case of the missing body: The 'Ormond College' case and the media. In A. Howe (Ed.), *Sexed crime in the news* (pp. 77–86). Sydney: Federation Press.

*Meyers, M. (1997). *News coverage of violence against women: Engendering blame.* Thousand Oaks, CA: Sage.

Miller, S. (Ed.). (1998). *Crime control and women: Feminist implications of criminal justice policy.* Thousand Oaks, CA: Sage.

Mills, C. W. (1959). *The sociological imagination.* London: Oxford University Press.

O'Brien, P. (2001). *Making it in the "free world."* Albany: State University of New York Press.

Owen, B. (1998). *"In the mix": Struggle and survival in a women's prison.* Albany: State University of New York Press.

Pollock, J. M. (1999). *Criminal women.* Cincinnati, OH: Anderson.

*Potter, G. W., & Kappeler, V. E. (Eds.). (1998). *Constructing crime: Perspectives on making news and social problems.* Prospect Heights, IL: Waveland Press.

*Potter, W. J. (1999). *On media violence.* Thousand Oaks, CA: Sage.

Price, B. R., & Sokoloff, N. J. (2004). *The criminal justice system and women: Offenders, prisoners, victims, and workers* (3rd ed.). Boston: McGraw-Hill.

*Reinarman, C. (1998). The social construction of an alcohol problem: The case of Mothers Against Drunk Driving and social control in the 1980s. In G. W. Potter & V. E. Kappeler (Eds.), *Constructing crime: Perspectives on making news and social problems* (pp. 193–220). Prospect Heights, IL: Waveland Press.

Rose, V. M. (1977). Rape as a social problem: A byproduct of the feminist movement. *Social Problems, 25* (1), 75–89.

*Sharrett, C. (Ed.). (1999). *Mythologies of violence in postmodern media.* Detroit: Wayne State University Press.

*Sparks, G. G. (2002). *Media effects research: A basic overview.* Belmont, CA: Wadsworth/ Thomson Learning.

Spector, M., & Kitsuse, J. I. (1973). Social problems: A re-formulation. *Social Problems, 21* (2), 145–159.

*Surette, R. (1998). *Media, crime, and criminal justice: Images and realities* (2nd ed.). Belmont, CA: West/Wadsworth.

Tierney, K. J. (1982). The battered woman movement and the creation of the wife beating problem. *Social Problems, 29* (3), 207–220.

Tjaden, P., & Thoennes, N. (2000). Full report of the prevalence, incidence, and consequences of violence against women. Washington, DC: National Institute of Justice and the Centers for Disease Control and Prevention.

Tomasulo, F. P. (1999). Raging bully: Postmodern violence and masculinity in *Raging Bull.* In C. Sharrett (Ed.), *Mythologies of violence in postmodern media* (pp. 175–197). Detroit: Wayne State University Press.

Wright, R. A. (1987). Are "sisters in crime" finally being booked? The coverage of women and crime in journals and textbooks. *Teaching Sociology, 15,* 418–422.

———. (1990). Ten recent criminology textbooks: Diversity without currency or quality. *Teaching Sociology, 18,* 550–561.

———. (1994). Twenty recent criminology textbooks: Continued diversity without currency or quality. *Teaching Sociology, 22,* 87–104.

———. (1995). Women as "victims" and as "resisters": Depictions of the oppression of women in criminology textbooks. *Teaching Sociology, 23,* 111–121.

*Wykes, M. (2001). *News, crime and culture.* Sterling, VA: Pluto Press.

Young, A. (1998). Violence as seduction: Enduring genres of rape. In A. Howe (Ed.), *Sexed crime in the news* (pp.145–162). Sydney: Federation Press.

PART II

DEBATING THE ISSUES
FEMICIDE AND SEXUAL TERRORISM

Femicide is a term that refers to the killing of women by men because they are women. It came into the study of violence against women by way of the *Ms. Magazine* article "Femicide: Speaking the Unspeakable" by Caputi and Russell (1990; see also Caputi & Russell, 1992). Their article is a critical response to press representations of the 1989 Montreal Massacre. Its description of the attack is short and to the point:

> During a half-hour rampage, [Marc] Lepine killed 14 young women, wounded 9 other women and 4 men, then turned his gun on himself. A three-page suicide note blamed all of his failures on women, whom he felt had rejected and scorned him. Also found on his body was a hit-list of 15 prominent Canadian women. (Caputi and Russell, 1990, p. 34)

At the time, press accounts attributed the incident to madness and characterized Lepine as a deeply disturbed individual. Caputi and Russell objected to the representation, arguing that systematic killings on the scale of the Montreal Massacre were never just the result of madness. The Montreal Massacre and subsequent public mass murders are rooted in misogynist attitudes, just as pogroms and lynchings resulted from anti-Semitism and racism, according to Caputi and Russell (1990). Like other such violations, femicide should be considered a hate crime, with enhanced punishment for its commission.

If Caputi and Russell were concerned by the skewed focus of press accounts of mass murder, then in Chapter 5, "Does Gender Make a Difference?," Clifford, Jensen, and Petee are uneasy about overgeneralizing on the basis of dramatic incidents. Not all killers who seek out public sites such as schools or malls necessarily target women, according to these authors. What bases do they have for concern? First, female victimization is overrepresented in nationally televised news accounts of public mass murders. As a result, the public is exposed to a disproportionate number of incidents with female victims, and some people may erroneously associate the two. Second, real-life women are killed in public mass murder incidents at higher rates than they are killed in normal homicides. The authors interpret the difference in light of routine activities theory: Women are more likely than men to be found in some public locations (e.g., malls) and just as likely as men to be found in others (e.g., schools). Hence, women are going to be among the victims of public mass murderers. It is a question of women being in harms way, according to Clifford, Jensen, and Petee.

In its original formulation, femicide—the intentional killing of women by men—represented one end of a sexual terrorism continuum that ranged from deliberate fatalities through physical and psychological abuse, the latter including sexual harassment, forced sterilization, female mutilation, and cosmetic surgery. When the consequence of these and related practices was the death of a woman, Caputi and Russell defined such incidents as femicides (Caputi & Russell, 1992, p.15). Hence, for these two feminists, a finding of elevated female fatalities in public mass murder incidents over regular homicides would be grounds for using the terms femicide and hate crime (Caputi & Russell, 1992; see also Danner & Carmody, 2001).

Hate crime solutions to problems such as femicide, however, depend on deliberate acts or those that meet the legal requirements for intentional homicide (see Douglas, 2001; Martin, 2002). Following Ellis and Dekeseredy (1997), the current emphasis in defining U.S. femicide is on motive and status; that is, on the male perpetrator's specific intention to kill a woman. As such, femicide tends to be applied to intimate violence fatalities in the United States (see Frye, Hosein, & Waltermaurer, 2005; Koziol-McLain et al., 2006). Outside the United States, particulary in areas of the world where femicide is culturally condoned or politically motivated (Russell & Harmes, 2001), media representations tend to emphasize consequences over perpetrator intentions.

We saw in the chapters in Section I, Gendering Constructions: Women and Violence, that media representations in the United States downplay real-life female victimization and that, when press accounts recognize it, female victims are presented from a masculine point of view. Women are located in the domestic sphere, where sex segregation is an illusion reinforced by media violence. Women are idealized or stigmatized depending on whether they are characterized as Madonnas or whores. Female victims are further stigmatized depending on other identities such as race, ethnicity, immigration status, or social class. Chapters 6, 7, and 8 build on these constructions to consider images of violence and women, including femicide in the context of a lawless Bangladesh and sexual terrorism in the former Yugoslavia and in Rwanda. Chapter 8 revisits ethnic cleansing, albeit through the lens of a police procedural.

In Chapter 6, "Rapist Freed, Victim Punished," Khondaker and Barlow assess media representations of violence against women based on news stories published in the on-line edition of an independent Bangladeshi newspaper. Violence against women is difficult to describe without also introducing "Purdah," the rigidly defined Bangladeshi system of sex segregation that imposes clear boundaries between the spheres of female domesticity and male work (Feldman & McCarthy, 1983; Ferree, 1990; Kabria, 1995). Moreover, the female victims of violence in Bangladesh are perceived as women who have violated male directives and are therefore justifiably subject to punishment. In Bangladesh, the injured party in rape cases is the victim's father, husband, or brother, all of whom have the traditional right to restore honor by punishing the victim (Schuler, Hashemi, Riley, & Akhter, 1996). Finally, in some cases, the female victims of violence are minority Hindu women, hence, the violence is strategic.

The social construction of femicide in Bangladesh is also affected by the general conditions of lawlessness (Schuler, Hashemi, Riley, & Akhter, 1996). As a failing or failed state, the Bangladeshi government has abdicated responsibility for public security, a situation unlike that in the United States, where government agencies fulfill mandates for crime control. Although it is true that the U.S. police have been a source of sexual violence against women (see, e.g., Kraska and Kappeler, 1995), lawlessness in Bangladesh goes far beyond official misconduct. In the examples cited by Khondaker and Barlow, we see police officers abduct, gang rape, and leave a young woman for dead. Evidence also points to the failure of the police to provide other basic services. In rural areas, citizens must bribe the police in order to get them to take a crime report. In the face of government failures, Bangladeshis seeking redress turn to traditional arbitration meetings, but these institutions have been used by Islamists to punish women. Islamist gangs linked to the ruling party (the Bangladesh National Party) are reported to be involved in the strategic use of sexual violence against the wives and daughters of leading members of the opposition party (the Awami League). Under these circumstances, the independent Bangladeshi press bears witness to all manner of violence and in particular to the injustices inflicted on Bangladeshi women. The journalists who report on violence against women do so at their own peril. This, too, bears on how we understand media representations and violence against women in Bangladesh.

Because Chapter 7, "Media Images of Wartime Sexual Violence," by Williams and Bower deals with "ethnic cleansing," this introduction provides background on the two crises described in the chapter. In Bosnia and Rwanda, ethnic cleansing describes efforts to eliminate and expel ethnic or racial minorities from a region or nation-state in order to make it more secure and homogeneous for the majority (Michels, 1998). Ethnic cleansing came to the attention of the U.S. public following the breakup of the former Yugoslavia and took on its present meaning amid ethnic and religious strife that erupted in a Serbian campaign to "cleanse" non-Serbs and Muslim minorities from Bosnia in 1992 (Cigar, 1995). Through local councils, Serbs coordinated mass rape, forced pregnancy, torture, and the murder of women in their campaign to terrorize non-Serbs and Muslims. The West was slow to respond: NATO did not intervene militarily until 1995. Peace accords of the same year called for the prosecution of war criminals. In 2001, the International Criminal Tribunal for the Former Yugoslavia convicted three Serbian leaders on war crimes charges for rape, torture, and enslavement of women. This was the first time that an international tribunal had held leaders responsible for wartime sexual violence against women.

The international community failed to intervene in Rwanda; the United Nations withdrew its meager peacekeeping forces in late 1994 (Nowrojee, 1996). Unchecked, the Hutu majority whipped up ethnic hatreds and unleashed a systematic campaign that massacred Tutsis (and moderate Hutus) beginning in December 1994. The killings lasted 100 days, stopping only when a Tutsi force reentered the country. The International Tribunal for Rwanda held Hutu war criminals accountable for ethnic cleansing and wartime sexual violence on the grounds that Tutsi women alone were targeted for rape or terrorism based on rape. The tribunal is scheduled to complete its work by 2009, but present-day officials, some of whom took part in the massacres, have prevented key trials from moving forward.

In Chapter 7, Williams and Bower's summary of the literature on ethnic cleansing is chilling. Wartime sexual violence comprises forced prostitution, sexual slavery, genital mutilation, rape, and torture, some of which produced fatalities. In many parts of the world, victims of these crimes would be shamed and their families dishonored enough to ostracize or kill them. Where bloodlines and ethnic identity are fused, however, sexual violence can have catastrophic consequences. Large numbers of women, the victims of sexual violence, are no longer in a position to transmit ethnic culture from one generation to the next or to center the community in any meaningful sense. Rape victims are a constant reminder to male relatives that they failed to protect their women. And lastly, the progeny of interethnic rape are understood as contaminating the entire racial or ethnic community.

Williams and Bower compare news coverage of wartime sexual violence in Bosnia and Rwanda. Anyone reading news accounts of the conflict in Bosnia (the former Yugoslavia) would have believed that the Bosnian campaign was more serious and had more casualties than the Rwandan situation. In reality, the reverse was true. The commonly accepted (mis)perception turned out to reflect selective reporting and differential elaboration in terms. In short, news articles about Bosnia far outnumbered those about Rwanda. Both crises were described as exterminations and massacres, but the Bosnian coverage also focused heavily on wartime sexual violence, rape, and sexual assault. The terms used to describe ethnic cleansing in Bosnia resonated with other Western atrocities such as the Holocaust, whereas the limited number of terms used to describe events in Rwanda were not symbolic. News coverage of both crises tended to avoid reference to human rights violations, a designation that had implications for mandated UN intervention. The coverage also avoided terms that would have described practices that forced rape victims to carry pregnancies to term.

Chapter 8, "The Haunting of Jane Tennison," by Adelman, Cavender, and Jurik is fictional. However, real wartime sexual violence in Bosnia provides the background for the two fictional London homicides that figure in "The Last Witness," the sixth episode in the British series *Prime Suspect*. The plot follows the conventions of a police procedural, but the series offers a surprisingly feminist approach to matters of crime and justice, according to Adelman, Cavender, and Jurik. First, the lead homicide detective is a woman, Jane Tennison, hampered by sexist colleagues. Gender, however, is both a weakness and strength in the series. As a woman, Tennison is an effective investigator because, in recognizing the value of female witnesses, she is able to elicit information that escapes her male colleagues. In "The Last Witness," Tennison's intuition enables her to sense a wider tragedy in the cigarette burns on the solitary corpse, that of a woman originally from Bosnia.

Second, the film offers a new victim narrative, one that exposes female marginality by recording the plight of women caught between the terror of wartime sexual violence and the promise of safety through immigration. As Muslim women, the two victims had survived torture and sexual slavery in Bosnia, where fear and shame had silenced them. In London, they toiled in low-paying jobs, invisible to the affluent clients they served. To avoid deportation, they hid in a Bosnian enclave, where police ignored immigrants and where their former Bosnian torturer found and killed them in order to cover up prior war crimes.

Third, "The Last Witness" illustrates the principles of moral fiction. In filling in the gaps between two London homicides and wartime sexual violence in Bosnia, it transforms the viewer's understanding of reality. We see the difference between shallow and deep justice. The arrest and prosecution of a Serbian war criminal for London murders is shallow justice. The realization that murder had roots in wartime torture and sexual slavery requires a deeper, but perhaps more elusive, kind of justice.

Because ethnic cleansing and wartime sexual violence continue to claim victims, the chapters in this section provide a starting point for investigating media representations of violence against women in other localities, including the Darfur region of western Sudan, where after years of civil war, the United States has condemned events as genocide. A July 2007 *Washington Post* article reports that rape is being used in Darfur as "a systematic weapon of ethnic cleansing" against ethnic minority and Muslim women by the [Sudanese] government-backed Janjaweed (Boustany, 2007, p. 9). Civil wars, however, are not the only crises that take a toll on women. There is another designation, that of failed or failing states such as Bangladesh, where public safety failures and governmental corruption—a condition described as lawlessness by Khondaker and Barlow—have exposed women to sexual terrorism and forms of violence that reflect an unforgiving and traditionally rigid patriarchy.

REFERENCES

Boustany, N. (2007, July 3). Janjaweed rape rising as "integral" weapon in Darfur, aid group says. *Washington Post*, p. A9.

Caputi, J., & Russell, D. E. H. (1990, September/October). Femicide: Speaking the unspeakable. *Ms. Magazine, 1* (2), 34–38.

———. (1992). *Femicide: The politics of woman killing*. New York: Twayne.

Cigar, N. (1995). *Genocide in Bosnia: The policy of ethnic cleansing*. College Station: Texas A&M University Press.

Danner, M., & Carmody, D. (2001). Missing gender in cases of infamous school violence: Investigating research and media explanations. *Justice Quarterly, 18*, 87–114.

Douglas, C. A. [Reviewer]. (2001). Femicide in global perspective. *Off Our Backs, 31*, 31–33.

Ellis, D., & Dekeseredy, W. W. (1997). Rethinking estrangement, interventions, and intimate femicide. *Violence Against Women, 3*, 590–610.

Feldman, S., & McCarthy, F. E. (1983). Purdah and changing patterns of social control among rural women in Bangladesh. *Journal of Marriage and the Family, 45*, 949–959.

Ferree, M. M. (1990). Beyond separate spheres: Feminism and family research. *Journal of Marriage and the Family, 54*, 866–884.

Frye, V., Hosein, V., & Waltermaurer, E. (2005). Femicide in New York City: 1900–1999. *Homicide Studies, 9*, 204–228.

Kabria, N. (1995). Culture, cash, and income control: Women garment workers in Bangladesh. *Gender and Society, 9*, 289–309.

Koziol-McLain, J., Webster, D., McFarlane, J., Block, R., Ulrich, Y., Glass, N., & Campbell, J. C. (2006). Risk factors for femicide-suicide in abusive relationships: Results from a multisite case control study. *Violence and Victims, 21*, 3–21.

Kraska, P. B., & Kappeler, V. E. (1995). To serve and preserve: Exploring police sexual violence against women. *Justice Quarterly, 12*, 85–112.

Martin, S. E. [Reviewer]. (2002). Femicide in global perspective. *Violence Against Women, 8*, 1004–1008.

Michels, P. (1998). Le nettoyage ethnique: Definitions et implications. *Canadian Review of Studies in Nationalism, 25*, 83–94.

Nowrojee, B. (1996). Shattered lives: Sexual violence during the Rwandan genocide and its aftermath. *Human Rights Watch/Africa*. New York: Human Rights Watch.

Russell, D. E. H., & Harmes, R. A. (2001). *Femicide in global perspective*. New York: Teachers College Press.

Schuler, S. R., Hashemi, S. M., Riley, A. P., & Akhter, S. (1996). Credit programs, patriarchy and men's violence against women in rural Bangladesh. *Social Science and Medicine, 43*, 1729–1742.

CHAPTER 5

DOES GENDER MAKE A DIFFERENCE?

The Influence of Female Victimization on Media Coverage of Mass Murder Incidents

Janice E. Clifford, Carl J. Jensen III, and Thomas A. Petee

Mass murder has immense appeal to the news media, which exploit many of its newsworthy features—randomness, extreme violence, multiple victims, and unlikely offenders—for public consumption. It might be argued that the violent content of news simply reflects the concerns, values, and interests of the intended audience (Zimring & Hawkins, 1997). Although violent news may be marketed like other consumer products, it has a number of effects that warrant inquiry. The premise that violent imagery has a potential for encouraging aggressive behavior among viewers has been the focus of a significant body of research (Comstock & Strasburger, 1990; Donnerstein, Slaby, & Eron, 1994; Huesmann, 1986). Some studies report that exposure to violence leads to aggressive behavior (American Psychological Association, 1993; Berkowitz & Geen, 1967; National Institute of Mental Health, 1982; Phillips, 1983, Surgeon General's Scientific Advisory Committee on Television and Social Behavior, 1972). Other studies suggest that viewers who are predisposed to aggressive behavior are attracted to television shows and movies that have violent content (Berkowitz, 1970, 1972). An alternative explanation sees media as a precipitating, but not a causal, factor (Phillips & Carstensen, 1986).

The news also has the power to shape public perceptions of social problems such as violence or mass murder. These perceptual effects, alternatively, have justified different lines of research, including process studies regarding the manner in which news workers construct the news, audience research that might shed light on the perceptual effects of the news, and content studies like this one.

One premise that has gained increasing acceptance in the popular media is that females are overrepresented as mass murder victims. According to at least some pundits, mass murder is a form of femicide in which perpetrators disproportionately seek out female rather than male victims (Palmer, 1998; Steinem, 1999). The focus of the present study is to examine how newspapers and television news networks handle mass murder incidents and, in particular, whether they fuel misconceptions regarding mass murder femicide. To that end, we examine whether news accounts accurately mirror official statistics regarding mass murder. We also analyze whether media coverage of mass murder events is skewed (i.e., whether victims' gender affects levels of reporting, coverage in the national as opposed to local outlets, and/or the amount of space or time devoted to the story).

Literature Review

Crime is a mainstay of newspaper reporting. Research findings reported by Chermak (2002) indicate that between 20% and 50% of the total space available in the media is allocated to coverage of crime. Most of this news focuses on crime incidents themselves rather than criminal justice policies or issues. Further, crimes are generally presented independently and not conveyed within the context of patterns or causality. Chermak (2002) argues that the news accounts about crime "do not accurately reflect the realities of crime" (Chermak, 2002, p. 1041). The news emphasizes violent acts, which in reality occur only rarely. For example, property crimes are much more prevalent than violent crimes, yet they are often ignored in media reports (Chermak, 1994). Several other studies (Chermak, 1994; Cohen, 1975; Sheley & Ashkins, 1981) have reached the same conclusion: News stories focus on personal crimes and, in particular, murder.

Crime is such an important part of daily news that coverage defies national trends. While national crime rates were declining during the 1990s, the media continued to emphasize violent events, according to Chermak (2002). Fedler and Jordan (1982) reported similar findings based on crime coverage in the *Orlando Sentinel Star* for a three-month period in 1980. Although violent crime represented only 22% of all felonies, it received 60% of the media coverage. Breaking down violent crime coverage further, the most common offenses (assault and robbery) received the least coverage, whereas less common events (murder and arson) received the most (Fedler & Jordan, 1982).

The media demonstrably skew the homicide problem, according to two important studies that looked at factors predicting whether homicides were covered (Sorenson, Manz, & Berk, 1998) or factors predicting the extent of coverage (length and number of articles) (Paulsen, 2003). By comparing official police records with articles from the *Houston Chronicle* for the period 1986–1994, Paulsen (2003) found that two-thirds (67%) of all homicides were included as news stories in that newspaper. Characteristics of the homicide incidents that received more rather than less coverage included familial or partner violence and multiple victims. Sorenson, Manz, and Berk (1998) compared media accounts of homicide and homicide victimizations in Los Angeles County in the 1990–1994 period. They found that homicides were more likely to be covered as news when certain factors were present. Incident characteristics that made it more likely that a homicide would be reported included multiple victims, no identified suspect, stranger victim–offender relationship, firearm use, occurrence outside a residence, and occurrence in neighborhoods with a median household income of at least $20,000.

Victim characteristics that influenced the extent of coverage included victims who were women, who were Asian, who were under age 15 or over 44, and who possessed greater than a high school education (Sorensen, Manz, & Berk, 1998). In addition, Paulsen (2003) reported that victim characteristics played a significant role in determining the level of news coverage. By comparing the actual incidents and news reports, Paulsen showed that news reports tended to emphasize female victims, victims under 18 years of age or over 51, and those who were either Asian or white. For example, women were victims in 17 homicide incidents, and 72% of these events were covered in the newspaper. In comparison, males were victims in 83 homicide incidents, but only 68% of the incidents received newspaper coverage. Moreover, cases involving young (under age 18) and middle-aged victims (over 51) received the largest percentage of coverage (73%), whereas in reality they represented 16% of all victims. Such an atypical pattern of victimization reveals that "unique, rather than the commonplace events" are the major feature of news (Sorenson, Manz, & Berk, 1998, p. 1514).

On the other hand, the effect of suspect traits on news coverage is less certain. Sorensen, Manz, and Berk (1998) found that suspect traits did not predict the likelihood that the homicide would receive coverage. Paulsen (2003) found that the offender's sex was a determinant in the extent of media coverage. Seven of the incidents that Paulsen (2003) analyzed involved a female offender. The incidents were slightly more likely to receive a greater percentage of coverage than the 72 homicides involving males (72% compared with 70% of actual incidents). Other offender traits were not as significant in predicting the proportion of coverage.

The length of an article in words and the number of articles define what Paulsen understood as the extent of coverage (Paulsen, 2003). Articles with the highest word counts featured female victims, female offenders, white victims, white offenders, younger victims and offenders, and multiple victims. Likewise, the homicides that involved female and white victims and those involving multiple victims produced a greater number of articles. Article placement (front page or buried in the back pages) was also affected by victim characteristics. A final measure of prominence was assessed by the location of articles written about the criminal event. Prominently displayed articles tended to involve females, Asians, young persons, multiple victims, and those incidents occurring in wealthy areas. In comparison, homicide events involving statistically common characteristics were more likely to be placed in the back sections of the newspaper. These cases included male victims, single victims, and crimes occurring in low- or median-income areas.

Duwe's (2000) study of "body count journalism" extended the analysis of the determinants of coverage of violence and homicide to include mass killings. Using a set of incidents drawn from newspapers, network television news, and weekly news magazines, Duwe was able to show that mass killings were covered more extensively in local rather than national media outlets. In addition, factors influencing the extent of coverage devoted to mass killings were similar to those that account for the coverage of homicide incidents. Mass killings that received relatively more coverage than others were likely to include a large number of victims, stranger victims, public and workplace locations, interracial incidents, and assault weapons (and, to a lesser extent, older offenders and general gun use).

Thus far, the studies reviewed are based on newspaper accounts of violence or mass murder. However, our study is based on television accounts. In spite of the different medium, we suggest that television coverage of mass murder events is subject to the same distortions exhibited by print coverage of those events. In this respect, Lipschultz and Hilt (2002) describe a twofold process in the social construction of television news. First, the newsroom makes decisions on what stories to cover and how to present those stories to the public. Second, the audience creates its own reality based on the association between the event and personal experiences. Thus, the viewer's perception tends to reflect the social construction rather than its underlying reality.

Television news, however, plays a more significant role than newspapers in constructing social problems. The extent of crime coverage on the local television news exceeds that in other types of media, including newspapers or nationally televised news (Surette, 1998). Televised news reaches a national audience, and Americans use television as a major source of news (Bollen & Phillips, 1982). Locally televised reports of crime are "part of the spectacle of everyday life" (Kidd-Hewitt, 1995, p.1). The public tends to believe that televised crime news causes crime: 55% of Americans viewed the emphasis on violent crime by the news media as a causal factor in the high homicide rates found in the United States, according to a 1994 Harris Poll reported by Maguire and Pastore (1994). Furthermore, a 1998 Harris Poll reported that 92% of respondents felt that violence on television is a cause of crime in the United States, and 81% felt that local TV news reports had some level of influence on the incidence of crime (Maguire & Pastore, 1999).

The literature reviewed here makes it plain that atypical victims play a role in both the likelihood and extent of news coverage of public mass murder incidents. Based on skewed reporting, the public may conclude that women have a greater risk of victimization in general and for homicide in particular. However, when looking at official crime statistics, we find that the female patterns of victimization are not substantiated.

Historically, the *Uniform Crime Reports* compiled by the Federal Bureau of Investigation (hereafter FBI) have constituted the "official statistics" regarding the incidence and distribution of crime in the United States. The Uniform Crime Reporting system was initiated in the 1930s, when the FBI was charged by Congress with the task of acquiring, collecting, and preserving crime records (O'Brien, 1985). The FBI collects crime report and arrest data on an annual basis from nearly 17,000 law enforcement agencies across the United States, which are subsequently published as *Crime in the United States*. While the adequacy of the data published in the *Uniform Crime Reports* has been questioned—largely because not all crimes are reported to the police and not all law enforcement agencies report to the FBI—they remain one of the most cited sources of crime data.

According to the *Uniform Crime Reports*, in 2002 an estimated 11,877,218 index offenses occurred in the United States.[1] The greatest percentage of offenses were property crimes (88%), whereas violent crime accounted for a much smaller percentage of the total (12%). Examining the prevalence of all index crimes, larceny-theft was the most prevalent (59.4%), whereas murder was committed least often (0.1%).

The FBI data on murder and nonnegligent manslaughter (which in tandem are identified as "homicide") are contained in an ancillary publication, the *Supplementary Homicide Reports* (*SHR*). Homicide includes murder and non-negligent manslaughter and is defined as the "willful (non-negligent) killing of one human being by another" (Federal Bureau of Investigation, 2003b). According to the *SHR*, in 2002 there were 16,204 homicides in the United States (Federal Bureau of Investigation, 2003a). However, not everyone has an equal likelihood of becoming a victim of homicide in the United States, as certain categories of people are more likely than others to become victims (MacKellar & Yanagishita, 1995). An individual's risk of becoming a victim of murder is dependent on a number of demographic characteristics, including race/ethnicity, gender, and age. Taken in conjunction with one another, these characteristics are critical in understanding the risk of victimization.

Men are much more at risk than women for becoming the victim of a homicide (Brewer & Smith, 1995; MacKellar & Yanagishita, 1995; Segall & Wilson, 1993). In 2002, males constituted nearly 78% of all homicide victims despite the fact that they comprised 49% of the population (Federal Bureau of Investigation, 2003a). It has been speculated that this is attributable to the kinds of activities in which men engage, which put them at risk for becoming victims of homicide (i.e., the routine activities approach). The gender gap for homicide victimization continues throughout life, although the difference narrows somewhat as people approach middle age and in their elder years (MacKellar & Yanagishita, 1995).

Age and race are associated with increased risk of victimization. Persons aged 18 and over represented 90.1% of all homicide victims in 2002, whereas juveniles, defined as those 17 years of age or younger, accounted for 9.9% of all homicides (Federal Bureau of Investigation, 2003a). Likewise, those 50 and older constituted a small percentage of homicide victims (12.6%). Whites and blacks were almost equally represented among homicide victims, at 48.7% and 48.5%, respectively. With blacks comprising approximately 12.7% of the total U.S. population in 2002 (U.S. Census Bureau, 2003), they are clearly overrepresented among homicide victims. Other racial and ethnic groups represented only 2.7% of all victims.

Examination of victim–offender relationships reveals that the offender was someone known to the victim in 43.2% of the cases. Of the incidents in which the homicide victim knew the offender, 22.8% were committed by an "acquaintance," 9.4% by an "intimate partner" (husband, wife, boyfriend, or girlfriend), 7.4% by a "relative, other than husband or wife," and 3.3% by "someone known to the victim, but not a relative." In only 13.9% of cases was the homicide offender a "stranger." A large proportion of the cases involved an "unknown" relationship between victim and offender (42.8%) (Federal Bureau of Investigation, 2003b). The location of the incident is not recorded in either official measure of crime (*Uniform Crime Reports* or the *SHR*), and therefore these patterns cannot be examined.

Mass murder, the focus of our study, is a special type of homicide. It is generally defined as the killing of three or more persons in one location at one time (see Petee, Padgett, & York, 1997). Mass murder is typically distinguished from other forms of multiple homicide, such as serial and spree murder, that are not limited in location and have different time parameters associated with them. There is usually some flexibility allowed in the definition of mass murder as long as the incident occurs in a limited area over a limited time period (i.e., a few hours at the extreme). Mass murders are rare in the United States—for example, in 2002, they constituted only 8% of all murders (Federal Bureau of Investigation, 2003a). However, there are some incidents of mass murder that generate a fair amount of media interest. For example, the school shootings that took place in Jonesboro, Arkansas, in 1998 and Littleton, Colorado, in 1999 were major national news stories that had extensive coverage. It is important to note that not all types or incidents of mass murder garner a high level of media scrutiny.

The more common form of mass murder takes place in a domicile and involves the murder of family members, most often a husband killing his wife and children (Petee, Padgett, & York, 1997). With the exception of a few notorious cases (e.g., Jeffrey MacDonald, John List, Ronald Gene Simmons), family murders rarely generate interest beyond the local media (Duwe, 2000). By contrast, the less common form of mass murder takes place in public places and involves the murder of strangers (Petee, Padgett, & York, 2001). Public mass murders generate a great deal more media coverage precisely because they are public acts of violence. The highly recognizable perpetrators—Charles Whitman, Colin Ferguson, James Huberty, Dylan Klebold, and Eric Harris—all killed their victims in public settings. Such incidents are prone to extensive and sometimes sensationalistic coverage (Petee, Padgett, & York, 2001). Duwe states that media outlets, driven by the need for ratings, cater to the public appetite for rare and sensationalistic events:

> The mass murders that garnered greater media exposure were more newsworthy largely because they were riveting, emotionally evocative incidents that epitomized news as theater—a morality play involving pure, innocent victims and offenders who seemingly went "berserk" in a public setting. (Duwe, 2000, p. 391)

Incidents such as the school shootings in Jonesboro, Arkansas, and Littleton, Colorado, attracted the media because the offenders were juveniles. Other incidents attract attention because they occur in the workplace (e.g., the Post Office Killings) or because the violence appears inexplicably random (e.g., the victims of George Hennard or Colin Ferguson). Mass murder events are generally not predictable or restricted to specific locations, and offenders can fall into any age group.

In the present study, we reviewed a broad array of research and data to specify our research questions. Our first question is rooted in the literature on violence and the determinants of news coverage: Does female victimization make a difference in the likelihood and/or extent to which a mass murder is covered by the media? More specifically, we are interested in the relationship between the proportion of female victims and the extent and type of news coverage of mass murders in public settings. Our second question flows from the suggestion in much of the literature that the media tends to inflate violence and exploit atypical incidents or victim characteristics. Here the questions concern accuracy: In cases of public mass murder, are women actually victimized at higher rates than they are for other types of murder? Answers to these questions will shed light on speculation, based on a few published reports, that mass murder is analogous to femicide (see Palmer, 1998; Steinem, 1999).

The Research

The present study addresses the question of whether mass murder incidents result in higher rates of female victimization than for homicide in general. Further, it investigates the relationship between the proportion of female victims and the extent and type of media coverage of mass murder events in public settings.

To examine the extent to which female victimization influences media coverage of mass murders, we constructed a dataset based on incidents that occurred in public places between 1980 and 2002. The dataset was derived from newspapers and television network archives. First, incidents meeting our criterion were identified through searches of newspaper indices and on-line newspaper databases (i.e., NewsBank, NewsFile) that contained national, regional, and some local newspapers. Also, the Lexis-Nexis databank was searched for incidents. Second, a list of incidents was compiled. Case references were used to search national, regional, and some local newspapers (using on-line and/or print versions) for articles reporting on mass murder incidents. Third, articles were then screened to ensure that criteria for defining an incident as a mass murder were met: (1) requisite number of homicides (at least three) and (2) the appropriate context (occurring in a public place). "Public place" was defined as any nondomicile location. For some cases, information was compiled from both a printed article and an on-line version. Fourth, for each article, information was collected on crime, victim, and offender characteristics. The dataset comprised information drawn primarily from newspaper articles appearing in the following newspapers: *Atlanta Journal-Constitution, Birmingham Post-Herald, Boston Globe, Chicago Tribune, Detroit News/Free Press, Houston Post, Los Angeles Times, Miami Herald, New York Times, New Orleans Times-Picayune, Pittsburgh Post-Gazette, San Francisco Chronicle, USA Today,* and *Washington Post.*[2]

A data code sheet was developed for the collection of all pertinent information (see Etten and Petee, 1995; Petee, Padgett, & York, 1997). Relevant data were extracted from newspaper articles and transcribed to the code sheet. The data consisted of indicators pertaining to the context of the homicide episode, offender characteristics and actions, and victimology.[3] The total sample included 119 incidents, 149 offenders,[4] and 1,266 total victims (648 killed and 618 wounded). The bombings of the

Murrah Federal Building in Oklahoma City, Oklahoma, and the World Trade Center in New York City in 1993, and all incidents from September 11, 2001 (World Trade Center, New York City; Pentagon, Arlington, Virginia; and western Pennsylvania), were excluded from our analysis because their high death counts and the nature of the events would have skewed the victimization data.

The last step in the data collection process involved searching the on-line Vanderbilt University Television News Archives. Nightly broadcast news shows were examined for each of the major networks (ABC, NBC, and CBS) to ascertain whether coverage of the mass homicides contained in the dataset was included in the broadcast the day the incident occurred and for two days after.

Results

Data were analyzed using contingency table analysis, with the chi-square statistic indicating the significance of the association between relevant variables. We examined the ratio of female to male victims in order to determine if a higher female victimization ratio had any impact on the level of television news coverage (i.e., local only, regional, or national). Our results indicate that, indeed, a higher ratio of female to male victims did affect whether coverage occurred only at the local level or at the national level ($\chi^2 = 13.48$, df = 6, $< .05$). Mass murder incidents limited in scope to only local news coverage were more likely to occur when the female to male victimization ratio was close to even (around 1.0). When that ratio was 2.0 or higher, the frequency of incidents receiving only local television news coverage was lower than expected based on chi-square analysis. By contrast, a female to male victimization ratio of 2.0 or more was much more likely to result in national news coverage, with the expected frequencies being lower than the actual number of cases of national news coverage for these ratio levels. Overall, coverage limited to the region of the country where the incident occurred was about what was expected based on the chi-square analysis.

As in previous studies, results reveal that a relationship exists between both incident and victim characteristics as they relate to the likelihood that a mass murder will receive any television news coverage. The total number of victims, both the wounded and the killed, makes it more likely that the incident will receive any level of television news coverage. Further, it was found that the proportion of female to male victims killed in each incident also influences the level of television news coverage. Events that had the highest proportion of female victims received the greatest extent of coverage with respect to reporting at the local, regional, and national levels.

Understanding Female Victimization Patterns in Mass Murder Incidents

After the mass murder that occurred in Jonesboro, Arkansas, in 1998, questions were raised about the targeting of females for victimization. In that incident, all five of the victims killed by Mitchell Johnson and Andrew Golden were female, and the offenders had apparently specifically targeted girls from their class. This attracted quite a bit of attention in the media, and there was some discussion of mass murder being equated with femicide (see Palmer, 1998; Steinem, 1999). According to these articles, women were much more likely to become the victims of mass murder compared with their risk of victimization for homicide overall. Moreover, these stories claimed that the increased risk of victimization was attributable to the misogynistic tendencies of the offenders, who were seeking vengeance against women for perceived wrongs. These claims were supported by examples where mass murder offenders had specifically targeted women for victimization, such as the 1991 case of George Hennard in Killeen, Texas, or the 1989 case of Marc Lepine in Montreal.

In fact, women are more at risk of becoming the victims of mass murder incidents. The FBI's *Supplemental Homicide Reports* indicate that from 1980 until 2002, 37.9% of all mass murder victims were female. In comparison, females represented 30% of all homicide victims during that same time period (Bureau of Justice Statistics, 2004).[5] At least in part, this can be explained by the high proportion of mass murder cases that occur in a domicile (see Petee, Padgett, & York, 1997). Most mass murders occurring in a home setting are domestic in nature and almost by definition will involve at least one female victim (i.e., wife or girlfriend). By contrast, mass murders occurring in a public setting do not have this bias, which is reflected by the fact that for mass murders in public places, females constitute 35.2% of the victims. However, on further reflection, these numbers are not unexpected. Unlike general homicide trends, where the risk of victimization is correlated with demographic criteria, which in turn are related to lifestyle factors (see MacKellar & Yanagishita, 1995), a mass murder occurring in a public place has a risk factor associated with the probability of being in a particular location at the time these incidents occur.

Essentially, one would expect the at-risk proportions to be representative of the distribution of males and females in the population in general. Statistics from 2002 indicate that the risk of a male becoming a murder victim was 3.4 times greater than for females (Bureau of Justice Statistics, 2004). Because mass murder has more of a random quality, the risk of victimization is likely the result of being in the wrong place at the wrong time. Consequently, the day-to-day activities of people could put them in situations where they are at risk of becoming the victim of such a crime.

Routine activities theory may be the key to understanding victimization patterns for mass murders in public places. As formulated by Cohen and Felson (1979), routine activity refers to the notion that certain kinds of crime result from day-to-day activities that take place in a community. Cohen and Felson (1979) contend that crime involving direct contact between a victim and offender is influenced by the convergence in time and space of motivated offenders and suitable targets in a context in which there is a relative lack of guardianship. In other words, these crimes will occur when the activity patterns of potential victims intersect those of offenders. In the case of mass murder, this means that victimization will more likely result when, because of their day-to-day activities, people are in a location where a motivated offender decides to perpetrate such an offense.

In this way, females may be at greater risk than in the past of becoming victims of a mass murder because their activity patterns put them in a place where these offenses occur—for example, a restaurant, retail store, or school. In these cases, one would expect to see a fairly high proportion of female victimization—certainly more than what occurs with homicide in general, where the context of murder is more dependent on other types of activities more directly associated with risk (i.e., getting into fights, being involved in other crimes) that are frequently linked with male victimization. Of course, with mass murder, some modification to the expected victimization rate would have to be made for specific contexts—for example, those mass murders occurring in the workplace would have to take into account female versus male participation in the labor force.

Conclusions

The results of the present study support other research that has found a bias in media reporting of mass homicide events. In particular, the total number of victims (both the wounded and the killed) and the proportion of female to male victims killed are positively related to the extent of media coverage at the national, state, and local levels.

Further, although the proportion of female to male victims in mass homicides is somewhat greater than in single homicides, we do not mean to suggest that perpetrators are intentionally seeking out females. Rather, we argue that female fatalities can be explained by the random nature of most mass homicide incidents and by the presence of women in public spaces. For this reason, we believe that routine activities theory offers the better explanation for the majority of public mass homicide victimizations.

Media reporting is important for many reasons; in the present context, its importance can be viewed with regard to the social construction of crime. The sheer volume of reporting influences the manner in which people view the world around them. The present study supports the findings of others who note that the reporting of public mass murder events is skewed to emphasize the sensationalistic or unique over the typical. This trend can be viewed as especially important given that the public depends almost exclusively on the media for information regarding mass homicide incidents. Unlike for more mundane crimes (e.g., burglary and robbery), most individuals do not have access to alternative sources of information regarding public mass homicide events (e.g., they have never been personally involved with or victimized by such an event) and are therefore totally dependent on the media (Graber, 1980). Individual perceptions, in turn, influence both public policy and behavior (Duwe, 2000).

Zaller (1999) contends that market forces greatly influence the manner in which media reporting occurs; the more competitive the market, the more likely it is that accuracy will be sacrificed for sensationalism. He further notes that local media outlets (the ones most likely to report about mass homicides) are the ones most affected by competition. If one accepts Zaller's line of reasoning, the rapid proliferation of the media in recent years to include 24-hour news channels, public access outlets, and the Internet may have a significant impact on reporters' behavior, tempting outlets to sacrifice quality for speed and ratings. To that end, market-driven forces may actually increase the level of reporting bias that favors the unique and sensational over the typical. Therefore, the results noted in this chapter may be but a prelude to the future.

NOTES

1. The Federal Bureau of Investigation (2003b) includes both violent crimes (murder, robbery, forcible rape, and aggravated assault) and property crimes (larceny-theft, motor vehicle theft, burglary, and arson) in the index crime category.
2. This methodology was based upon that employed by Levin and Fox (1985). In one case (that of Thomas McIlvane), the newspaper sources were supplemented by a report (U.S. House of Representatives, 1992). Although newspapers constitute another type of media source (and hence a potential contributor to the stereotype for mass murder), it is our contention that they are more likely to provide in-depth factual information and are less prone to engage in sensationalistic or superficial reporting on mass murder events than other forms of popular media.
3. These data are descriptive in nature, as the purpose of the present study is to describe and differentiate between various types of mass murder occurring in public places. Whereas many studies that employ newspaper accounts of events are concerned with rhetorical analysis, this is not within the scope of this study.
4. The reported total number of offenders is a minimum, given that there were some incidents where the exact number of offenders was unknown or the specific names of the offenders were not reported in the news accounts. Although obviously there have been a number of incidents involving multiple offenders, there is one instance of a single offender (Eric Leonard) who was involved in two separate mass murder incidents that occurred exactly one week apart.
5. The authors would like to thank Greg Weaver for his assistance with statistical procedures.

REFERENCES

American Psychological Association Commission on Violence and Youth. (1993). *Violence and youth: Psychology's response.* Washington, DC: Public Interest Directorate, American Psychological Association.

Berkowitz, L. (1970). The contagion of violence: An S-R mediational analysis of some effects of observed aggression. *Nebraska Symposium on Motivation, 18,* 95–135.

———. (1972). Words and symbols as stimuli to aggressive responses. In J. F. Knutson

(Ed.), *Control of aggression: Implications from basic research* (pp. 113–144). Chicago: Aldine-Atherton.

Berkowitz, L., & Geen, R. (1967). Stimulus qualities of the targets of aggression: A further study. *Journal of Personality and Social Psychology, 5*, 364–368.

Bollen, K., & Phillips, D. (1982). Imitative suicides: A national study of the effects of television news stories. *American Sociological Review, 47*, 802–809.

Brewer, V. E., & Smith, M. D. (1995). Gender inequality and rates of female victimization across U.S. cities. *Journal of Research in Crime and Delinquency, 32*, 175–190.

Bureau of Justice Statistics (2004). Homicide trends in the United States. Washington, DC: U.S. Department of Justice. Retrieved July 21, 2005, from http://www.ojp.usdoj.gov/bjs/homicide/gender.htm.

Chermak, S. (1994). Body count news: How crime is presented in the news media. *Justice Quarterly, 11*, 561–582.

———. (2002). Media. In D. Levinson (Ed.), *Encyclopedia of crime and punishment* (pp. 1040–1044). Thousand Oaks, CA: Sage.

Cohen, L. E., & Felson, M. (1979). Social change and crime rate trends: A routine activity approach. *American Sociological Review, 44*, 588–608.

Cohen, S. (1975). A comparison of crime coverage in Detroit and Atlanta newspapers. *Journalism Quarterly, 52*, 726–730.

Comstock, G., & Strasburger, V. (1990). Deceptive appearances: Television violence and aggressive behavior. *Journal of Adolescent Health Care, 11*, 31–44.

Donnerstein, E., Slaby, R., & Eron, L. (1994). The media and youth aggression. In L. Eron, J. Gentry, and P. Schlegel (Eds.), *Reason to hope: A psychosocial perspective on violence and youth* (pp. 219–250). Washington, DC: American Psychological Association.

Duwe, G. (2000). Body-count journalism. *Homicide Studies, 4*, 364–399.

Etten, T., & Petee, T. (1995, November). Mass murder in public places: Questioning the validity of episode-motivated crime policy. Paper presented at the meeting of the American Society of Criminology, Boston, MA.

Federal Bureau of Investigation. (2003a). *Supplementary Homicide Reports (SHR)*, 2002. Ann Arbor, MI: Inter-University Consortium for Political and Social Research.

———. (2003b). *Crime in the United States, 2002: Uniform Crime Reports*. Retrieved November 1, 2004, from http://www.fbi.gov/ucr/02cius.htm.

Fedler, F., & Jordan, D. (1982). How emphasis on people affects coverage of crime. *Journalism Quarterly, 17*, 474–478.

Graber, D. (1980). *Crime news and the public*. New York: Praeger.

Huesmann, L. R. (1986). Psychological processes promoting the relation between exposure to media violence and aggressive behavior by the viewer. *Journal of Social Issues, 42*, 125–139.

Kidd-Hewitt, D. (1995). Crime and the media: A criminological perspective. In D. Kidd-Hewitt & R. Osborne (Eds.), *Crime and the media* (pp.1–24). London: Pluto Press.

Levin, J., & Fox, J. A. (1985). *Mass murder: America's growing menaice.* New York: Plenum.

Lipschultz, J., & Hilt, M. (2002). *Crime and local television news: Dramatic, breaking and live from the scene.* Mahwah, NJ: Lawrence Erlbaum Associates.

MacKellar, F.L., & Yanagishita, M. (1995). *Homicide in the United States: Who's at risk?* Washington, DC: Population Reference Bureau.

Maguire, K., & Pastore, A. (Eds.). (1994). *Sourcebook of criminal justice statistics, 1994.* U.S. Department of Justice, Bureau of Justice Statistics. Washington, DC: U.S. Government Printing Office.

———. (1999). *Sourcebook of criminal justice statistics, 1998.* U.S. Department of Justice, Bureau of Justice Statistics. Washington, DC: U.S. Government Printing Office.

National Institute of Mental Health. (1982). *Television and behavior: Ten years of scientific progress and implications for the eighties, summary report* (Vol. 1). Washington, DC: U.S. Government Printing Office.

O'Brien, R. M. (1985). *Crime and victimization data.* Beverly Hills, CA: Sage.

Palmer, I. D. (1998, April 26). Women frequently the victims of mass murders. *New Orleans Times-Picayune,* p. A28.

Paulsen, D. (2003). Murder in black and white. *Homicide Studies, 7,* 289–317.

Petee, T., Padgett, K., & York, T. (1997). Debunking the stereotype: Examination of mass murder in public places. *Homicide Studies, 1,* 317–337.

———. (2001). Mass murder. In D. Peck and N. Dolch (Eds.), *Extraordinary behavior: A case study approach to understanding social problems* (pp. 241–251). Westport, CT: Praeger.

Phillips, D. (1983). The impact of mass media violence on U.S. homicides. *American Sociological Review, 48* (4), 560–568.

Phillips, D., & Carstensen, L. (1986). Clustering of teenage suicides after television news stories about suicide. *New England Journal of Medicine, 315,* 658–659.

Segall, W. E., & Wilson, A. V. (1993). Who is at greatest risk in homicides: A comparison of victimization rates by geographic region. In A. V. Wilson (Ed.), *Homicide: The victim/offender connection* (pp. 343–356). Cincinnati, OH: Anderson Publishing.

Sheley, J., & Ashkins, C. (1981). Crime, crime news, and crime views. *Public Opinion Quarterly, 45,* 492–506.

Sorenson, S., Manz, J., & Berk, R. (1998). News media coverage and epidemiology of homicide. *American Journal of Public Health, 88,* 1510–1514.

Steinem, G. (1999, August/September). Supremacy crimes. *Ms. Magazine, 9,* (5), 44–47.

Surette, R. (1998). *Media, crime and criminal justice* (2nd ed.). Belmont, CA: Wadsworth.

Surgeon General's Scientific Advisory Committee on Television and Social Behavior. (1972). *Television and growing up: The impact of televised violence.* Washington, DC: U.S. Government Printing Office.

U.S. Census Bureau. (2003). *National population estimates: Annual resident population estimates of the United States by sex, race and Hispanic or Latino origin: April 1, 2001 to*

July 1, 2002. Retrieved November 15, 2004, from http://www.census.gov/popest/ archives/2000s/vintage_2002/NA-EST2002–ASRO-02.html.

U.S. House of Representatives. (1992). *A Post Office tragedy: The shooting at Royal Oak*. Report of the Committee on Post Office and Civil Service, House of Representatives Investigation into the Events of the Shooting on Thursday, November 14, 1991 at the U.S. Post Office at Royal Oak, MI (Print 102-7). 102nd Congress, 2nd Session. Washington, DC: U.S. Government Printing Office.

Zaller, J. (1999). Market competition and news quality. Paper presented at the meeting of the American Political Science Association, Atlanta, Georgia.

Zimring, F., & Hawkins, G. (1997). *Crime is not the problem: Lethal violence in America*. New York: Oxford University Press.

CHAPTER 6

RAPIST FREED, VICTIM PUNISHED

*Newspaper Accounts of Violence against
Women in Bangladesh*

Mahfuzul I. Khondaker and Melissa H. Barlow

Media representations are an important subfield in criminology, but rarely have Western social scientists considered the ways in which non-Western media socially construct violence against women. In an effort to remedy this deficiency, we focus on Bangladesh and on Southeast Asian perspectives on women, violence, and the media. In Bangladesh, violence against women is attributed to Purdah, a rigidly conservative form of patriarchy that excludes Bangladeshi women from public roles and subordinates them to men. Violence is exacerbated by political instabilities that stem from corruption, failures in security, and factionalized elites. Under these conditions, the independent press serves to witness social problems—violence against women, corruption, repression of opposition, and persecution of minorities—that ruling parties would suppress. We believe that an analysis of Bangladeshi news promises to expand the thinking of Western readers about violence against women and its representations in the news.

The exploration is organized into several sections. We provide background about violence against women, the criminal justice response, Purdah, and the role of journalists in Bangladesh. Next, we lay out our research and describe our findings based on a sample of news articles taken from the on-line edition of the *Daily Star*, an independent, English-language paper published daily in Bangladesh. Our discussion of dowry killings, rape, and, among other things, abductions, returns to the issues of Purdah, political repression, political instabilities, and the role of an independent press.

Background

In Bangladesh, domestic violence occurs at higher rates and is more severe than in many parts of the world (Garcia-Moreno et al. 2006). This is the conclusion of a ten-nation survey sponsored by the World Health Organization. The survey looked at domestic violence in both cities and provincial sites. The lifetime prevalence of physical partner violence is 42% (Bangladesh provincial site), a high-end figure in a range where most sites fall between 23% (Thailand city) and 49% (Ethiopian provincial) (Garcia-Moreno et al. 2006, Table 4). Moreover, just under one-half of the women who had ever been victimized characterized the physical violence as severe. Severe violence includes being hit with a fist or other object; being dragged, kicked, or beaten up; being intentionally choked or burned; and facing a perpetrator who threatened to use or used a gun, knife, or other weapon. The lifetime prevalence for severe physical violence is almost half, which places Bangladeshi figures at the highest end of a range running from 4% (Japanese city) to 49% (Peruvian province) (Garcia-Moreno et al. 2006, Fig. 1). In Bangladesh, as elsewhere, severe domestic violence is part of a continuing pattern of abuse.

Women in Bangladesh, however, rarely disclose domestic violence (Navel, 2006; Rosenberg, 2006). In one survey of rural women, 66% of abused women never discussed their victimization with anyone (Rosenberg, 2006). They remained silent for several reasons. Women believed that their husbands had a right to use violence against them, they wanted to avoid the stigma of being an abused wife, or they feared greater harm by talking about what happened to them (Rosenberg, 2006). In the same survey, women who disclosed their victimizations talked to parents, siblings, and neighbors, all of whom provided some measure of help. A small portion (2%) sought help from formal authorities, but respondents said that they received no assistance (Rosenberg, 2006).

In the West, police and other formal authorities play a key role in responding to domestic violence.[1] Public service is not the guiding principle among police in Bangladesh, which ranks among the most corrupt countries in the world according to the Corruption Perception Index (CPI) published by Transparency International, an anticorruption watchdog organization (Transparency International-Bangladesh, n. d.). The CPI ranks nations according to the degree to which corruption is perceived to exist among public officials and politicians. From 2001 to 2004, Bangladesh ranked among the nations with the highest levels of corruption. Although most people reported avoiding the police, 10% said that they had had some contact with them (United Nations, 2003). Of those who had had contact with police, 84% complained of police corruption. In order to report domestic violence or other crimes, citizens are expected to pay on average 2,000 taka ($29), which is a huge portion of respondents' average yearly salary of 5,016 taka ($73) (Transparency International-Bangladesh, n. d., but see also Transparency International-Bangladesh, 2006).

In addition to corruption, police are also a source of violence against women in rural Bangladesh (Schuler, Hashemi, Riley, & Akhter, 1996). In the villages, when police are unable to make an arrest or find evidence, "they [police] harass, beat, or rape women members of the household" (Schuler, Hashemi, Riley, & Akhter, 1996, p.1734). In times of unrest, police camps that are intended to establish order are a source of villagers' complaints about theft, violence, and the harassment of village women (Schuler, Hashemi, Riley, & Akhter, 1996).

Lastly, police are believed to be complicit in the ruling party's efforts to suppress the political opposition and to persecute minorities, Hindus, and other non-Muslims. Writing in *Time Asia*, the Asian equivalent of *Time Magazine*, journalist Aravind Adiga argued that ordinary Bangladeshis "believe the cops are only lackeys in a system in which the chief criminal beneficiaries are a handful of powerful gang lords with important political connections" (Adiga, 2004, para. 6). In other words, ordinary people take systemic corruption for granted; major criminals are protected by police and well-placed politicians. In making a second point, Adiga reiterates a remark made by former Bangladeshi president Chowdhury (1991–2001), who characterized the political instability following the elections of 2001: "Some politicians have cultivated gangs of armed youths in order to intimidate their opponents" (Adiga 2004, para. 6). Ordinary people also believe that leaders in the ruling party (the Bangladesh National Party and its Islamist allies) have recruited and armed youth gangs in order to persecute political opponents and minorities.

With formal authority compromised, women have little hope of justice in Bangladesh. Cultural practices that regulate male and female relationships are largely responsible (Kabria, 1995, p. 289). The lives of Muslims in Bangladesh are given shape by Purdah, norms that restrict women to the home, that exclude them from visible social roles, and that involve the wearing of a burka (Feldman & McCarthy, 1983). When girls reach puberty, their mobility becomes limited, and in the household where they are confined, girls are placed under the supervision of older female relatives (Feldman & McCarthy, 1983). Because marriage determines adult status for women, the socialization of girls aims at fulfilling Muslim expectations about sexual virtue, obedience to male authority, and an uncomplaining attitude toward hard work. Upon marriage, girls or young women go to live and work in their husbands' homes. One effect of the physical move is to separate brides from the protection of their own families and to subject them to the authority of older women and male relatives in the joint family (Kabria, 1995). What in the West would be domestic violence is an accepted means for a husband or his family to discipline the wife.

Sexual violence and rape are also understood differently in Bangladesh than in the West. In going out or in failing to wear the burka, a daughter or wife violates Purdah and is therefore responsible for any subsequent victimization and for the dishonor that a sexual attack brings on the family. According to Bangladeshi culture, the victim's family is the injured party, and the family or its surrogates have the right to ask elders to convene a village council (shalish) to review the matter and issue a ruling that in punishing the victim would restore family honor (Schuler, Hashemi, Riley, & Akhter, 1996, p. 1735). Although such fatwas are illegal, rulings have been issued for the public whipping of women (Helie-Lucas & Kapoor, 1996; Schuler, Hashemi, Riley, & Akhter, 1996, p. 1735).

An important step in telling the stories of abused women of Bangladesh took place almost a decade ago. In 1999, internationally acclaimed freelance journalist Sumi Khan first wrote about "a maid who had been raped by her boss and kicked off his balcony. The maid broke her leg in the fall. Writing about the scandal had huge ramifications within Khan's newspaper, where 'some of the higher-ups at the paper were friends of the businessman,' she says. Although some male reporters also covered this story, Khan was the only one to lose her job over it" (Simpson, n.d.).

Working for other newspapers and magazines, Khan continued to write about the "floating women," those living in abandoned buildings or on the street, and women held in virtual bondage by employers (Simpson, n. d.). Her stories exposed violence against women, encouraged victimized women to report it, and set a standard for reporters to follow. All of this made her a target for Islamists who had come to power with the Bangladesh National Party in 2001 (Simpson, n.d.). In 2002, Kahn was detained for having met with a foreign TV team covering the rise of fundamentalist Islam (Reporters Without Borders, 2003). In April 2004, she was attacked and nearly killed for writing about the involvement of religious groups and political leaders in attacks on minorities (Piddy, 2005). The Press Freedom Index, compiled and published by Reporters Without Borders, ranks Bangladesh as among the worst abusers of press freedoms in the world (151st out of 165) (Reporters Without Borders, 2004).

Patriarchy, police corruption, and governmental repression all contribute to violence against women and the way the media represent it. To ascertain the nature of the influence, we asked three questions. First, we wanted to know something about the nature of violent incidents reported in newspapers. Second, we asked who the victims and assailants were. Last, we focused on official criminal justice responses to violence against women and asked questions about arrests and punishments.

Methods

This study is based on news accounts from the on-line edition of the *Daily Star: Journalism without Fear or Favor*, a national English-language daily newspaper with a reputation for independent reporting.[2] In 1997, the current editor and publisher, Mahfuz Anam, launched the Internet edition, which publishes from 100 to 110 news items—fewer items than appear in the print version of the paper. From the Internet version, we collected 178 news articles over a 14–month period during 2003–2004. The news articles were read and coded for the nature of the crime, victims and perpetrators, and the criminal justice response. We report categories of attacks on women and types of perpetrators. In reporting the criminal justice response, we focus on arrests and convictions.

Findings
Violence, Perpetrators, Justice

We identified 11 categories of violence against women. The categories include crimes that are familiar in the United States: rape, abduction, stalking, and teasing (harassment). Other forms of violence, however, are unique to Southeast Asia: dowry-related violence (killing and torture) and acid attacks, which will require some explanation.

Dowry killings account for the largest grouping of news stories about violence against women. They are motivated by money, especially in villages where dowry is a source of income for poor families. The Dowry Prohibition Act of 1980 prohibits the practice, but, in rural areas, the bride's family is expected to pay or promise to pay the groom's family a negotiated sum in money or property. Because unmarried daughters are a financial drain, parents of older girls are willing to pay a dowry in order to secure marriage contracts. Trouble arises when parents are unable to make good on their promises or when husbands make additional and repeated dowry demands on the bride's family. If threats or beatings fail to induce the bride's family to pay, the husband may simply kill his wife and seek another bride and additional dowry.

Dowry-related abuse or torture is widely perceived as a private matter, but a dowry-related death requires an official response. The deaths, however, are accepted by police as accidents or suicides, which limits public exposure to all but the most egregious cases. For example, the following news account mixes motherhood, murder, and greed. A wife's family refused or could not meet additional dowry demands, so the wife's husband beat her—although she was pregnant and the mother of his two children—until she was dead (*Daily Star*, January 12, 2005). The sum in question, 10,000 taka, or about $145, comes close to the average annual income for a family. As a widower whose wife died by accident or suicide, the husband would have been free to remarry and to receive additional dowry payments. The financial incentive for dowry killing is one reason that such murders are subject to the death penalty.

In addition to dowry killings, another type of news story features rape perpetrated by groups and single individuals. Such news underscores perpetrators' contempt for their victims. In the following excerpt, several men raped their victim and then left her for dead.

> They took her to a grocer shop owned by one Mohid and gang raped her. The criminals tied her mouth and hands with cloth and left her in a nearby field. She was rescued next morning in an unconscious state and taken to Shingra hospital. She was later shifted to Manikganj Sadar Hospital. (*Daily Star*, September 11, 2004b)

Not all victims who are cast aside as if they were waste are rescued. Many die, which means that murder charges accompany some rapes. Victims who survive these attacks, however, bear a heavy cultural burden. Some rape victims take their own lives. A 35-year-old village housewife victimized by gang rape was reported to have committed suicide because she was unable to "bear her brunt of humiliation" (*Daily Star*, September 6, 2004c). The details of the attack make it plain that she was not responsible.

> A gang of four youths led by local terrorist Rahimuddin intercepted [the victim] . . . while going to her father's house at night with her husband Aminur Rahman, police said. Later tying up her husband with a rope, [the gang] violated her by turns. As local people hearing their screams rushed to the spot, the miscreants fled. (*Daily Star*, September 6, 2004c)

A man who is unable to protect his wife from rapists is diminished as a man; the loss of masculine prowess is attributed to the victim. In believing that she is the source of stigma, the housewife who took her own life restored the family's honor.

Not all families abandon rape victims. A few families sought justice, but in news accounts, criminals easily stopped them. Following an incident in which a 30-year-old villager broke into a house and raped a young girl, "influential people at the village organized an arbitration meeting and fined . . . [the rapist] 20,000 taka in his absence [$296]" (*Daily Star*, June 16, 2004g). Arbitration meetings are part of an informal system of courts that are mandated to resolve minor disputes. In practice, arbitration meetings are the default option for rural villagers without access to the police or courts; hence the reference to the "influential people" who convened the meeting. These meetings lack enforcement powers or personnel, judging from what happened next. The rapist refused to comply with the judgment and threatened to kill the rape victim's father unless he sent his daughter away. Fearing for his life, the father moved his daughter to Dhaka, the capital city. The practice of sending rape victims into hiding, however, does not necessarily protect them from further assault. As in the first example, a father frightened by a rapist's threats of retaliation sent his daughter into hiding, where she was attacked again, this time by a neighbor, who also threatened to attack the family should they decide to seek legal action against him (*Daily Star*, September 11, 2004b).

Abductions represent a third major type of news story in which retaliation or money is the motive. A suitor may resort to abduction when the prospective bride or her family rejects his marriage proposal. In these cases, abductions restore the suitor's honor or provide the means of getting even. When they are motivated by ransom, the victims tend to come from wealthy families. In one case, a man who abducted the daughter of a chemistry professor was her cousin. He demanded 10 lakh, or about $148,000, before he would release her (*Daily Star*, September 21, 2004a).

Acid attacks are the final category of news stories about violence against women. Throwing acid on the face of a woman may not kill her, but facial disfigurement has lifelong consequences and reduces her chances in marriage, which defines a woman's adult status. Family feuds and land disputes motivate these attacks, but acid throwing is also used in dowry disputes and as retaliation for perceived infractions by women. A man who attempted but failed to rape a woman, for instance, was reported by a news story to have taken revenge by throwing acid on her (*Daily Star*, July 31, 2004e). Similarly, a rejected suitor took his frustrations out on his neighbor for refusing his proposal of marriage (*Daily Star*, June 29, 2004f). Rejected suitors, jilted lovers, and ex-husbands are among those who are described as having thrown acid in this way.

Perpetrators: Family, Police, and Political Henchmen

In the majority of news stories, victims are related to or know the perpetrators. Of the perpetrators known to the victim, over half are husbands and about a third are neighbors or friends. In-laws and relatives and employers or co-workers àre also represented as perpetrators. In the incidents of dowry assaults or killings, the perpetrators are the husband and his family, the very people who have a legal obligation to protect the bride. Among the attackers not known to victims, some (30%) are police officers and political henchmen. In this category, police officers commit rape and police officials attempt to cover it up. Police officers in the next example were tried in 1997 and executed in 2004 (*Daily Star*, September 2, 2004i); the underlying event illustrates the problem. In August 1995, three police officers approached a young girl who waited by the side of the road and offered to drive her home. Once in the police van, the 13-year-old girl was raped and killed; the police officers threw her body into the street. When the public organized mass demonstrations to protest police violence, local police shot into the crowd, killing seven protesters (*Daily Star*, September 2, 2004d).

Islamist gangs tied to ruling politicians (Bangladesh National Party) used sexual violence in the post-2001 election drive to persecute minorities (e.g., Hindus and other non-Muslims) and terrorize the opposition political party, the Awami League. In a *Daily Star* story referencing these campaigns, police dropped an investigation into the involvement of "protection officers" associated with the ruling party (BNP) in the rape and strangulation of the 8-year-old daughter of the village leader for the Awami League (*Daily Star*, February 5, 2004h). Among other incidents, Amnesty International (2003) reported allegations that men linked to the BNP had gone into the homes of Hindu families belonging to the Awami League; these henchmen tied up the men and raped the women (Amnesty International, 2003).

Arrest and Punishment

What do the news accounts tell us about the Bangladeshi response to violence against women? Even though the police have full investigative authority along with prosecutorial responsibilities for minor crimes, they do not make many arrests. They ignore criminal complaints, take reports only when bribed, and reclassify fatalities as accidents or suicides. In the news accounts we examined, police investigations produced arrests about 40% of the time. Because it may take several years for an arrest to come to trial, the low arrest rate may be the product of a limited period of data collection. Nonetheless, based on the seriousness of the offenses reported in *Daily Star*, the clearance rate is quite low, but it is consistent with police corruption. The criminal courts, however, appear to do better. In cases that reach the point of sentencing, over 90% of defendants were sentenced to death or life imprisonment. This involves less than 20% of the cases, and in half of these, the defendants were tried and sentenced in their absence. On the face of it, severity in sentencing is symbolic. What passes as justice is a blend of capital punishment and police corruption.

In summary, the main types of violence that we observed are dowry killings, rape, abduction, and acid throwing. According to Purdah, responsibility for the attacks falls to the victims, who also bear (or fail to) the humiliation of having also dishonored their families. Family members, police, and political henchmen are among the perpetrators of violence against women. Although the motives may differ, the common disdain for women runs through male violence against women, police corruption, and political campaigns to repress minorities. Victims and their families forgo justice, fearing retaliation from criminals and police. Most criminals escape justice, having little to fear from the police.

Discussion and Conclusion

In the West, representations of violence against women may send a chilling message to women. In Bangladesh, the representations send a similar message. Stranger rape is an image that externalizes the threat of violence, locating it in the public rather than the private sphere. In the *Daily Star*, one finds horrific accounts of stranger attacks on women, which may be understood as reinforcing traditional gender boundaries. The entrance of women into the Bangladeshi garment industry as wage workers has weakened sex segregation at the same time as unemployment has diminished male economic power. In emphasizing the lack of safety for women who venture outside the home, stranger rape can be expected to frighten women into complying with traditional forms of Purdah. We can also see that numerous news reports about dowry killings may serve to terrify families into redoubling their efforts to pay. The tragedy is that dowries do not safeguard daughters in Bangladesh. In rural areas, dowry payments, especially in small amounts increase the risks of domestic abuse, beatings, rape, murder, or abandonment (Suran, Amin, Huq, & Chowdury, 2004, p. 12).

Social control explanations, however, do not fully describe media representations of violence against women in Bangladesh. The conspiracy of silence about domestic violence is both cultural and institutional. Women in Bangladesh do not disclose domestic violence. The one study on this point suggests that in rural areas up to two-thirds of the victims say nothing because they believe that husbands have the right to discipline wives, because they wish to avoid humiliation, or because they believe that disclosure will make matters worse. In addition, police bribery is a disincentive for those who suspect foul play. Police notice dowry-related fatalities, but officers record them as unnatural deaths, accidents, or suicides, which require no further action (Farouk, 2005, p. 12).

Alternatively, a critique of the general state of lawlessness goes a long way in explaining news representations in the *Daily Star*. Rated as the most corrupt country in the world by Transparency International, police corruption in Bangladesh is deeply ingrained and widespread. Police bribery is one manifestation, although it was not picked up in the news stories we examined. Opportunistic police violence against women, however, found its way into news reports in the *Daily Star*. Schuler and colleagues described the rape and sexual harassment of rural village women at the hands of police (Schuler, Hashemi, Riley, & Akhter, 1996). Moreover, news reports tapped into deeper instabilities in Bangladesh. In 2001, the Bangladesh National Party, in coalition with Islamist parties, took control of the government and unleashed a wave of violence that included the strategic use of sexual violence. Islamist gangs targeted the wives and daughters of the Awani League leadership.

In a December 2006 editorial, the *Daily Star* took issue with the nation's system of justice. The editorial praised traditional arbitration courts (shalishes), and their rulings (fatwas) functioned as no-cost alternatives to official institutions in a country where most villagers lack the money required to bribe the police or bring charges in court (*Daily Star* [editorial], December 20, 2006b). At the same time, the editorial called on the government—led by the Bangladesh National Party—to take a stand against the use of arbitration courts by Islamists to impose religious law (shariah) (*Daily Star* [editorial], December 19, 2006a).

In the one news account that referred to an arbitration court, the court fined a man who had raped a young woman (*Daily Star*, June 16, 2004g). As described, the meeting is striking: In taking up the matter of rape, it exceeded its traditional authority to rule in minor disputes. In practice, however, it is believed that shalish courts rule on two-thirds of the cases that would have normally gone to the criminal courts (Farouk, 2005, p.11). The meeting is also striking because the court did not issue a fatwa against the rape victim, suggesting that this particular court had not been taken over by Islamists, for under Shariah the victim would have been sanctioned. Also, the rapist fled, easily evading the fine, suggesting that compliance with court rulings is voluntary. In contrast, where Islamists have assumed control of arbitration courts, the enforcement of religious law is swift and efficient, although women are the ones who are targeted for public punishment (see, e.g., Riaz, 2005).

Bangladesh is at risk of becoming a failed state (see Foreign Policy and the Fund for Peace, 2006).[3] Extensive corruption and violence, factionalized elites, and failures in the state's security apparatus are indicative of a state that no longer controls its territory, provides basic functions, or protects public safety. Jalal Alamgir, a political scientist at the University of Massachusetts, dates current failures to the 2001 elections that swept the Bangladesh National Party into power (Alamgir, 2007). Throughout the period, the BNP blocked investigations—many demanded by the independent press—into government-sponsored persecutions. When the BNP attempted to rig the 2007 elections, the military stepped in to create a caretaker government. After a brief period of support, the caretaker government has again cracked down on the opposition, abrogated civil liberties, and proposed an alternative government that centralizes authority and that would improve Islamists' prospects for political advancement (Alamgir, 2007).

In a climate of lawlessness and repression, the journalists who write for independent newspapers such as the *Daily Star* face considerable risk in exposing violence against women and other injustices. The Bangladesh National Party as well as the current caretaker government have carried out repressive campaigns to suppress this information. But journalists like Sumi Khan, who began by writing about the plight of women (Simpson, n. d.; Piddy 2005), soon realized that attacks on women, police corruption, and political violence were sometimes linked. In bearing witness to these links, independent journalists face harassment, intimidation, physical attack, and death. At one level, the meaning of the news about violence against women in Bangladesh is that it is testimony, at considerable risk to those who give it, about the cruel injustices that women face in a failed state and where Islamists are expected to gain power (Reporters Without Borders, 2006).

NOTES

1. In the United States, the news about crime is based on police or justice sources. The U.S. "crime beat" places reporters in contact with various offices in the criminal justice system, from which they learn about crime events and the cases that are moved through the criminal justice system. In Bangladesh, however, police accounts, police records, court filings, and sentencing information are suspect; consequently, the news has a unique status as being both a representation and an established data source. Journalists who cover crime in Bangladesh may use official sources, but they pursue independent leads in developing many news stories about the plight of women.

2. An expatriate readership is the presumed audience for the on-line edition of the *Daily Star*. Judging from letters to the editor, Bangladeshi expatriates, living and

working or going to school in the United States, Canada, Australia, and South Africa define the readership for the Internet edition. As a group, the "expats" are more literate, educated, and affluent than most people who stay in Bangladesh. Most people in Bangladesh cannot read—the literacy rate for women is 38%—but even men who cannot read gather in cafés and tea stalls where someone else reads aloud. The discussion of events so reported is a male activity.

3. This statement is based on the Failed State Index, a ranking of over 100 countries using a dozen military, political, and social indicators to assess their vulnerability to violent internal conflict and societal dysfunction. By these rankings, Bangladesh is a failed or failing state brought to this condition by corruption, factionalized elites, and among other things, the persecution of minorities (see Foreign Policy and the Fund for Peace, 2006).

REFERENCES

Adiga, A. (2004, April 9). State of disgrace. *Time Asia.* Retrieved April 10, 2004, from http://affiliate.timeincmags.com/time/asia/magazine/printout/0,13675,501040412-607842,00.html.

Alamgir, J. (2007). Bangladesh: Democracy saved or sunk? *Foreign Policy.* Retrieved July 7, 2007, from http://foreignpolicy.com.

Amnesty International. (2003). *Amnesty International report 2003.* Retrieved December 5, 2004, from http://web.amnesty.org/report2003/bgd-summary-eng.

Daily Star. (2004a, September 21). One-year-old girl rescued. Retrieved September 23, 2004, from http://thedailystar.net/2004/09/21/d40921012625.htm.

———. (2004b, September 11). Gang raped school girl fighting for life. Retrieved September 12, 2004, from http://thedaily star.net/2004/09/11/d40911070872.htm.

———. (2004c, September 6). Gang-raped housewife commits suicide. Retrieved September 12, 2004, from http://thedailystar.net/2004/09/06/d40906012725.htm.

———. (2004d, September 2). Yasmeen Rape, Murder: 2 cops walk gallows in Rangpur jail. Retrieved September 3, 2004, from http://thedailystar.net/2004/09/02/d40902 01044.htm.

———. (2004e, July 31). Acid thrown on woman in Khulna. Retrieved August 1, 2004, from http://thedailystar.net/2004/07/31/d40731100379.htm.

———. (2004f, June 29). One to die for throwing acid on sister-in-law. Retrieved July 2, 2004, from http://thedailystar.net/2004/06/29/d40629060264.htm.

———. (2004g, June 16). Woes of 2 rape victims. Retrieved June 17, 2004, from http://thedailystar.net/2004/06/16/d40616070569.htm.

———. (2004h, February 5). Daughter of AL leader raped, strangled. Retrieved February 7, 2004, from http://thedailystar.net/2004/02/05/d40205012020.htm.

———. (2005, January 12). Violence against women on the rise. Retrieved February 4, 2005, from http://thedailystar.net/2005/01/12/d50112100174.htm.

————. [editorial]. (2006a, December 19). The curse of the fatwa. Retrieved July 3, 2007, from http://www.europe-solidaire.org/spip.php?article4365.

————. [editorial]. (2006b, December 20). A parallel system of justice cannot be allowed. Retrieved July 3, 2007, from http://www.europe-solidaire.org/spip/php?article4365#tweak_sommaire_1.

Farouk, S. A. (2005). Violence against women in Bangladesh: A statistical overview, challenges and gaps in data collection and methodology and approaches for overcoming them. Paper presented at the Expert Group Meeting on Violence Against Women, Economic Commission for Europe and the World Health Organization, Geneva, Switzerland, April 11–14. Retrieved July 3, 2007, from http://www.un.org/womenwatch/daw/egm/vaw-stat-2005/docs/expert-papers/Farouk.pdf.

Feldman, S., & McCarthy, F. W. (1983). Purdah and changing patterns of social control among rural women in Bangladesh. *Journal of Marriage and the Family, 45*, 949–959.

Foreign Policy and the Fund for Peace. (2006). *The Failed States Index* (May/June). Retrieved July 1, 2006, from http://www.foreignpolicy.com/story/cms.php?story_id=3420.

Garcia-Moreno, C., Jansen, H. F. M., Ellsberg, L., Heise L., & Watts, C. H. L. (2006, October 7). Prevalence of intimate partner violence: Findings from the WHO multi-country study on women's health and domestic violence. *Lancet, 368* (9543) 1260–1269.

Helie-Lucas, A. M., & Kapoor, A. K. (1996). *Fatwas against women in Bangladesh*. Grabels: Women Living Under Muslim Law.

Kabria, N. (1995). Culture, cash, and income control: Women garment workers in Bangladesh. *Gender and Society, 9* (3), 289–309.

Navel, R. T. (2006). Physical violence by husbands, magnitude of disclosure, help seeking behavior of women in Bangladesh. *Social Sciences and Medicine, 62* (12), 2917–2929.

Piddy, H. (2005, March 2). I wasn't scared, they were afraid of me. The *Guardian*. Retrieved July 10, 2007, from http/:www.guardian.co.uk.

Reporters Without Borders (2003). *2003 Annual Report—Bangladesh*. Retrieved June 14, 2007, from http://rsf.org

————. (2004). Third annual worldwide Press Freedom Index: East Asia and Middle East have worst press freedom records. Retrieved June 14, 2007, from http://www.rsf.org/IMG/pdf/Asia_index_Eng_2004.pdf.

————. (2006). *2006 Annual Report—Bangladesh*. Retrieved June 14, 2007, from http://rsf.org.

Riaz, A. (2005). Traditional institutions as tools of political Islam in Bangladesh. *Journal of Asian and African Studies, 40* (3), 171–196.

Rosenberg, J. (2006). Update: Bangladeshi women rarely seek help for abuse. *International Family Planning Perspectives, 32* (3), 108.

Schuler, S. R., Hashemi, S. M., Riley, A. P., & Akhter, S. (1996). Credit programs, patriarchy and men's violence against women in rural Bangladesh. *Social Science and Medicine, 43* (12), 1729–1742.

Simpson, P. (n. d.). *Uncovering violence in Bangladesh.* Washington, DC: International Women's Media Foundation. Retrieved June 14, 2007, from http://iwmf.org.

Suran, L., Amin, S., Huq, L., & Chowdury, K. (2004). Working papers: Does dowry improve life for brides? A test of the bequest theory of dowry in rural Bangladesh. (No. 195, pp. 1–26). New York: Population Council: Policy Research Division.

Transparency International—Bangladesh (n. d.). *Social movement against corruption: CPI [Corruption Perceptions Index].* Retrieved June 18, 2007, from http://www.ti-bangladesh.org/.

———. (2006, November 6). Corruption Perception Index 2006. Press release, Dakar, Bangladesh. Retrieved July 8, 2007, from http://www.ti-bangladesh.org/.

United Nations. (2003). Corruption in Bangladesh: A household survey, 2002. Retrieved June 6, 2007 from unpan1.un.org/intradoc/groups/public/documents/APCITY/UNPAN015435.pdf.

CHAPTER 7

MEDIA IMAGES OF WARTIME SEXUAL VIOLENCE

Ethnic Cleansing in Rwanda and the Former Yugoslavia

Yaschica Williams and Janine Bower

The most insidious form of news control is silence. Silence is a form of rewriting history; it transforms events into non-events.

Erlich, 1999, p. 329

Conflicts involving ethnic cleansing, such as those that occurred in the former Yugoslavia between 1992 and 1996, in Rwanda in 1994, and more recently in Sudan's Darfur region, have all involved the systematic rape and sexual mutilation of females. As a weapon of war, sexual violence devastates local victims and has been used to destroy entire ethnic communities. International bodies have recognized systematic sexual violence as a form of genocide in Rwanda and the former Yugoslavia. In the United States, however, the public responded quite differently to these conflicts: Yugoslavian ethnic cleansing was seen as important, involving U.S. interests; the others, arising in Africa, were viewed as unimportant, being outside the areas of American engagement. The incongruity between the uniform horror of ethnic cleansing and the American tendency to select one but not the other led us quite naturally to ask questions about the role of news media in shaping or reinforcing perceptions of genocide. In seeking to answer such questions, our research has led us through the literatures on sexual violence and ethnic cleansing, on the media and public perceptions, and on the civil wars in the former Yugoslavia and Rwanda.

A working knowledge of the two conflicts can be gleaned from some basic facts. Between 1992 and 1996, the period of civil war in the former Yugoslavia, Bosnian Serbs attempted to drive Muslims out of Bosnia and Herzegovina in order to seize their lands and thereby establish an ethnically pure state. In the course of this conflict, over 130,000 Bosnian Muslims were murdered and over 30,000 young girls and women were raped by Bosnian Serbs (UNIFEM, n. d.). Ethnic diversity was a factor in the civil war: 37.1% of the population were Serbian, 48% were Bosniak,[1] and 14.3% were Croat. The population was divided along religious lines, too: 40% of the population were Muslim, 31% were Orthodox, and 15% were Roman Catholic (Central Intelligence Agency, 2004a).

In the Rwandan crisis, the Hutus attempted to gain control over populated areas and natural resources, which required driving out or killing Tutsis (Central Intelligence Agency, 2004b). In a three-month period in 1994, over 500,000 Tutsi were murdered and over 250,000 young Tutsi girls and women were raped by [Hutu] soldiers and civilians (UNIFEM, n. d. a). At the time of the conflict, 84% of the population were Hutus, whereas the minority Tutsis accounted for 15% of the population. Roman Catholics made up 56.5% of the population, Protestants represented 26%, 11% of the population were Adventists, and 4.6% of the population were Muslims.

Literature Review
Sexual Violence and War

Ethnic cleansing has shown how limited individual explanations of rape can be. The "sexual urge" argument assumes that rape serves as an outlet for sexual desire, but it has been questioned on grounds that rape occurs even when soldiers have alternative means for satisfying sexual urges. The "biological argument" assumes that elevated levels of testosterone or a genetic predisposition are responsible for male sexual aggression against women. Both theories falter because they fail to explain the increased incidence of rape during wartime and to account for variations in the prevalence of rape from one society to another. Sexual attacks on women "are not the sum total of a couple of hundred thousand genetic predispositions for aggressiveness" (Seifert, 1996, p. 36). Nor is wartime rape an unfortunate "by-product" of war, as we are keenly aware that rape and sexual violence against "enemy" civilian females has been invoked as a strategy of war (Price, 2001).[2]

Mass rape as a strategic tool of war has accompanied the major conflicts of the twentieth century. Table 7.1, giving a history of sexual violence during times of war, provides rough estimates of the scope of the problem (see Skjelsbaek, 2001b, pp. 70–79). The summary begins in 1932

TABLE 7.1

History of Sexual Violence During Times of War

Year	Victimized Group	Incident
1932–1945	Korean Women ("comfort women")	200,000 women forced into prostitution by Japanese military personnel. Women were forced, lured, and kidnapped into sexual slavery in all areas occupied by the Japanese.
1937	Chinese women	20,000 Chinese women were raped, sexually tortured, and murdered in Nanking following the Japanese takeover of the city in 1937. There were reports of 10 gang rapes a day.
1944–1945	German women	90,000–110,000 women were raped by Russian forces in Berlin during the final days of WWII.
1960–1996	Mayan women	State authorities sponsored rape in Guatemala during its civil war. Guatemalan soldiers systematically raped Mayan women.
1970–1980	Ugandan women	Ugandan women were forced to marry men in the rebel forces in order to provide them with sexual favors for free.
1980s	Central and Latin American women	During interrogation and detention, Latinas were sexually tortured, gang raped, or raped repeatedly. Victims came from Argentina, Chile, El Salvador, Guatemala, Peru, Colombia, and Uruguay.
1986–1990	Serbian women	In Kosovo, Albanian men were accused of raping Serbian women on a massive scale.
1990s	Somali refugees	As a means of punishment, female prisoners were stripped naked in front of males who lived in their villages.
1991–1993	The former Yugoslavia	As a means of ethnic cleansing, Serbs raped Muslim and Croatian women, forcing them to migrate elsewhere.
1992–1996	The former Yugoslavia	From 10,000 to 60,000 women of various ethnic groups were raped.
1994	Rwanda	As many as 500,000 women were raped during the 1994 genocide in Rwanda. Hutu men raped Tutsi women in order to destroy Tutsi culture.

Year	Victimized Group	Incident
Ongoing	Palestinian Women	In Israeli-occupied territories, Israeli security guards sexually humiliate Palestinian women by fondling them and threatening them with sexual violence.

Source: Skjelsbaek (2001b), pp. 70–79.

with the "comfort women," when the Japanese military forced 200,000 Korean women into prostitution. In all areas occupied by the Japanese, women were forced, lured, and kidnapped into sexual slavery. Mayan women were systematically raped by soldiers; the Guatemalan military, which controlled the police and courts, condoned rape, protecting soldiers from prosecution and criminalizing those whom soldiers had victimized (Hastings, 2002). The summary ends with the continued humiliation of Palestinian women in the "occupied territories" at the hands of the Israeli military.

One can see from Table 7.1 that the events in Rwanda (1994) and those in the former Yugoslavia (1992–1996) are more recent. In Rwanda, "political propaganda played on stereotypes of Tutsi women," suggesting that Hutu soldiers might be exploited by the beautiful, sexually more desirable Tutsi females (Skjelsbaek, 2001b, p. 73). "These stereotypes, coupled with the view of women as men's possessions, made Tutsi women particularly vulnerable to sexual violence" (Skjelsbaek, 2001b, p. 73; see also Mamdani, 2001). In the former Yugoslavia's civil war, a Serbian strategy was to establish rape camps for women, where women of the intelligentsia and of higher social status were among those initially targeted for selection (Albanese, 2001). Events in the former Yugoslavia are what brought wartime sexual violence to international attention, according to Seifert (1996, p. 35; see also Lindsey, 2002). Skjelsbaek (2001a, 2001b) agrees, noting that sexual violence "appeared to play a new strategic role in the wars of the 1990s, a role the international community was not able to identify nor had adequate response to" (2001b, p. 69). The failure to respond may have been a failure to see sexual violence as political persecution: "Rape is generally not considered political persecution, and public revelations of rape are individualized and depoliticized by state authorities. Women who include their experiences of rape in testimonies of violence are thereby viewed primarily as victimized women rather than as persecuted citizens" (Hastings, 2002, p. 1175).

In the context of war, sexual violence is not limited to acts of rape; it frequently includes "forced prostitution, sexual slavery and genital mutilation," according to Skjelsbaek (2001b, p. 70). In addition, it is usually followed by other forms of violence, such as torture or killings, making it hard to isolate the unique consequences of rape (Skjelsbaek, 2001b, p. 79). The targets of wartime sexual violence are typically women because mothers keep communities and families together and are often the primary transmitters of culture (Einhorn, 1996). Through rearing children, women ensure that cultural norms and values are transmitted from one generation to the next. In this way, "the primary target for sexual violence in war is not the individual victims themselves, but the social identity they represent" (Skjelsbaek, 2001b, p. 72).

Wartime sexual violence requires us to understand the relationship between rape and national identity (Einhorn, 1996; Gellner, 1983). The social construction of national identity may rest on a sense of common origin or common destiny as in the United States (Yuval-Davis, 1996). Or it may rest on polarized distinctions between a majority group as "us" and a minority group as "them." The conversion of "them" to "stranger" marks a pivotal point on the road to genocide and ethnic cleansing, as the stranger, who does not belong, is vulnerable to attack (see Dunne & Wheeler, 1999). In and among some societies, the line of demarcation between us and them and the stranger is marked by origin (i.e., birth): "When nationalist and racist ideologies are interwoven, [being born into] may be the only way to join and those who do not comply are excluded" as the "other" (Yuval-Davis, 1996, p.17). Alternative means of joining may include intermarriage, but even then, intermarriage may be considered a source of contamination for an otherwise "pure" race or ethnicity.

A nationalist discourse that is preoccupied with the pureness of the majority group is also by necessity concerned with sexual relations among and between ethnic or racial groups (Holter, 2002; Yuval-Davis, 1996). The systematic victimization of women, particularly sexual victimization, has the potential for destroying national identity along with its social fabric. The political construction of women as bearers of members of the nation and bearers of culture makes women's bodies the battleground on which racial and ethnic differences and nationalist ideology are fought.

In the case of the Rwandan conflict, the "imagined community" (Anderson, 1983) is scripted by conceiving the "Hutu nation" as unified, bounded, and distinct from the Tutsis, and this way of thinking results in the bodies of women becoming the "highly contested terrain" through which national identity is forged (Baines, 2003). Rwandan women had been valued according to their maternal role, fertility, and the number of children they produced. Indeed, the average number of births per woman prior to the 1994 genocide was among the highest in the world (Nowrojee, 1996). Many women who had been subjected to sexual violence (violent or repeated rape, genital mutilation) were no longer able to bear children. As a result, Tutsi women lost a core feature of their identity, their standing as creators of the collective identity, and Tutsis as a group lost the biological basis to reproduce themselves. In addition, wartime sexual violence sends a symbolic message to males that they are incapable of protecting "their women" from men of the opposing ethnic group. The symbolism rests on basic cultural assumptions that construct men as protectors of women, who are objectified as vulnerable to assault by the stranger (Meznaric, 1994). For men, the failure to live up to the ideal of protector is a source of demoralization.

Pregnancy, enforced through rape, contaminates the collective identity (Carpenter, 2000). The "enemy seed" takes demoralization one step further. The Hutu assault on the Tutsi and Muslim women that resulted in live births threatened the biological basis of ethnic identity (Stanley, 1998). Estimates indicate that between 2,000 and 5,000 children were born out of the roughly 250,000 rapes that occurred over the three-month period in the Rwandan conflict. Called "children of hate," "enfants non-desires" (unwanted children), or "enfants mauvais souvenir" (children of bad memories), these children have in many cases been abandoned or killed by their mothers, and children of hate have been rejected and isolated by their relatives (Nowrojee, 1996). In the former Yugoslavia, Muslim women were often tortured into revealing whether they used some form of contraception; women impregnated by Serbians received milk and generally received better treatment than women who had not conceived or those with unconfirmed pregnancies. Serbians detained women carrying Serbian fetuses past the point of abortion, thereby improving the chances for live births (Lewis, 1994). The cruelty inherent in such practices is obvious, but as a strategy it "is being practiced on the bodies of these girls and women, in an unspeakably cruel way, in that these women—whose own social and personal existence has been destroyed—are made to generate the future of that other community by extinguishing the present of their own community" (Seifert, 1996, p. 40, quoting Wobbe, 1993).

News Media and the Social Construction of Problems

We now turn to the American news media and consider issues associated with the social construction of wartime sexual violence. Scholars who have looked into how the media shape public perceptions stress a few key points. Direct experience plays a role, but because we don't directly experience problems like genocide or ethnic cleansing, we have to rely on the media, especially the news, for information about them. Moreover, news is not information; rather, the news is a social construction that follows identifiable rules.

One set of rules concerns selectivity: The press has the capacity to determine what is and is not, and what is important and what is not, simply by covering or emphasizing one set of events. Another set of rules concern objectivity, the standard by which people judge news as credible. The authority of the news source (typically a government agency) and a balance (quotations from opposing sides) define objectivity (see Erlich, 1999; Fishman, 1980; and Tuchman 1972). In this way, a news story "takes on the appearance of 'objectivity'" (Erlich, 1999, pp. 319–321), which legitimates the story as authoritative and nonbiased for the reporter and news organization (Erlich, 1999, p. 320) as well as the reading public. A final consideration is word selection. Effective news stories exploit the full potential of the English language. Some words convey neutrality and objectivity (e.g., "in a UN document reporting abuse"); others are more emotive, conveying a sense of horror (e.g., "committed mass atrocities") or urgency (e.g., "impending famine"). In this way, a news story has a unique emotive tone that may not be obvious to the casual reader.

Our observation that U.S. citizens tend to recognize ethnic cleansing in the former Yugoslavia but not in Rwanda led us to review two very different bodies of literature. The literature on wartime sexual violence leads us to ask questions about the degree to which the news focuses on the systematic use of rape and torture, ethnic cleansing and genocide, human rights, and the meaning of rape and forced pregnancy for national identity. On the other hand, the literature on the media suggests that we consider news stories about wartime sexual violence in the context of the selection of events, the relative emphasis and deemphasis placed on different events, and the language choices used to convey emotional tone. Both bodies of literature lead us to ask questions about the explanations the media provide for wartime sexual violence.

The Study

Our study is cross-sectional, exploratory, and designed to compare news coverage of wartime sexual violence in Rwanda and the former Yugoslavia. In both countries, sexual violence functioned as a tool in broader ethnic cleansing campaigns. To investigate news representations of wartime sexual violence, we selected two American newspapers noted for their coverage of foreign affairs, the *New York Times* and the *Washington Post*, and relied on the Lexis-Nexis search engine to select relevant news articles. Lexis-Nexis provides access to major newspapers and permits media researchers to download and print selected articles for later analysis. Our search focused on articles published during the 1994 conflict in Rwanda and during the much longer civil war in the former Yugoslavia (1992–1996). Search terms are broadly conceived and include "weapon of war, rape"; "war crimes, rape"; "ethnic cleansing, rape"; "genocide, rape"; "rape camps"; "forced pregnancy"; "rape, military"; "sexual violence, war"; "forced prostitution"; "Rwanda"; "the former Yugoslavia"; and "Bosnia-Herzegovina." Using these terms, we identified the 139 news articles used in this study. Note that about 60% of the sample was drawn from the *Washington Post*.

The articles were coded according to content analysis techniques developed by Stempel and Westley, who describe them as "a research technique for the objective, systematic, and quantitative description of the manifest content of communication" (Stempel & Westley, 1989, p. 125). As a technique, it is well suited for use with newspaper accounts. Meyers (1997), for example, notes that current indexes make it easier to search through newspapers than other electronic media. She suggests also that stories printed in newspapers serve as the foundation for other forms of media such as radio, television, and magazine news stories. On the other hand, content analysis is open to criticism for its tendency to reduce meaning to a few terms or words, hence taking them out of context. However, we address this problem by taking into consideration *how* a term is used and by paying attention to the descriptive words and phrases that accompany terms.

A central idea in content analysis is that many words in a text can be classified into fewer content categories (Weber, 1990). In our case, we used key words from our search as a starting point, and by going back and forth between the news descriptions and search terms, we were able to reduce the number of categories to just seven. In this sense, our coding categories are derived from the content of the articles. We read each article, paying attention to terms and concepts related to sexual violence against women. We considered the emotive value of words; that is, whether they were neutral or objective words or whether the words carried an emotional message with respect to the event, victims, and victimization. Explicit terms were fairly easy to identify, whereas implicit terms were coded based on their level of implication, which we determined subjectively.

A term or concept was counted only once because this gave a simple but adequate method for identifying the range of terms that composed broader constructions. In describing torture and sexual violence in Rwanda and the former Yugoslavia, do the news articles adopt a common list of terms or do they use different words? Does the news about the conflict in Rwanda incorporate fewer terms than the news about the civil war in the former Yugoslavia Republic? Do the data support a conclusion that the news had developed a more elaborate vocabulary for events in the former Yugoslavia than in Rwanda?

Researchers independently coded terms or concepts in each article from the *New York Times* or the *Washington Post*. In order to reduce potential bias, the coding instrument included terms, phrases, or concepts that may be found in the newspaper text. We constructed the list of terms from a convenience sample of articles covering both conflicts that we reviewed prior to the data collection for this study. Furthermore, we randomly exchanged articles to assess intercoder reliability. We found there were no inconsistencies between each of our codings for the randomly selected articles.

Finally, we look at the explanations offered by the sample of news articles for wartime sexual violence against women. At one extreme, biological explanations, which relate torture and sexual violence to sexual urges or testosterone levels, focus on the individual. Here one would expect to find terms or concepts related to sex drive. At the other extreme, ethnic cleansing explanations, which relate torture and sexual violence to the demoralization of an entire ethnic community, shift the focus from individual propensity to the deliberate and strategic use of rape in wartime. Here one anticipates a set of terms that link sexual violence to the goals of war. Reality may fall somewhere between the two extremes.

Our data analysis techniques are descriptive. We compare the number of articles about wartime sexual violence in the Rwandan conflict and the civil war in the former Yugoslavia (Table 7.2). We compare emergent categories that describe wartime sexual violence in Rwanda and the former Yugoslavia (Table 7.3). We list the actual terms used to describe wartime sexual violence by category and compare how the terms apply to ethnic cleansing in the two conflicts (Table 7.4). Finally, we present our findings on explanations offered by the news for torture and sexual violence.

Findings

Table 7.2 summarizes findings on the number of articles about wartime sexual violence that the *New York Times* and the *Washington Post* published during conflicts in the former Yugoslavia and Rwanda. Generally speaking, the number of articles about sexual violence in the former Yugoslavia exceeded those about rape or torture in Rwanda. Of the 56 *New York Times* articles, 26% (15) covered events in Rwanda. Of the 83 *Washington Post* articles, 8% (7) pertained to Rwanda. We considered that the conflict in Rwanda did not take place until 1994 and ended the same year, whereas the conflict in the former Yugoslavia began in 1992 and ended in 1996. However, in 1994, during the height of the Rwandan conflict, coverage of the then two-year-long war in the former Yugoslavia still received the lion's share of the news coverage. In subsequent years, the Rwandan conflict continued to receive substantially less news coverage compared with that in the former Yugoslavia. Even following the cessation of both conflicts, the coverage of the civil war in the former Yugoslavia continued to receive the most media attention.

TABLE 7.2

News Articles about the Civil Wars in the Former Yugoslavia and Rwanda[a]
by Newspaper, 1992–2000

	NEW YORK TIMES			WASHINGTON POST		
Year	Total[b]	Rwanda	Both[c]	Total[b]	Rwanda	Both[c]
1992	3	0		10	0	
1993	14	0		21	0	
1994	3	0		5	0	1
1995	9	2		13	1	3
1996	9	2	2	5	0	
1997	5	2	1	2	0	
1998	7	3	3	10	1	
1999	3	0		12	0	
2000	3	0		5	1	
Totals	56	9	6	83	3	4

[a]The Rwandan crisis began in 1994
[b]Totals include articles about the crises in the former Yugoslavia and in Rwanda.
[c]Both refers to articles that included information about both crises.

Five categories of wartime sexual violence against women emerged from our data. They are listed in Table 7.3 beneath the heading, "Terms and Concepts Describing Acts in the Conflicts." They include rape and sexual assault; ethnic cleansing and related terms (genocide, extermination, or massacre); torture; crimes against humanity; and forced pregnancy. Table 7.3 identifies the terms and concepts that apply to acts in the conflicts in both Rwanda and the former Yugoslavia and then lists the terms separately for the two conflicts. Table 7.3 also shows that specific terms used to describe acts in the conflict in the former Yugoslavia fall into the categories of sexual assault (33%), ethnic cleansing (44%), torture (16%), and forced pregnancy (5%). In contrast, most terms specific to the Rwandan conflict fall into a single category, ethnic cleansing (60%).

Table 7.4 lists the actual terms used to describe torture and sexual violence in news accounts about the civil wars in Rwanda and the former

TABLE 7.3

Terms and Concepts Used in News Accounts to Describe Acts in Civil Wars in the Former Yugoslavia and Rwanda

| | NEWS STORIES | | | | | |
| | About Former Yugoslavia and Rwanda | | About Former Yugoslavia | | About Rwanda | |
Terms and Concepts Describing Acts in the Conflicts	n	%	n	%	n	%
Rape and sexual assault	8	42	31	33	3	
Ethnic cleansing, genocide, extermination, or massacre	8	42	41	44	6	60
Torture	0		15	16	1	
Crimes against humanity	2		2		0	
Forced pregnancy	1		5	5	0	
Total terms and concepts	19	100	94	100	10	100

Source: One hundred thirty-nine news articles about torture and wartime sexual violence against women in Rwandan and Yugoslavian conflicts, 1992–2000 were published in the *New York Times* or the *Washington Post*.

Yugoslavia. The terms are arranged by category (e.g., rape and sexual assault or ethnic cleansing, genocide, extermination, or massacre). Within each category, we have separated out the terms used to describe both civil wars from those that apply specifically to Rwanda or the former Yugoslavia. Consider first the common terms used to describe sexual assault and ethnic cleansing. Taken together, the common terms tend to emphasize the scale of violence ("mass rape" and "mass killing [murder]"), its organization ("rape camps" and "detention camps"), and its systematic use ("systematic rape" and "systematic killings"). Emotional terms such as "sexual slavery" or "sexual mutilation" and "bloodletting" or "barbaric slaughter" add to the sense of brutality. Other common terms ("enforced pregnancy," "violation of human rights," and "atrocities") contribute to the construction of events as ethnic cleansing.

Second, we draw attention to the specific terms used to describe events in each country. With regard to rape and sexual assault, one is struck by the large number of descriptive terms associated with the conflict in the

TABLE 7.4

The Terms and Concepts Used to Describe Categories of Torture and Sexual Violence in News Accounts of the Civil Wars in Rwanda and the Former Yugoslavia

RWANDA	THE FORMER YUGOSLAVIA

RAPE AND SEXUAL ASSAULT

Common terms

Mass rape, sexual slavery, gang rape, (sexual) mutilation, systematic rape, rape and murder, rape camps, forced prostitution

Specific terms

Domestic violence, instruments used to rape, enforced sterilization	Rape to raise fighter morale, sexual humiliation, brutal rape, an old clime of war, rape, motel used as prison for Muslim women, systematic assaults, sexual abuse of men in detention camps, rape used as a weapon of war, women of reproductive age missing, held captive, sadistic, rampage against women, wartime rape, race as tactical form of warfare, rape used by Serbs as a weapon of terror, Rape of Bosnia, organized rape, repeatedly raped, sexual atrocities, weapons of genocide, rape as a form of ethnic cleansing, rape used to destroy an ethnic group, acts of unspeakable brutality, strategic [rape], human rights violations, death rape camps, raped to death, military strategy, rape as torture, rape as crime against humanity

ETHNIC CLEANSING, EXTERMINATION, OR MASSACRE

Common terms

murder, mass killing, bloodletting, barbaric slaughter, ethnic slaughter (violence), detention camps, extermination, systematic killings (murder)

Specific terms

Eliminate, planned slaughter, planned genocide, tragedy, genocide attempt, half million people killed	mass murder, mass executions, butchered, mass graves, death camps, concentration camps, internment camps, genocidal policy, killing, executed, Muslims missing, prison camps, Nazi era, carnage, atrocities, communal warfare, Holocaust, evil, Nazi style, Hitler, ethnic hatred, Nazi concentration camps, horror, forced relocation, wanton killing, willful killing, wanton butchery, wanton murder, ethnocide, demoralize, death, slaughter like cattle, depopulation, public murder, terrorist attack, mass expulsion, expelled, extinguished, Stalin, persecution, savagery

RWANDA	THE FORMER YUGOSLAVIA
ACTS OF TORTURE	
Common terms	
no common terms	
Specific terms	
torture	criminal brutality, terror, brutality, starvation, hostage/ rape, inhumanity, imprisonment, savagery, labor camps, beatings, systematically beaten, maiming of children, mass torture, psychological terror/torture, calculated cruelty
CRIMES AGAINST HUMANITY	
Common terms	
violation of human rights, atrocities	
Specific terms	
no specific terms	criminal responsibility, human rights abuses
FORCED PREGNANCIES	
Common terms	
enforced pregnancy	
Specific terms	
no specific terms	forced paternity, forced to bear offspring, seeds of evil, created Serbian babies, impregnate

Source: Sample of news accounts about wartime sexual violence against women in Rwanda and the former Yugoslavia, 1992–2000

former Yugoslavia, many of which refer to rape as a weapon of war. Rape raises the morale of soldiers. It has tactical or strategic value in effecting genocide and ethnic cleansing and in destroying an ethnic community. Moreover, the emotional quality of the terms is more intense in describing events in the former Yugoslavia, as indicated by such phrases as "raped to death" and "unspeakable brutality." "The Rape of Bosnia" implies not only the widespread nature of the offenses but the demoralization of a people and the destruction of a collective entity. In contrast, the smaller number of phrases that apply specifically to sexual assaults in Rwanda is unrelated to war. "Domestic violence," a more neutral term, is a criminal offense that involves intimates, not parties to ethnic cleansing. Although terms refer to instruments used to effect rape, the instrumental value of rape in effecting genocide is ignored in the coverage of Rwanda. The single reference to "enforced sterilization" is, however, open to interpretation as a biological method of ethnic cleansing.

Shifting to the next category in Table 7.4, ethnic cleansing, genocide, extermination, and massacre, one is again impressed by the number of descriptive terms associated with the conflict in the former Yugoslavia. Terms specific to the Yugoslavian conflict underscore and elaborate the scale, organization, and systematic use of the killings. "Mass graves," "mass executions," and "mass expulsions" are terms that underscore "mass murder," one of the terms used to describe conflicts in both countries. "Death camps," "concentration camps," "internment camps," and "prison camps" all reinforce "detention camps," a term applied to both conflicts. "Genocidal policy" raises the stakes on "systematic killing," another of the common terms. In particular, we point out that the language used to describe ethnic cleansing in the former Yugoslavia is reflective of the Holocaust, evoking powerful emotions associated with terms such as Nazi and the leadership of Hitler and Stalin. In contrast, the scant number of phrases that apply to ethnic cleansing in Rwanda carry far less emotional baggage. Whereas terms such as "planned slaughter" or "planned genocide" reinforce common descriptions of ethnic cleansing as deliberate, the terms that reinforce scale ("half million people killed") are too few and too neutral to convey the enormity of the tragedy.

Consider terms associated with the remaining categories: torture, human rights violations, and enforced pregnancy. There are no torture-related terms that apply to both Rwanda and the former Yugoslavia. Whereas acts of torture were reported in Rwanda, the reports from the former Yugoslavia involved a broader range of terms, ranging from "criminal brutality" to "calculated acts of cruelty." Torture may not be a neutral term, but it is far less inflammatory than the smaller acts (e.g., maiming children) that constitute it. Moreover, there appears to be a narrow band of terms ("violation of human rights" and "atrocities") that apply human rights violations in Rwanda and the former Yugoslavia. "Human rights abuses," a legal term requiring documentation, occurred in the former Yugoslavia but not in Rwanda, where the United Nations failed to act. Finally, the term "enforced pregnancy" applied to both conflicts, but specific terms applied only to the former Yugoslavia, where related terms such as "forced paternity" and "forced to bear offspring" reinforced the idea that rape and sexual assault were instruments for destroying and demoralizing ethnic communities.

The news articles we examined placed wartime sexual violence against women in the context of ethnic cleansing. We note that articles avoided biological explanations, such as soldiers' sexual urges or their testosterone levels, although in the case of the former Yugoslavia, references to sadism and the morale of soldiers come closer to individual propensity than one would expect. On the other hand, the tendency to place wartime sexual violence amid ethnic cleansing did not yield uniform explanations. Admittedly, a common set of terms about the scale, organization, and systematic character of violence appears to apply to both tragedies. Beyond basic description, however, the explanations are dramatically different. The Rwandan crisis was underreported, accounts of it were narrowly conceived, and terms fell disproportionately in the ethnic cleansing category. Descriptive terms, however, were poorly elaborated, being based on comparatively fewer terms in all categories. Significantly, the emotive value of any of these terms paled in comparison with the symbolic message conveyed by references to the Holocaust, Nazis, and Hitler.

Discussion and Conclusion

From the vantage point of the media, our findings suggest that the newspapers surveyed emphasized rape and sexual violence as war crimes in the former Yugoslavia, lending these crimes a reality that the equally horrific Rwandan offenses lacked. This is not just a matter of the number of articles published. The press created or drew on an extensive vocabulary to describe rape and ethnic cleansing in the former Yugoslavia and dramatically restricted the number of terms to describe these same events in Rwanda. In every category, the descriptions of events in the former Yugoslavia were emotional. In the former Yugoslavia, one reads about Stalin, Hitler, and concentration camps, the clearly defined enemy for those who grew up in the shadow of World War II, but in Rwanda, planned slaughter is just that, another atrocity without the sorts of symbols that might have stirred action. It should be noted that the articles surveyed contained no references to individualized motives, such as sexual urges or genetic predisposition, and that they treated the problem in relation to larger political events. Generally speaking, articles emphasize sexual assault and ethnic cleansing, themes that evoke public reaction, but without also stressing other important issues. Torture and crimes against humanity were deemphasized in our sample, and this minimized any public understanding of the legal bases for allegations of human rights violations against Serbs or Tutsis. Forced pregnancy and the children of hate are the least developed category in the articles reviewed; it is undoubtedly the most important in the context of ethnic cleansing.

Rape victimizes women and destroys both their standing as transmitters of culture and the community. It sends a message to the men that they are unable to protect their women against transgressors. In the midst of an ethnic community, enforced pregnancy results in the birth of children fathered by one's enemy. Estimates indicate that between 10,000 and 60,000 women were raped in the former Yugoslavia, whereas in the Rwandan civil war, as many as 500,000 women were raped. On this basis alone, one would have expected coverage to have tilted in the direction of rape in Rwanda. That it did not is a subtle reminder that shifts in press coverage have the capacity to determine what exists and what does not and what is important and what is not. If the crisis in Rwanda existed at all for U.S. citizens, it was decidedly less important than the civil war in the former Yugoslavia.

On the international stage, ethnic cleansings in Rwanda and the former Yugoslavia are treated quite differently. For one thing, the crisis in Rwanda involved an estimated 500,000 rapes, a figure that greatly exceeds the 10,000 to 60,000 rapes in the former Yugoslavia. The United Nations, for example, acknowledged the gravity of crises in both nations. It created the International Tribunal for the Former Yugoslavia (1993) and a second one for Rwanda in 1994. The tribunals set legal precedent. As a matter of international law, they recognized rape as a crime against humanity and a violation of the laws and customs of war. With evidence that the rapes are perpetrated for the purpose of destroying an ethnic group, they can be prosecuted as genocide (see Schiessl, 2002).

Where the average news consumer's knowledge of the social world is

limited, the emphases, word choices, and explanations that we have identified shape public perceptions (see Barak, 1998). That wartime sexual violence in the former Yugoslavia registered with the public and the events
in Rwanda did not may be attributed to the manner in which the news
constructed those events. Building on this study of wartime violence, we
plan to replicate our project using a larger number of ethnic and regional
conflicts and a larger sample of news outlets, and we intend to examine
the effects of race and ethnic differences among victims on the social construction of rape and sexual torture.

NOTES

1. The term "Bosniak" has replaced "Muslim" as an ethnic term in part to avoid confusion with the religious term "Muslim," an adherent of Islam.
2. For example, a Serbian strategy in the war in the former Yugoslavia was to establish
rape camps for women, where women of the intelligentsia and of higher social status were among those initially targeted for selection.

REFERENCES

Albanese, P. (2001). Nationalism, war, and archaization of gender relations in the Balkans.
Violence Against Women, 7, 999–1023.

Anderson, B. (1983). *Imagined communities.* London: Verso.

Baines, E. K. (2003). Body politics and the Rwandan crisis. *Third World Quarterly, 24,* (3),
479–493.

Barak, G. (1998). *Integrating criminologies.* Boston: Allyn and Bacon.

Carpenter, R. C. (2000). Surfacing children: Limitations of genocidal rape discourse.
Human Rights Quarterly, 22, 428–477.

Central Intelligence Agency (2004a). *The world factbook.* Bosnia and Herzegovina. Retrieved
October 22, 2003, from http://www.cia.gov/cia/publications/factbook/geos/bk.html.

———. (2004b). *The world factbook.* Rwanda. Retrieved October 22, 2003, from http://
www.cia.gov/cia/publications/factbook/geos/rw.html.

Dunne, T., & Wheeler, N. (1999). *Human rights in global politics.* Cambridge: Cambridge
University Press.

Einhorn, B. (1996). Links across difference: Gender, ethnicity, and nationalism. *Women's
Studies International Forum, 19,* 1–3.

Erlich, H. J. (1999). Reporting ethnoviolence: Newspaper treatment of race and ethnic
conflict. In F. Pincus & H. J. Erlich (Eds.), *Race and ethnic conflict: Contending views
on prejudice, discrimination, and ethnic conflict* (2nd ed. pp. 319–330). Boulder, CO:
Westview Press.

Fishman, M. (1980). *Manufacturing the news.* Austin: University of Texas Press.

Gellner, E. (1983). *Nations and nationalism.* Ithaca, NY: Cornell University Press.

Hastings, J. A. (2002). Silencing state sponsored rape in and beyond a transnational Guatemalan community. *Violence Against Women, 8*, 1153–1181.

Holter, O. G. (2002). A theory of gendercide. *Journal of Genocide Research, 4*, 11–38.

Lewis, P. (1994, June 12). Word for word: The Balkan war-crimes report. *The New York Times*, pp. 4, 7.

Lindsey, R. (2002). From atrocity to data: Histographies of rape in former Yugoslavia and the gendering of gendercide. *Patterns of Prejudice, 36*, 59–78.

Mamdani, M. (2001). *When victims become killers: Colonialism, nativism, and the genocide in Rwanda.* Princeton, NJ: Princeton University Press.

Meyers, M. (1997). *News coverage of violence against women: Engendering blame.* Newbury Park, CA: Sage.

Meznaric, S. (1994). Gender as an ethno-marker: Rape, war, and identity politics in the former Yugoslavia. In V. M. Moghadam (Ed.), *Identity politics and women: Cultural reassertions and feminisms in internal perspective* (pp. 76–97). Boulder, CO: Westview Press.

Nowrojee, B. (1996). Shattered lives: Sexual violence during the Rwandan genocide and its aftermath. *Human Rights Watch/Africa.* New York: Human Rights Watch.

Price, L. S. (2001). Finding the man in the soldier-rapist: Some reflections on comprehension and accountability. *Women's Studies International Forum, 24*, 211–227.

Schiessl, C. (2002). An element of genocide: Rape, total war, and international law in the twentieth century. *Journal of Genocide Research, 4*, 197–210.

Seifert, R. (1996). The second front: The logic of sexual violence during war. *Women's Studies International Forum, 19*, 35–43.

Skjelsbaek, I. (2001a). Sexual violence and war: Mapping out a complex relationship. *European Journal of International Relations, 7*, 211–237.

———. (2001b). Sexual violence in times of war: A new challenge for peace operations? *International Peacekeeping, 8*, 69–84.

Stanley, A. (1998, July 9). Semantics stall pact labeling rape as a war crime. *The New York Times*, p. A3.

Stempel, G. H., & Westley, B. H. (Eds.). (1989). *Research methods in mass communication.* Englewood Cliffs, NJ: Prentice-Hall.

Tuchman, G. (1972). Objectivity as strategic ritual: An examination of newsmen's notion of objectivity. *American Journal of Sociology, 77*, 660–679.

United Nations Development Fund for Women (UNIFEM) (n. d.). Gender profile of the conflict in Bosnia and Herzegovina. Retrieved October 22, 2003, from www.women warpeace.org/bosnia/docs/bosnia_pfv.pdf.

———. (n. d.-a.) Gender profile of the conflict in Rwanda. Retrieved October 22, 2003, from www.womenwarpeace.org/rwanda/docs/rwanda_pfv.pdf.

Weber, R. P. (1990). *Basic content analysis* (2nd ed.). Thousand Oaks, CA: Sage.

Wobbe, T. (1993). Die grenzen des geschlechts. *Konstruktionen von Gemeinschaft und Rassismus Mitteilungen des Instituts für Sozialforschung Frankfurt, 2*, 98–108.

Yuval-Davis, N. (1996). Women and the biological reproduction of 'the nation'. *Women's Studies International Forum, 19*, 17–24.

CHAPTER 8

THE HAUNTING OF JANE TENNISON

Investigating Violence against Women in Prime Suspect

Madelaine Adelman, Gray Cavender, and Nancy C. Jurik

Prime Suspect is a popular series of made-for-TV films that feature the exploits of Jane Tennison, a fictional detective with the London Metropolitan Police. These award-winning films air in the United States on the Public Broadcasting System (PBS). The series is something of an anomaly in contemporary television programming. The films not only feature a female lead in a crime genre program but offer a sensibility different from such very successful programs as *Law and Order*. In addition to crime drama, the *Prime Suspect* series offers plots that deal with social problems, especially issues that address populations who are largely ignored by mainstream television programming. In this chapter, we focus on "The Last Witness" (2004), the sixth film in the series. The film, which deals with the murder of two immigrant women, offers an opportunity to consider how a television crime program might meaningfully address a contemporary social problem (i.e., the plight of immigrants in London) and the justice issues that surround it.

We first discuss what makes the *Prime Suspect* series different from other police procedurals. Next, we offer a methodological note, a synopsis of "The Last Witness," and a brief overview of the Bosnian situation that is the film's backstory. Then we turn to our analysis. Throughout much of the film, we see Tennison haunted by persons and events from the past that include the torture and rape of Bosnian Muslim women in a war 11 years earlier. By being attuned to these "ghosts," she challenges her own taken-for-granted reality as well as that of her police colleagues, the government, and perhaps her viewers as well. Our study highlights the ways in which her investigation makes invisible lives and issues visible and as a result promotes a deeper sense of justice than that developed in most other crime genre programs. Although the sense of justice that the film promotes is limited in some respects, we argue that "The Last Witness" represents a work of moral fiction (Cavender & Jurik, 2004).

Prime Suspect and Deep Justice

Genres are classifications of cultural production. Crime is one of the most popular and enduring genres. It transcends media and moves with equal popularity across literary fiction, film, radio, and television (Cavender & Fishman, 1998). There are many explanations for the popularity of the crime genre, including fascinating detectives, the adventure of the quest to discover "whodunit" and why, or the righting of wrongs (Cawletti, 1976, p. 145; Klein, 1992; Knight, 1980, p. 83). This interest in the righting of wrongs goes to notions of justice, and indeed some critics argue that a sense of justice, in the character of the detective and in a deeper societal sense, is at the heart of the crime genre (Vernet, 1993).

Crime genres tend to favor a shallow sense of justice, one that focuses narrowly on the criminal justice system and that reproduces the dominant social order (Knight, 1980, p. 4). In contrast, our analysis of the genre moves toward a deeper understanding of the complexities of social and economic justice, (including injustice, inequality, domination, and subordination) (Cavender & Jurick, 2007). We argue that some crime genres convey a deep sense of justice, which may "illuminate the impact of structural oppression" and empower others to challenge "unjust social arrangements and organizations" (see Cavender & Jurik, 2004, p. 212).

The PBS *Prime Suspect* series is an especially interesting phenomenon because it conveys a deeper sense of justice. This British series of made-for-TV films began in 1992. Films in the series are police procedurals, and, as is standard in that subgenre, the focus is on the police organization as it tries to discover the identity of criminals and procure their arrest. The films differ somewhat from the norm; the lead character is a woman, Jane Tennison, played by Helen Mirren. In the early films, Tennison is a detective chief inspector (DCI) of the London Metropolitan Police. By virtue of her rank, she directs a team of detectives in criminal investigations. The police procedural as a subgenre traditionally has been resistant to women as lead characters (Klein, 1995); however, the *Prime Suspect* series presents many features that are consistent with works of progressive feminist crime fiction (see Klein, 1992; Reddy, 2003). Although the films deal with crimes, often murders, there is less overt violence than in other versions of police procedurals. Moreover, both in character development and plot, the films are relevant to women. Tennison is depicted as a strong-willed character who fights individual and institutional sexism to succeed in her investigations and her career. The films also address a variety of additional contemporary social problem issues.

Indeed, many of the films in the series deal with justice-related issues, for example, problems of sexism, racism, and economic injustice. "Prime Suspect 1" is a compelling portrayal of how women are discounted in the criminal justice system. The justice issue in "Prime Suspect 2" pertains to matters of race. In "Inner Circles," the plot deals with social class. Subsequent films in the series address other justice-related issues. In "Prime Suspect 3," the plot revolves around issues of sexuality. "The Lost Child" deals with the plight of a single mother whose child has been abducted. Thus, unlike other television crime genre programs and especially police procedurals, the *Prime Suspect* series addresses current social problem issues. More specifically, the films deal with populations that are often devalued in society and that are to a degree invisible. With respect to film plot, their invisibility is manifested in a virtual unwillingness by the police to address their victimization. But if these populations are unworthy victims to the police, Tennison takes up the gauntlet on their behalf, acting as a kind of justice provocateur.

Jane Aiken (2001) uses the concept of "provocateur for justice" to describe her training pedagogy for law students. We apply this concept to our analysis of fictional work because "provocateur for justice" is highly consistent with our concept of moral fiction[1] elaborated elsewhere (Cavender & Jurik, 2004). Justice provocateurs instigate and inspire others to work for human dignity and social justice. Provocateurs may work with the law but also understand the limitations of law; they know that neither law nor the state are neutral agents and that there are few absolute answers. However, provocateurs are not satisfied with legal relativism or a sense of cynicism or powerlessness. They are ready to take a stand and support their position in ways that do justice and, where possible, work for social transformation. Accordingly, like moral fiction, justice provocateurs identify inequality and injustice and feel empowered to try to promote change.

"The Last Witness" confronts issues of immigration and nationalism, and the victimization of women that often accompanies these movements. The problems addressed in the film, particularly the plight of immigrants—their fears and the invisibility and degradation associated with the work that they do, as well as the torture and rape inflicted on the minds and bodies of women in the name of nationalist struggles—has not been sufficiently recognized by international tribunals (Human Rights Watch, 2001) or popular film and television. Avery Gordon (1997) argues that such problems and the people affected by them are kinds of "ghosts" in our world—things seen and unseen that serve as symptoms of something missing from social reality. The ghost usually represents a loss, sometimes of life and sometimes of a path not taken. Being haunted by ghosts meddles with taken-for-granted realities, and investigating their haunting can lead the audience to a transformative recognition of an oppressed past and a more hopeful future. As an example, Gordon discusses *He Who Searches* [1977] (1979), Luisa Valenzuela's novel about a system of state terror in Argentina in the 1970s known as disappearance. Gordon argues that "illegal abduction by the police, military and paramilitary squads, detention in secret centers, torture and murder, improper burial, and denial by the authorities were characteristics of this organized system of state repression" (Gordon, 1997, p. 72).

Gordon recommends that we explore hauntings and reckon with ghosts "graciously out of a concern for justice" (Gordon, 1997, p. 64). Thus, much as earlier films served as vehicles for understanding the crime genre in terms of gender and race (Cavender & Jurik, 1998, 2004), "The Last Witness" addresses issues ranging from the devalued and invisible community of immigrants to ghostly signs of past atrocities.

Methodology, Film Synopsis, and Historical Background

Our discussion is based on an in-depth qualitative analysis of "The Last Witness." Each of us viewed the film twice. After the first viewing, we discussed the episode and identified emergent themes for our analysis. During the second viewing, we replayed scenes and took extensive notes about the plot, visual images, and dialogue. We again discussed the film in general and specific themes and scenes in depth. We reviewed each other's notes and quotations from the film. We also examined the film description, interviews with the actors, writers, and producers, and fan mail that appeared on the "Prime Suspect 6" Website (n. d.). After this work and a review of literature related to our research subject area, we finalized our major analytic themes. We then organized our film notes according to these themes. We begin our analysis with a synopsis of "The Last Witness" and follow with a brief overview of the real historical conflicts that form the backdrop to the film. Then we turn to a discussion of our three analytic themes: invisibility, haunting, and investigation. In closing, we discuss the tensions of the film and its significance as a piece of moral fiction that might evoke in viewers a sense of deep justice and empowerment to help promote progressive social change.

Synopsis of "The Last Witness"

"The Last Witness" opens with two scenes juxtaposed. The first scene is an extreme close-up shot of someone examining a body. Jane Tennison is undergoing a physical exam. She is completing 30 years of service and is under pressure to retire. The second scene is of a group of men anxiously awaiting the arrival of vans. They are global immigrants, day laborers hoping for work. At a worksite, before one group can begin their tasks, the body of a young woman is discovered (later identified as Samira Blekic, a Bosnian immigrant). An accompanying soundtrack features evocative Southeastern European music. Later, during an autopsy, the pathologist calls Tennison's attention to cigarette burn marks on the victim, saying they are similar in pattern to old burn scars: Samira was tortured as a young girl.

DCI Simon Finch leads the murder investigation. The investigation is politically sensitive due to anti-immigration sentiments among British politicians. Finch is relegated to second-in-command status when Tennison, his superior and now a detective chief superintendent (DCS), decides to lead the investigation. Finch suspects that Samira was murdered because Kasim Ibrahimivic, her sister Jasmina's fiancé, is connected to a Bosnian Mafia cigarette smuggling operation. Finch thinks that Samira was murdered as a warning to Kasim, who was trying to start his own smuggling operation. Unaware of the smuggling investigation, Tennison searches for Jasmina, who works as a hospital janitor. The search brings her into contact with immigrants who work invisibly in menial jobs and who fear deportation. Tennison locates Samira and Jasmina's apartment and finds Jasmina hiding there. Jasmina tells Tennison that she and Samira were victims of an atrocity 11 years before in Bosnia, when a Serbian paramilitary unit murdered Muslims.

Tennison's investigation produces a suspect: Duscan Zigic, a security guard. Zigic, aided by an interpreter (Milan Lukic), denies any knowledge of the murder. Zigic is released because of a lack of evidence. Jasmina is murdered at the hospital where she works. Acting on a tip, the police capture Zigic. Tennison seeks aid from friend and former lover Robert West, a photojournalist with experience in Bosnia. West secures a video of the atrocity that Jasmina recounted. Against orders, Tennison and West go to Bosnia. Despite little help from locals, they locate the killing site, a large, empty building.

In Bosnia, Tennison learns that the interpreter she called Milan Lukic is in fact Dragon Yankovic, the sadistic leader of a Serbian paramilitary group. The real Lukic is missing. Tennison presumes that Yankovic saw Samira as he left a London hotel where he had had a tryst and she entered her nearby workplace. He killed Samira to hide his past. British Intelligence orders Tennison not to pursue Yankovic, an informant who has led them to other war criminals. Tennison drops the case until her dad encourages her to do what she believes is right.

Tennison redirects her efforts, focusing on Yankovic's wife, Susan, who knows nothing of his past. Detective Constable Greaves tips DCS Larry Hall, Tennison's superior, that she is still working the case against Yankovic, and Hall removes Tennison from the case. She pursues it on her own. She again interviews Susan Lukic, and secretly tapes the conversation; Susan reveals that her husband is an informant. Tennison plays the tape for Zigic, the man who spared the sisters 11 years earlier. He admits that Yankovic had him kill the real Lukic, and he shows the police where the body is buried. Tennison now has a murder case under her jurisdiction. She arrests Yankovic as British Intelligence is about to relocate him. He surrenders after briefly taking his own daughter hostage.

Historical Background of Wartime Atrocities
in the Former Yugoslavia

"The Last Witness" introduces its viewers to real wartime atrocities that occurred in the 1991–1995 period in the former Yugoslavia. The film provides glimpses into this historical reality but does not provide sufficient background for viewers to understand why Bosnian Muslim women like Samira and Jasmina Blekic were raped, tortured, and killed by Bosnian Serbian men like Duscan Zigic and Milan Lukic.

Blueprints for the war can be traced to the growing expression in Yugoslavia of Serbian expansionist nationalism, which was articulated in statements produced in 1986 by the Serbian Academy of Sciences and Arts and the Serbian Orthodox Church (Cohen, 1996). Within a year, the leader of the Serbian Communist Party, Slobodan Milosevic, came to power in the Republic of Serbia. He rallied his nationalist supporters and escalated minority Serbian dissent against the majority ethnic Albanian population in Serbia's autonomous Kosovo province. Despite a lack of evidence, Milosevic's state-controlled media campaign lamented the uncertain future of the Serbian people and framed ethnic Albanian men as rapists of Serbian women (Silber & Little, 1997). During the same period, Serbia criminalized political rape, "the sexual assault on citizens of different nationality" (Meznaric, 1994, p. 86). Distinctions within the multiethnic/national region were further heightened and reconfigured in mid-1991 when Serbia unsuccessfully attacked Slovenia but then occupied much of Croatia and Bosnia-Herzegovina. By August 1992, stories of mass expulsion and systematic rape perpetrated by Serbs against local residents began to be leaked to the media, human rights organizations, and the United Nations by Muslim (Bosniak) and Croat survivors and witnesses in Bosnia-Herzegovina (Allen, 1996).

Serbs established quasi-governmental regimes in a quest to establish a "pure" Serbian state in much of Yugoslavia. To that end, Serbs abducted their neighbors and placed them in detention centers where they were "detained, tortured, raped and either expelled, killed or 'disappeared'" (Human Rights Watch, 1998). Serbian civilians along with members of regular and irregular military forces specifically targeted women with genocidal rape in their effort to create a Serbian polity (Allen, 1996). They raped girls and women in front of family and community members to terrorize and instigate the exile of the non-Serb population; they also systematically tortured, raped, and killed Bosnian Muslim women held in detention camps (Allen, 1996). Women described how they were "gang-raped, taunted with ethnic slurs and cursed by rapists who stated their intention to forcibly impregnate women as a haunting reminder of the rape" (Human Rights Watch, 1993). A popular slogan at the time, "rodit ces cetnik" ("you will give birth to a Chetnik soldier"), reflected Serbian logic according to which such pregnancies, when combined with expulsion and death, would ultimately result in the erasure of non-Serb nationals from the region (Allen, 1996, p. xiii; see also Stiglmayer, 1994).

This "recognizable pattern . . . has come to be known as 'ethnic cleans-ing'" (Human Rights Watch, 1993).

U.S. and European responses were late and politically ambiguous—perhaps because the U.S. Gulf War, the breakup of the Soviet Union, and the emerging European Union preoccupied the world powers (Cushman & Mestrovic, 1996; Williams, 2001). For example, George H. W. Bush's Secretary of State, James Baker, argued, "We don't have a dog in that fight" (Silber & Little, 1997, p. 30). The United Nations dealt with Bosnian victims by introducing peacekeeping (but not peacemaking) troops into the region and by forming the International Criminal Tribunal of the Former Yugoslavia (ICTY). The ICTY convicted some Serbs (and Croats) for crimes against humanity, though the majority of indicted men remain free. Notably, "these cases marked the first time in history that an international tribunal brought charges solely for crimes of sexual violence against women . . . and the first time that the ICTY found rape and enslavement as crimes against humanity" rather than simply as war crimes (Human Rights Watch, 2001). However, global attention quickly diminished. Ten years after the formation of the ICTY, the General Secretary of the State Commission for Gathering Facts on War Crimes in the Republic of Bosnia-Herzegovina referred to them as "forgotten victims" (Tokaca, 2004). Despite the millions of postwar dollars flowing into Bosnia, no national strategy emerged to rebuild the lives of the survivors.

We observe the atrocities in the former Yugoslavia as a powerful example of how women's bodies mark and are marked by nationalism. By this we mean that rather than consider "the nation" as derived from a primordially determined collectivity, we join other scholars of nationalism to argue that this sense of belonging and the delineation of borders between "us" and "them" is a cultural construction. Within this construction, women often symbolically and materially reproduce the nation. Not surprisingly, then, national movements sustain and are sustained by violence against women (Adelman, 2003; Aretxaga, 1997). Cynthia Enloe explains that "rapes have been reported as violations of 'our' women's honor, as threats to 'our' manhood as fathers, husbands and sons, challenges to 'our' collective masculinized honor as an ethnic community, as a nation . . . [rape is] the mortar that has kept the bricks of patriarchal international politics in place" (Enloe, 1994, p. 220). In other words, rape as a weapon of war is not a new phenomenon. In the conflict in the former Yugoslavia, as in most wars, the rape of women (actual or purported) rationalized the use of force to defend the integrity of nationalized groups and advance their agenda (Korac, 1998). Our analysis of "The Last Witness" that follows focuses on how survivors embody the mass rape and "ethnic cleansing" they endured during the war.

Themes of Invisibility, Ghosts and Hauntings, and the Police Organization
Invisibility

A recurrent theme in "The Last Witness" is the invisibility of Samira, Jasmina, and others like them. This invisibility characterizes work and personal lives. Even in death, they assume an air of local and international unimportance. The London Metropolitan and Bosnian police, British and Bosnian government officials and records, British and Bosnian citizens, and even the victims themselves are complicit in this invisibility.

Feminist scholars have long discussed the "invisibility" of women in the workplace. Women's work in caring for others, particularly in dealing with the concrete bodily needs of husbands and children, often goes uncounted and unnoticed. The more effectively such care work is done, the more invisible it becomes (Oakley, 1974; Smith, 1979). More recently, feminist analyses have examined the unequal division of labor among women along the lines of race, ethnicity, and class. This employment structure is both cause and outcome of a social hierarchy wherein poor women of color and immigrant women are disproportionately charged with the low-paid dirty work of cleaning up after others and tending to their bodily needs. These jobs entail long hours of back-breaking labor that are supposed to remain unnoticed. However, such work plays a vital role in "liberating" mostly middle-class and elite white women from domestic responsibilities so that they can compete for the higher-paying professional, "skilled," and "knowledge intensive" jobs (Romero, 2002). The first victim in "The Last Witness," Samira, works in a low-paid, service sector position. She was a housekeeper in a London hotel.

After Samira's death is reported, the police receive a call from her coworker, Stephen Abacha. Tennison and a sergeant go to the luxury hotel where Samira and Stephen were employed. The hotel manager takes them through several levels of basements where the housekeeping staff work.

Most of the staff are persons of color. Tennison and her sergeant follow the manager through rooms of staff sorting trash, putting cleaning chemicals on carts, and sorting, washing, drying, and folding avalanches of hotel laundry. The manager actually gets lost and has to ask the cleaning staff how to find Stephen Abacha. They direct him to Stephen's work assignment, cleaning urinals. These scenes give the viewers a sense of the dungeon-like setting in which Samira labored for 12-hour shifts, six days a week, keeping the hotel pleasant in a style typically taken for granted by its luxury guests. After her shift each night, Samira had an hour's walk home because she could not afford public transport.

In the conversation with Stephen, the viewers also learn of Samira's Bosnian Muslim nationality and get a glimpse of her strong desire to be invisible. Stephen tells the police that Samira had worked in her job for quite some time, whereas "most do not stick it out [the job] for more than a few months." He adds, "She was too intelligent for this, but she said she felt safe here underground." He also described Samira as "permanently troubled." When asked if the hotel would have an address for Samira, Stephen says, "Yes, but it will be false."

Stephen directs the police to Jasmina, Samira's older sister, who although training to be a doctor in Bosnia now works as a cleaner in a London hospital. The police go to question Jasmina at the apartment where she lived with Samira. In this scene, we again get a glimpse of the two sisters' desires to remain hidden from "outsiders." When the police arrive, there appears to be no one in the apartment. However, after Tennison sends her two police subordinates away, pieces of the floor come up, and Jasmina rises out of the ground, armed with a knife. Later, at the police station, Jasmina begins to detail the torture she and Samira endured in Bosnia 11 years earlier. She tells Tennison that she and her sister built the space underground in their apartment because Samira remained frightened. Jasmina says, "It gave Samira something to do . . . she was making herself safe." When Samira was missing and later found dead, Jasmina did not report it to the police because she and her fiancé, Kasim, were afraid of being deported.

When the police later go to find Jasmina at work, we see another series of scenes deep in the underground bowels of the hospital. The police run through the underground caverns of cleaners, unable to locate Jasmina. Managers do not even know for certain who or where Jasmina is. Tennison finds her, but it is too late: Jasmina has been shot while cleaning hospital toilets.

Themes of invisibility and devaluation recur throughout the film—the invisibility and devaluation of immigrants, refugees, day laborers, and the homeless people on the streets of London. Their supervisors at work know neither who they are nor where they came from. At one point, DCI Finch questions a foreman about the identities of his employees at the construction site where Samira's body was found. The foreman reports that the day workers fled when the police arrived. He says, "I don't know them, don't mix with them; they just work for me, they're just casual workers." The London newspapers identify Samira as Albanian, and a politician fulminates about "the Balkan Mafia, illegal immigrants" and about London being "swamped by foreign criminals." The police have difficulty tracking down victims and witnesses, and they cannot pronounce their names correctly. Throughout the early stages of the investigation, police officers make insulting jokes about immigrants. In one such instance, Tennison warns a sergeant about his disdain of immigrants, saying, "Look, I don't know what kind of ideas you have about the community we serve, but they'd better expand to include Jasmina and Kasim."

Kasim and Jasmina fear and resent the police. Jasmina angrily responds to Tennison's questions about Samira's life: "No, she was not a prostitute. . . . She was honest and she was hardworking. . . . We lost our parents and our house and we came here because we thought it would be safe. And in ten years, she [Samira] has not taken a penny from you. I know how you despise us, how you think we are less than you because we do the filthy jobs, but we're not!" When Jasmina speaks of "you," it is clear that she is referring not only to Tennison but to the entire nonimmigrant, "native-born" British community.

When Tennison requests an investigation of the war crime that she believes led to Samira's death, the war crimes unit reports that there is no record of an atrocity fitting the details Jasmina described. As with so many women who were raped and tortured in nationalist conflicts (Enloe, 1994), the victimization of Samira and Jasmina is deemed insignificant and made invisible by the state. Afterward, when Tennison and West travel to Bosnia to investigate the scene of the atrocity that Jasmina described, neither local police nor citizens living near the site will acknowledge that these events occurred. The police advise Tennison and West to go back to London, and Bosnian citizens the two attempt to question are openly hostile and refuse to talk with them. Again, the viewers are given glimpses of efforts aimed at making Samira, Jasmina, and other victims and their torture invisible both in life and in death.

Ghosts and Haunting

Samira and Jasmina function in a way that is both a presence and an absence in British and Bosnian societies. Despite their own best efforts to remain hidden and safe, the past continues to haunt them, and they, in turn, haunt Tennison and other characters in "The Last Witness." The film's portrayal of the lives and deaths of Samira, Jasmina, and other immigrant refugees resonates strongly with the concept of haunting outlined in Avery Gordon's (1997) *Ghostly Matters*. Gordon's analysis accentuates the ways in which the past exists within the lives of survivors and how ghosts inhabit our construction of reality. Gordon argues:

> If haunting describes how that which appears to be not there is often a seething presence, acting on and often meddling with taken-for-granted realities, the ghost is just the sign, or the empirical evidence . . . that tells you a haunting is taking place. . . . The ghost . . . is one form by which something lost, or barely visible, or seemingly not there to our supposedly well-trained eyes, makes itself known or apparent to us. (Gordon, 1997, p. 8)

Tennison's haunting begins during the autopsy of Samira's body. The framing of this scene and what unfolds during it sets the tone for the rest of the film. Tennison and the pathologist, a woman, are in the operating chamber, while DCI Finch and other detectives are seated in a gallery (separated by glass) above them. With a shot-from-above camera angle, Samira's body, displayed on an operating table, is surgically revealed like the overlays in an anatomy text. The camera moves in closer, framing Samira's body in a way that briefly parallels the camera shots of Tennison's physical exam shown earlier. The pathologist describes forensic information: Samira's hands and feet were bound by wire, and she suffered cigarette burns.

Then, the scene almost magically slips into a liminal space that consists of Tennison, the pathologist, and Samira's remains. For a moment, the detectives in the gallery disappear and it is as if the pathologist and Tennison are alone, two women talking. The pathologist tells Tennison that Samira's body reveals deep scars from cigarette burns suffered long ago, burns that are in the same pattern as the current ones. Tennison seems to glimpse something—perhaps the ghost of Samira's past—and she visibly opens herself to it, moving closer to Samira as if to see her better. The dialogue becomes almost wistful.

TENNISON: "So, she was tortured before?"
PATHOLOGIST: "Yes, I think she was."
TENNISON: "She would have been quite young."
PATHOLOGIST: "Yes."

Taking Tennison's perspective, the camera moves to a close-up of Samira's face as the haunting soundtrack music begins.

TENNISON: "She was beautiful."
PATHOLOGIST: "Yes, she was very beautiful indeed."

Tennison and the pathologist, both prickly professional women, are haunted by Samira's body and the ghosts that she reveals.

Tennison moves into the world of the immigrant community as she searches for Jasmina. She interviews Stephen Abacha, Samira's friend and co-worker. He tells Tennison that he and the Blekics are ghosts: "We do not exist." They hide from the state and from their own pasts. Yet, they live in fear, digging holes under the earth to hide in their own home if necessary. For a time, they are safe, until the day that Samira phoned home and left a message with their young neighbor, Haweeya, to tell Jasmina that she had "seen the devil."

As Tennison increasingly opens herself to the haunting, she learns why the Blekic sisters and others like them are forced to hide. Jasmina was raped again and again by her captor, who burned Samira with cigarettes whenever Jasmina did not act as if she enjoyed the forced sexual intercourse with him. Other Muslims in their community were murdered, but their captor's subordinate (Zigic) went against his orders to shoot Samira and Jasmina. He allowed them to hide among the dead bodies of their friends and relatives. Jasmina stops talking to Tennison when Kasim, her fiancé, enters the room; it appears that he does not know that she was raped.

Following Jasmina's murder, Tennison's haunting intensifies. She visits her dad at his retirement home and sees a woman mopping the floor. The charwoman is a ghostly presence, who in Gordon's terms is "quiet and understated" (Gordon, 1997, p. 206). Tennison is so visibly distracted that her dad asks, "Seen a ghost?" Although Tennison does not reply, her truthful answer would be yes, the ghost of Jasmina, whom she failed to protect, and a ghostly, invisible worker (like Jasmina) who formerly Tennison might not have noticed.

Later, when Tennison is being pressured to drop the case, her dad reveals his own ghosts. As a medic during World War II, his unit discovered a young girl, alive, hiding in a mound of bodies at a concentration camp. They were ordered to search for survivors through thousands of other bodies. Haunted by the experience, her dad recounts that after the war he opted for a normal life away from the evil of those camps and the mounds of bodies. He then relates glimpses of Tennison's own past that perhaps explain her adult personality. He tells her that until age 12 (coincidentally Samira's age when she was tortured), she was an angel. But after that, she could not leave anything alone. He had hoped that Tennison could retire and move away from evil, but now (with this case) she has to deal with it again. He adds, "But you will, you know what's right."

The audience is haunted in this film as well. We never actually see the video of the atrocity, but we do see its horrible reality conveyed through Tennison's expressions as she watches it and through music that sounds at times as though voices are crying out in pain. We see the site where the atrocity took place, but it is years later and the building is empty and decayed. We see the bullet holes in the building wall and seconds of film images of bodies massacred, and we again hear echoes of cries of pain deep in the past.

The Police Organization and the Investigation

Within the crime genre, a part of the audience's pleasure is to follow the detective's quest to solve a crime. In this quest, detectives use different methods of investigation. Sherlock Holmes employed rational deduction. Sam Spade and Philip Marlowe's investigations were characterized by a dogged determination that included a willingness to take a beating but to stay on the trail. In the action film *Die Hard*, physical prowess and technical competence allow police detective John McClane to overcome a heavily armed gang. Whatever the method, in finding the solution, the detective resolves the tension that was caused when crime disrupted the social equilibrium and in so doing produces some form of justice in the story's denouement. In this quest, the detective confronts many obstacles. The detective story resembles the classic adventure narrative that follows the hero on a journey that is fraught with peril (Cawletti, 1976). The resolution of these perils is as much a part of the audience's pleasure as the successful completion of the quest.

Gordon's (1997) conceptualization of haunting advances our understanding of Jane Tennison's intense commitment to pursue the ghosts in this case and her willingness to place her body in the location and position of the war victims. The examination of haunting transcends the mind/body split so often found in traditional understandings of victimization (Scarry, 1985). The bodies of the dead have been buried or lost, and physical trauma may have ceased for the living, but the body remembers and the terror continues. Yet, more than entangling bodies and minds, the haunting forces the reader to integrate history and memory and past with present. Gordon (1997, p. 58) quotes Derrida's recommendation about how best to deal with ghosts: "To exorcize not in order to chase away the ghosts, but this time to grant them the right . . . to . . . a hospitable memory . . . out of a concern for justice" (Derrida, 1991, p. 175). Tennison tries to do just this in her investigation: Almost as if it is a method of detection, she opens herself to the haunting and seeks to uncover the silenced voices of the victims in her case. Also consistent with Gordon's discussion, Tennison faces a number of obstacles in her quest to unravel the stories of Samira and Jasmina Blekic and their murders.

The first set of obstacles is occasioned by the police organization itself. "The Last Witness" depicts the London Metropolitan Police as an organizational labyrinth filled with twists and turns, any one of which can stymie Tennison's investigation. In the opening scene, the physical examination and the questions that follow subject Tennison to a close, invasive scrutiny of her body and her life. Although the process supposedly is designed to help her "understand her options," it is really designed to pressure her toward an involuntary retirement.

Tennison confronts other organizational obstacles in terms of situations and colleagues. These include DCI Simon Finch, her subordinate, who leads the murder investigation. Finch is an aggressive careerist (like Tennison in the earlier films) and a threat to her command. He pursues his own theory of the case and his own prime suspect, and he withholds relevant information from Tennison. Moreover, he enjoys the support of DCS Larry Hall, his mentor and Tennison's superior. As members of the same soccer club, Finch and Hall share an easy camaraderie, a form of male bonding, that excludes Tennison.

"The Last Witness" depicts other dimensions of life within the police organization. Given the sensitivity of this high-profile case, there is an organizational imperative to produce quick results. When Tennison decides to head the investigation, DCS Hall tells Finch that he discussed the matter with Tennison and agreed with her decision because Finch was making no headway: "You were five days in [the investigation] and had no leads." In any case, Tennison's decision to take charge strains her working relationship with Finch. Tennison also has strained relations with other lower-echelon detectives. These include detective sergeant (DS) Alun Simms, who is biased against immigrants, and detective constable (DC) Lorna Greaves. Later, as payback and to further her own career, DC Greaves tips DCS Hall that Tennison is pursuing the case despite orders to drop it.

The depiction of the police organization as an impediment is not uncommon in the genre: The heroic police detective is often ordered by a superior to drop a case. But "The Last Witness" brings these organizational dimensions into sharp relief. It not only portrays the organization as complicit in chasing away the ghosts but depicts it as a minefield, and in a manner that employs an important characteristic of the genre: realism. This workplace reality may be a reason that the series resonates with the audience, many of whom are professionals. They, too, work in organizations that demand more work and faster productivity, and they experience the potential to be undercut by competitive colleagues.

Gordon (1997, p. 206) argues that the state and its representatives deny ghosts and what they symbolize and constantly narrow what counts as evidence of the harms and indignities that people experience in their lives. This repeatedly is the case in "The Last Witness." Although Tennison opens herself to the haunting, and the ghosts that it symbolizes, others refuse to do so. DCI Finch tells Tennison that he can find no evidence of the atrocity that Jasmina recounted and that maybe she made it up. Similarly, when Tennison shows the video of the atrocity to DCS Hall, her superior almost seems to open to the ghosts but then stifles such feelings and once again becomes the organization man. He orders Tennison, "No way you're going to Bosnia."

Perhaps the most striking example of Gordon's argument about how the state and its representatives constrict the evidence to deny ghosts comes in a scene in which Tennison is confronted by an MI6 (British Intelligence) agent who initially appears as a nondescript woman. As Tennison signs an Official Secrets Act document, she refers to the female agent:

TENNISON: "And are we going to be introduced?"
AGENT: "Oh, I'm not important, I just brought the forms."

However, after Tennison lays out her case against Yankovic, the agent takes control of the meeting and even assumes an imperial tone with Tennison. She tells Tennison that there are no records that connect Zigic and Yankovic and therefore there is no connection:

AGENT: "We [spoken with an imperial emphasis] have come to the conclusion that Zigic acted alone."

She also denies that an atrocity occurred and offers an insulting explanation for why Tennison accepts its reality: Some people desire to associate themselves with a historical tragedy because it gives them "a sense of self-worth, of self-importance." The agent reminds Tennison that the Official Secrets Act precludes her from using any information that she learned at the meeting or from even discussing the meeting. As the agent speaks, she refers to Tennison as "Detective Chief Superintendent Tennison," a pointed reference to the state's hierarchy of rank and its power to deny the existence of the atrocity and the meeting and to block Tennison's investigation.

Tennison is unlike the other detectives. As her dad predicted, she will not let go. Against orders and despite obstacles, she and West travel to Bosnia to find the site of the atrocity. Once inside that bullet-riddled building, the haunting ceases to be quiet and understated; there, where the atrocity occurred, the haunting becomes, in Gordon's terms, "dramatic and deafening" (Gordon, 1997, p. 206). We see a mound of bodies and the aftermath: women gesturing in a manner that passes far beyond sadness as they see their murdered loved ones.

Tennison pursues the investigation and discovers that the real Lukic was murdered and that Dragon Yankovic, the sadistic paramilitary commander, assumed his identity. Possessed by the haunting, Tennison's investigation reveals the facts that were the ghostly visages: the atrocity; what Yankovic dismissed as "the reality of war," which in fact was a horrible brutality; and the reality, identified years ago by Susan Brownmiller (1975), that in war rape is a brutal political tool. Before her murder, Jasmina tells Tennison, "That's why they rape you, so you are always, always ashamed." This forces the victims to deny their victimization.

Jasmina and Samira tried to forget their brutal victimization at the hands of Yankovic until the day that he and Samira recognized each other on a busy London street. Tennison relives their encounter as she retraces the route from the hotel where Yankovic met his mistress to his place of work. On that route, he passed by the hotel where Samira worked. In this chance encounter, Yankovic sees that Samira is still alive and could identify him—the two sisters are murdered to hide his past.

In the final scene of "The Last Witness," Tennison is on the patio outside of Yankovic's house. Like the classic detective, she has solved the case: Yankovic may be an informant, but MI6 cannot shield him from a charge of murdering Lukic. There is no dialogue (only the soundtrack), so we do not know what Tennison is thinking. Perhaps she is thinking of Samira and Jasmina, of the others who were murdered in that building in Bosnia, or of Stephen Abacha and the other ghosts. Whatever her thoughts, Tennison opened herself to the haunting and by doing so revealed those hidden realities that the ghosts symbolized. As she told West earlier in the film, you do the best you can do. But there is more to it than this. Gordon (1997) notes that the ghost represents a future possibility, a hope, and that one opens oneself up to it out of a concern with justice. Perhaps this is why Tennison became a justice provocateur.

Conclusion: The Possibility of Deep Justice

The *Prime Suspect* series repeats a pattern of dealing with marginalized communities, alternately criminalized or rendered invisible and about whom few are aware or care. Tennison, often relying on intuition or empathy, tries to see and understand members of such marginalized communities. Similarly, "The Last Witness" presents complex and competing images of justice. The film contains a conventional story of shallow justice. A relatively rare but extreme form of crime is committed, the suspect is identified, and the criminal justice system is proceeding according to its well-established rules of prosecution and punishment. Tennison has once again proved her mettle and gotten her man—and she remains a lone provocateur of justice.

Following Gordon (1997), Tennison uniquely presents haunting as a method to better understand immigrants' lives. "The Last Witness" reveals to a mostly uninformed audience the ghostly life of immigrants, a population haunted by violence and injustice, whom viewers are intended to now recognize and attend to. Viewers are seeing the hidden lives of immigrants and their underground world, perhaps for the first time. The writers indicate that sympathy is necessary to begin to understand the lives of these immigrants. Yet Tennison pushes beyond a sympathetic viewing of invisible immigrants and attempts an empathic stance toward asylum seekers and victims of gendered crimes against humanity. She tries multiple times to embody Samira's victimization: observing her physical injuries, subjecting herself to the killer's gaze, listening intently to Jasmina's descriptions, and transporting herself to see the atrocities in situ. The film even tries to bring the viewer to the site after Tennison herself has exited, with its shot of the haunted "empty" building riddled with bodies and bullet holes. Empathy is not easily obtained, however—Jasmina argues with Tennison that the experience of wartime atrocities is knowable only to its immediate participants: "Please don't tell me you understand. *You* wake up every morning for ten years terrified, then you can tell me that."

"The Last Witness" is a police procedural, and thus hoping for an unconventional ending may be unrealistic. However elusive, the possibility of deep justice remains. This notion of deep justice moves viewers away from a focus on criminal justice and toward more robust social and economic forms of justice. Tennison, for example, is circumscribed by her position within the criminal justice system to pursue a rather shallow or narrow form of justice in which individual suspects are pursued and (sometimes) convicted. But the camera does not move away from the underlying issues that inform such criminal acts, an approach Cavender and Jurik (2004) call progressive moral fiction.

Progressive moral fiction looks at how private issues are publicly produced and thus (should) become social concerns. According to moral fiction, individual pathology cannot fully explain inequality, oppression, or violence. Still, progressive moral fiction points to but does not sink under the weight of structural causes of oppression. Progressive moral fiction is not a hopeless documentation of suffering and victimization. Rather, progressive moral fiction presents a politics of hope by making viewers and readers live vicariously through its characters and have them feel empowered to do something to address identified public concerns.

As justice provocateur, Tennison embodies a hopeful vision. She did not shrink or become paralyzed in the face of state protection of nationalist violence—she stuck it out to provoke a new form of justice. Without blaming the victim, by making oppressive structures visible, and despite her estranged position within the police organization, she is nonetheless able to identify and connect with other like-minded provocateurs of justice, such as Robert West. Generations of individuals like Tennison and her father have recognized the need to actively advance such a deep sense of justice.

Ironically, Lukic seems to most persuasively point to the potential location of deep justice. Referring to the killings he perpetrated during the war, Lukic states to Tennison, his interrogator, "I believe we are all responsible for many deaths one way or another." Will viewers see themselves in Lukic's statement or will they continue to push the ghosts away and refuse to heed their knowledge?

NOTE

1. We have used the term "progressive moral fiction" to refer to "fictional works that illuminate the impact of structural oppression in everyday lives and offer visions and hope for collective challenges to these oppressions" (Cavender & Jurik, 2004, p. 212). Typically, moral fiction (1) "draws on insights from experiences of those who are socially marginalized"; (2) "locates the experience within a larger social context"; (3) "reveals fissures in the predominant ruling apparatus"; and (4) "offers a vision or hope for collective empowerment to unjust social arrangements and organizations" (Cavender & Jurik, 2004, p. 212).

REFERENCES

Adelman, M. (2003). The military, militarism and the militarization of domestic violence. *Violence Against Women, 9*, 1118–1152.

Aiken, J. (2001). Provocateurs for justice. *Clinical Law Review, 7*, 287–306.

Allen, B. (1996). *Rape warfare: The hidden genocide in Bosnia-Herzegovina and Croatia.* Minneapolis: University of Minnesota Press.

Aretxaga, B. (1997). *Shattering silence: Women, nationalism and political subjectivity in Northern Ireland*. Princeton, NJ: Princeton University Press.

Brownmiller, S. (1975). *Against our will: Men, women and rape*. New York: Simon and Schuster.

Cavender, G., & Fishman, M. (1998). Television reality crime programs. In M. Fishman & G. Cavender (Eds.), *Entertaining crime: Television reality programs* (pp. 3–15). New York: Aldine de Gruyter.

Cavender, G., & Jurik, N. (1998). Jane Tennison and the feminist police procedural. *Violence Against Women, 4*, 10–29.

Cavender, G., & Jurik, N. (2004). Policing race and gender: An analysis of *Prime Suspect 2*. *Women's Studies Quarterly, 32*, 211–230.

Cavender, G., & Jurik, N. (2007). Scene composition and justice for women. *Feminist Criminology, 2*, 277–303.

Cawletti, J. (1976). *Adventure, mystery, and romance: Formula stories as art and popular culture*. Chicago: University of Chicago Press.

Cohen, P. J. (1996). Role of intellectuals in planning war. In T. Cushman & S. G. Mestrovic (Eds.), *This time we knew: Western responses to genocide in Bosnia* (pp. 39–64). New York: New York University Press.

Cushman, T., & Mestrovic, S. G. (Eds.). (1996). *This time we knew: Western responses to genocide in Bosnia*. New York: New York University Press.

Derrida, J. (1991). Geopsychoanalysis: . . . and the rest of the world. *Americas Imago, 48*, 199–231.

Enloe, C. (1994). Afterword: Have the Bosnian rapes opened a new era of feminist consciousness? In A. Stiglmayer (Ed.), *Mass rape: The war against women in Bosnia-Herzegovina* (pp. 219–230). Lincoln: University of Nebraska Press.

Gordon, A. (1997). *Ghostly matters: Haunting and the sociological imagination*. Minneapolis: University of Minnesota Press.

Human Rights Watch. (1993). Rape in Bosnia-Hercegovina. Retrieved February 4, 2005, from http://www.hrw.org/about/projects/womrep/General-25.htm.

———. (1998). Bosnia and Hercegovina: A closed, dark place: Past and present human rights abuses in Foca. Retrieved February 4, 2005, from http://www.hrw.org/reports98/foca/.

———. (2001). Bosnia: Landmark verdicts for rape, torture, and sexual enslavement: Criminal tribunal convicts Bosnian Serbs for crimes against humanity. Retrieved February 4, 2005, from http://www.hrw.org/english/docs/2001/02/22/bosher256_txt.htm.

Klein, D. (1992). Reading the new feminist mystery: The female detective, crime and violence. *Women and Criminal Justice, 4*, 37–62.

Klein, K. (1995). *The woman detective: Gender and crime* (2nd ed.). Urbana: University of Illinois Press.

Knight, S. (1980). *Form and ideology in crime fiction*. Bloomington: Indiana University Press.

Korac, M. (1998). Ethnic-nationalism, wars and the patterns of social, political and sexual violence against women: The case of post-Yugoslav countries. *Identities: Global Studies in Culture and Power, 5*, 153–181.

Meznaric, S. (1994). Gender as an ethno-marker: Rape, war and identity politics in the former Yugoslavia. In V. Moghadam (Ed.), *Identity politics and women: Cultural reassertions and feminisms in international perspective* (pp. 76–97). Boulder, CO: Westview Press.

Oakley, A. (1974). *The sociology of housework*. New York: Pantheon Books.

Prime Suspect 6. (n. d.). Production notes. Retrieved January 23, 2005, from http://www.pbs.org/wgbh/masterpiece/primesuspect6/notes.

Reddy, M. (2003). *Traces, codes and clues: Reading race in crime fiction*. New Brunswick, NJ: Rutgers University Press.

Romero, M. (2002). *Maid in the USA*. New York: Routledge.

Scarry, E. (1985). *The body in pain: The making and unmaking of the world*. New York: Oxford University Press.

Silber, L., & Little, A. (1997). *Yugoslavia: Death of a nation*. New York: Penguin Books.

Smith, D. (1979). A sociology for women. In J. Sherman and E. Beck (Eds.), *The prism of sex: Essays in the sociology of knowledge* (pp. 135–187). Madison: University of Wisconsin Press.

Stiglmayer, A. (1994). The rapes in Bosnia-Herzegovina. In A. Stiglmayer (Ed.), *Mass rape: The war against women in Bosnia-Herzegovina* (pp. 82–169). Lincoln: University of Nebraska Press.

Tokaca, M. (2004, April 22). Comments at The Hague before the Board of Directors for the International Criminal Court's Trust Fund for Victims. Retrieved February 23, 2005, from http://www.icc-cpi.int/press/video.html.

Valenzuela, L. (1979) [1977]. *He who searches (como en la guerra)*, Helen Lane (Trans.). Elmwood Park, IL: Dalkey Archive.

Vernet, M. (1993). Film noir on the edge of doom. In J. Copjec (Ed.), *Shades of noir* (pp. 1–31). London: Verso.

Williams, P. (2001). The international community's response to the crisis in the former Yugoslavia. In B. Magas and I. Zanic (Eds.), *The war in Croatia and Bosnia-Herzegovina* (pp. 273–281). London: Frank Cass.

PART III

CHANGING THE IMAGE
FEMINIST CRITICS AND CRITICISM

Standpoint theory begins from the premise that female subordination yields understandings of reality that are fundamentally different from those of men and that the premise holds up when multiple forms of female subordination and male domination are considered (Collins, 2004; Harding, 2006; Wood, 2005). Sexual harassment in the workplace, for instance, reduces stress for men, who believe that sexual jokes or unwanted touching do not cross the boundaries of women they claim to know. For women, however, sexual jokes or touching violate boundaries, leading them to seek protection in groups (Dougherty, 2001). In studies based on college students, psychologists have repeatedly found that women are more likely than men to hold rape perpetrators responsible and that women are less likely than men to blame victims (Langhinrichsen-Rohling, Shlien-Dellinger, Huss, & Kramer, 2004). Gendered differences in experience do not automatically translate into what feminists call a standpoint (Wood, 2005). A standpoint involves reflection about gendered differences in power and the development of a critical perspective toward female subordination. A reflexive standpoint, however, is not the same thing as understanding how to combine experience and theory to criticize existing power relations and the gender inequalities that they produce (Wood, 2005). This last step defines a political consciousness in which feminist critics understand that individual experience is part of and is shaped by structural and historical realities. It is the starting point for criticism.

In this section, we consider two issues related to standpoint theory. The first concerns strategies for changing gendered images and the standpoint of those involved in the process of producing media representations. Contributors take the position that the viewpoint associated with writers' gender and with the expertise of news sources can make a difference in representing victims. The second issue concerns the role feminist critics play in defining a critical stance, in resisting and transcending the gendered terms of debate, and in testing the limits of gender analyses.

The Role of Sources and Writers

In Chapter 9, "Victims and Sources," Heeren and Messing address domestic homicides with multiple victims to show that differences in news sources affect how female victims are represented in news reports. They identify different kinds of victims: Women killed by intimates are often blamed, whereas children or hapless bystanders are characterized in positive terms. Attributions of blame appear to be related to a reporter's reliance on police sources. As the official version of events, the police standpoint is determinative.

In general, police officers have mixed views about domestic violence. Some are quite knowledgeable and are prepared to respond proactively; others are fatalistic, believing that such incidents are unpredictable and inevitable. Police may not blame all victims, but in responding to repeated calls from the same address, they wonder about the mental health of women who stay with abusive partners. They have experienced chaotic domestic scenes frequently enough to think that arresting both parties is a good option, and they are frustrated when victims refuse to press charges.

The reliance on police sources has other consequences. In a study that compared perpetrators of intimate partner violence by agency (police, victim advocacy agency, and batterers' intervention program), news reports that quoted police sources overrepresented people of color (McCloskey, Sitaker, Grignsby, & Malloy, 2006). Reality-based television shows such as *Cops* rely exclusively on police sources. They represent the police as helpful but leave the impression that domestic violence is concentrated in poor areas of a city or town (Consalvo, 1998).

In contrast to police sources, domestic violence experts have strong views on abuser accountability, according to Heeren and Messing. They stress the perpetrator's deliberate planning and his need for control. Lethal violence is understood by domestic violence counselors as the predictable outcome of a cycle of violence; it is not inevitable or unpredictable. Moreover, domestic violence advocates are critical of police and the courts for failing to take action and for allowing abuse to escalate to murder. They tend to validate the experience of women as legitimate victims—as opposed to police sources, which tend to blame victims. And, when quoted in news reports, their comments are more likely to include information that would help at-risk women in dealing with their own situations.

Teaching reporters about domestic violence is a practical strategy for improving the news. In one such project, reporters were presented with a handbook on domestic violence. An experiment compared news reports on domestic violence before and after the guidebook's introduction. In the post-guidebook period, reports written by reporters tended to label homicide incidents as domestic violence and to cite domestic violence advocates as sources (Ryan, Anastario, & DaCunha, 2006). Reports about "unpredictable private tragedies" were replaced by reports about "social problems warranting intervention" (Ryan, Anastario, & DaCunha, 2006). A workshop for student reporters yielded similar results. Student reporters exposed to a domestic violence presentation were less likely to excuse perpetrators and less inclined to blame victims (Park & Gordon, 2005).

In Chapter 10, "Running Out of Oxygen," Lenning and Kowitz consider the role played by writers, directors, and producers responsible for made-for-television films. Their contribution provides support for the claim that the stories created by women better reflect women's experiences. Lenning and Kowitz link the female writers and producers at the Lifetime network to films that situate victims in a totality of life experiences. As such, their stories steer clear of victim blaming and avoid framing violence as a single inexplicable act. Although the Lenning-Kowitz results are provisional, they are consistent with other research on writers' gender. Lauren and Dozier (2004, p. 496), for example, have shown that female writers are more likely than their male counterparts to represent male and female characters as having equal occupational power and equal leadership roles and to be equally goal oriented. In addition, female reporters are more likely than males to use multiple sources, to avoid stereotypes, and to write positive stories (Lauren & Dozier, 2004; Rodgers & Thorson, 2003). Such differences may, however, reflect gendered assignments: "'Soft' issues like culture and the arts are mainly consigned to women media practitioners, whereas 'hard' and therefore 'serious' issues like finance, economics and politics are more likely to fall within the purview of their male counterparts" (Turley, 2006, p.12).

Feminist Critics and Criticism

Scholars take on critical roles when the implications of their work point to changes; For example, what to change (sources) and how to change it (hire female screenwriters). Feminists also define critical perspectives. In the second part of their chapter, Lenning and Kowitz draw on standpoint theory to consider this very problem. Focusing on cable networks—Lifetime, Oxygen, and WE—the authors analyze women-in-jeopardy films created for television. As a genre, these films involve a crisis, frequently criminal victimization, from which a heroine extricates herself with or without the help of companions or a love interest. Although such films have been dismissed as mundane, Lenning and Kowitz take them as legitimate objects of inquiry.

Lenning and Kowitz use a technique called "positive redescription" to reimagine the violent crisis from the victim's perspective. What is the meaning of violence for the victim? What is the nature of the victim's struggle to acknowledge an incident or to disclose it to others? What are the institutional obstacles that stand between the victim and the possibility of justice? How do victims experience these obstacles? What justice do they achieve? Insofar as these questions capture the victim's viewpoint, answers to them promise to provide the basis for positive redescriptions. According to Lenning and Kowitz, positive redescription has the "potential for countering the idea that victimization is an isolated act and for broadening perceptions of victimization to include the cruelties imposed by institutional response."

In addition to establishing a critical edge, feminist critics frequently take on the opposition. Deborah Jermyn takes on masculine presumptions that have structured British debates about the media and their effects on increasing fears about crime, especially among women. In reading Jermyn's "Making Sense of a Female Malady" (Chapter 11), keep in mind that research has repeatedly shown that the more people are exposed to media violence, the more likely they are to fear crime. In Britain and the United States, a series of government surveys beginning in the 1980s confirmed that fear of crime was on the rise and that this increase was tied to the growing popularity of reality-based crime programs on television. In both countries, these findings put the television industry in a difficult position: Violence attracted audiences to television programs and sold the products featured in commercials, but the same violence increased fears and opened television to the implicit threat of government regulation or censorship. The Federal Communications Commission (FCC) in the United States moved to impose a rating system that allowed parents to better monitor children's viewing choices. In Britain, debate also focused on the effects of violent programs on women.

Surveys indicated that groups with low victimization rates registered higher levels of fear in response to questions like, "Do you feel safe walking around your neighborhood at night?" Because women experienced relatively low victimization rates (as measured by the surveys) and because they registered elevated fear levels, questions immediately arose about the rationality of women. In response, U.S. and U.K. feminists argued that most of what women experienced as victimization was not tapped by crime survey questionnaires (see, e.g., Stanko, 1988). Questions probing sexual harassment, domestic violence, stalking, sexual assault, and rape were not included in fear-of-crime surveys; nor were questions included about the vulnerabilities experienced daily by women. If these items had been included in such surveys, women's fear of crime would have been better aligned with their experiences of victimization. More recently, perceived social threat (defined by perceived racial composition of the neighborhood, not perceived risk or actual threat of male aggression) has been cited as an important mediating factor in the link between television viewing and fear of crime in the United States (Eschholz, Chiricos, & Gertz, 2003).

In Britain, researchers looked more deeply at the crime-related anxieties experienced by women exposed to television violence. A pioneering study, *Women Viewing Violence* (Schlesinger, Dobash, Dobash, & Weaver, 1992), showed a variety of television programs to a focus group of women and then monitored their reactions. In response to watching *Crimewatch UK* (a crime-reconstruction program discussed by Jermyn in Chapter 11), a third of the women said the program made them afraid and half said it increased their fears (Schlesinger, Dobash, Dobash, & Weaver, 1992, p. 55). Schlesinger and his colleagues concluded that *Crimewatch UK* increased women's anxieties about crime and that it reinforced a "culture of peril" (Schlesinger, Dobash, Dobash, & Weaver, 1992, pp. 28–39, 63–64). Investigation of television and women's anxieties focused on generalized crime fears, messages about female vulnerability, and coping strategies (see also Holloway & Jefferson, 1997).[1] In drawing on this study, Jermyn's account of women's responses to episodes of *Crimewatch UK* offers micro-level analyses of audience engagement, in contrast to the large surveys that characterize research in the United States.[2]

Jermyn begins her chapter with a brief summary of British producers' reactions to allegations that reality-based television shows exacerbated the fear of crime. From these debates, she proceeds by analogy. She draws a historical parallel between Victorian images of female hysterics (circa 1890) and contemporary ideas about women whose fears of crime are also presumed to be baseless. Just as a feminist literary tradition reclaimed the female hysteric as an icon of oppression, Jermyn sets out to free contemporary women from the burden of male beliefs about the paralyzing effects of crime-related fears. To this end, she offers "an accumulation of anecdotes" to build a picture of how potent *Crimewatch UK* is in the lives of women. In the process, she also describes women's engagement in using the media to cope with fears. Is catharsis, the purging of troubling emotions, a factor in women's exposure to *Crimewatch UK*? Jermyn refers to a cathartic function but notes that the televised aggression aimed at women is not a likely pretext for the wholesale release of anxiety. In any case, the persistence of fear following exposure to violent television imagery would suggest that the effects are situational. Alternatively, are women's responses to televised violence a matter of managing complex but persistent fears? In answering this question, Jermyn contrasts women who manage their fears and masculine assumptions about women cowed by fears of crime. Although empowerment would not apply to cowering women, it may be more aptly applied to women who in the safety of a familiar television format use violent television imagery to manage complex fears and afterward to get on with the business of living, which is likely to reactivate such fears.

Critics also test the limits of the feminist approach to gender. Chancer's work in Chapter 12, "Victim Blaming through High-Profile Crimes," is more reflective of standpoint theory in its focus on race, class, and gender than Jermyn's focus on female viewers. Chancer interviewed journalists, attorneys, politicians, and others who followed the high-profile cases of "the provoking assault variety." These are distinguished by three characteristics. First, they are symbolic of social problems such as racial injustice and gender inequalities that had festered in the United States. Second, they blur the distinction between legal case and social cause. Third, they reframe symbolic issues through a process called "partialization." As defense attorneys and prosecutors lay out their cases, they inevitably reduce complex realities into a simplistic, two-sided contest.

Also partialized are the informal conversations of observers who followed the trials.

Under normal conditions, observers would be inclined to accept the prosecutor's view, holding the defendant accountable and sympathizing with the victim. High-profile cases of the provoking assault variety, however, do not describe normal conditions. All the choices are freighted by the symbolic character of the trial and the complexity of observers' emotions, ambivalence, anger, or suspicions. A belief in a defendant's guilt may signify to the observer that racists have succeeded in railroading a black man. Or a belief in the defendant's innocence may mean that another female victim has been sacrificed in the name of class privilege. Under such circumstances, observers are likely to take positions based on "substituting" and "reversing," two social-psychological processes that recall displacement and reaction formation, defense mechanisms that people use to handle troubling emotions.

In "substituting," observers may displace complex feelings about a defendant onto the victim, who they blame for their own victimization. For example, observers quoted by Chancer blamed Nicole Simpson, a safer target for ambivalent feelings than O. J. Simpson, who represented to black observers a successful black man, a credible suspect, and the likely victim of U.S. racism. In "reversing," observers stifle latent suspicions about a defendant's guilt and adopt an oppositional stance; in this case, they come to see the defendant as a victim. Observers interested in the trial on rape charges of William Kennedy Smith may have harbored doubts about his claim of consensual sex but came to see Smith as a scapegoat in a justice system bent on proving that race was not a factor in bringing charges against O. J. Simpson.

NOTES

1. The results of a Belgian study failed to support the mood management hypothesis that frightened people watch more crime on television in order to learn how to cope with their fears. The study provided support for the cultivation hypothesis, that is, that television viewing increases fears (Van Der Buick, 2004). The study did not consider subgroup differences (e.g., male vs. female); nor did it include mediating conditions such as social threat or culture of peril.
2. U.S. researchers have tested a number of hypotheses about the fear–television association. The cultivation hypothesis predicts that the more a group watches television, the more members of that group will fear crime. Although research supports the cul-

tivation effect (Chiricos, Eschholz, & Gertz, 1997; Romer, Jamieson, & Aday, 2003; Van Der Buick, 2004), current work addresses more clearly specified hypotheses. The substitution hypothesis, which is most relevant to groups with low victimization rates, posits that television violence has a greater impact on increasing fears among young people, the elderly, and women because they substitute television violence for experience with crime (see Eschholz, Chiricos, & Gertz, 2003).

REFERENCES

Chiricos, T., Eschholz, S., & Gertz, M. (1997). Crime news and fear of crime: Toward an identification of audience effects. *Social Problems, 44*, 342–357.

Collins, P. H. (2004). *Black feminist thought: knowledge, consciousness, and the politics of empowerment* (2nd ed.). New York: Routledge.

Consalvo, M. (1998). Hegemony, domestic violence, and cops. *Journal of Popular Film and Television, 26*, 62–71.

Dougherty, D. S. (2001). Sexual harassment as (dys)functional process: A feminist standpoint analysis. *Journal of Applied Communications, 29*, 372–402.

Eschholz, S., Chiricos, T., & Gertz, M. (2003). Television and fear of crime: Program types, audience constraints, and the mediating effects of perceived neighborhood racial composition. *Social Problems, 50*, 395–415.

Harding, S. (2006). *Science and social inequality: Feminism and postcolonial issues.* Urbana: University of Illinois Press.

Holloway, W., & Jefferson, T. (1997). The risk society in an age of anxiety: Situating fear of crime. *British Journal of Sociology, 48*, 255–266.

Langhinrichsen-Rohling, J., Shlien-Dellinger, R. K., Huss, M. T., & Kramer, V. L. (2004). Attributions about perpetrators and victims of interpersonal violence. *Journal of Interpersonal Violence, 19*, 484–498.

Lauren, M. M., & Dozier, M. D. (2004). Evening the score in prime time: The relationship between behind the scenes women and onscreen portrayals of female and male characters. *Journal of Broadcasting and Electronic Media, 48*, 484–500.

McCloskey, K., Sitaker, M., Grignsby, N., & Malloy, K. A. (2006). Overrepresentation of people of color as intimate partner violence perpetrators: The case for examining multiple points of contact. *Journal of Aggression, Maltreatment and Trauma, 13*, 19–40.

Park, G., & Gordon, B. (2005). Domestic violence presentation raises awareness in student reporters' stories. *Newspaper Research Journal, 26*, 113–118.

Rodgers, S., & Thorson, E. (2003). A socialization perspective on male and female reporting. *Journal of Communications, 63* (4), 658–675.

Romer, D., Jamieson, K. H., & Aday, S. (2003). Television news and the cultivation of fear of crime. *Journal of Communications, 53* (1), 88–104.

Ryan, C., Anastario, M., & DaCunha, A. (2006). Changing coverage of domestic violence murders: A longitudinal experiment in participatory communication. *Journal of Interpersonal Violence, 21* (2), 209–228.

Schlesinger, P., Dobash, R. E., Dobash, R. P., & Weaver, C. K. (1992). *Women viewing violence.* London: British Film Institute.

Stanko, E. A. (1988). Fear of crime and the myth of the safe home: A feminist critique of criminology. In K. Yllo & M. Bograd (Eds.), *Feminist perspectives on wife abuse* (pp. 75–88). Newbury Park, CA: Sage.

Turley, A. (2006). Who makes the news? Promoting gender equality in and through news media. *Pacific Journalism Review, 12,* 10–14.

Van Der Buick, J. (2004). Research note: The relationship between television fiction and fear of crime: An empirical comparison of three causal relationships. *European Journal of Communications, 19,* 239–248.

Wood, J. T. (2005). Feminist standpoint theory and muted group theory: Commonalities and divergences. *Women and Language, 28,* 61–64.

CHAPTER 9

VICTIMS AND SOURCES

Newspaper Reports of Mass Murder in Domestic Contexts

John W. Heeren and Jill Theresa Messing

Although reporters strive for objectivity and, in their view, render a version of reality that is not far removed from "what really happened," a sizable body of research attests to distortion in the news about crime. Criminologists explain that media distortions are in part due to the reporters' heavy reliance on a single official source, the police. This chapter focuses on the news reporting of 41 purposively selected cases of multiple domestic homicide that occurred in the United States between 1994 and 1999. Within these stories, reporters focus on official sources to detail the events surrounding the homicide. However, alternative sources—such as domestic violence professionals, family, and friends of the victims—are also used and may contradict the police version of events. Although police stress the causal role of individual pathology in offending, domestic violence professionals attempt to educate the reader about the nature of intimate partner violence and contradict the police claim that the events could not be predicted. In addition, reporters often use alternative sources to establish a point of view, to add evocative details, or to describe and classify victims. News sources and their impact on the representation of victims and violence against women are considered in this chapter.

Literature Review

According to Schudson (1978), objectivity has been the standard in American journalism since the early part of the twentieth century. Modeled on the procedures of scientific knowing, objectivity takes form as a commitment to impartiality. Although among journalists the claim has come under fire (Surette, 1998), scientific knowing and objectivity continue to guide reporters' work (Ericson, Baranek, & Chan, 1987; Gans, 1979). Tuchman (1972, 1978) suggests that objectivity is a matter of strategic rituals that when followed allow reporters to claim impartiality. Among these rituals are the reliance on authoritative sources, presentation of opposing claims, and the careful use of quotations in order to distance the reporter from the report.

When justice officials make statements, reporters can report them as objective fact. The announcement of an arrest is treated as objective fact—source and fact being indistinguishable. However, a defense attorney's claim that the evidence points to an alternate suspect is treated as a point of view. To avoid the appearance that the reporter has taken one side against another, both statements require quotation marks, which maintain an appearance of impartiality. The preferred sources, according to Tuchman (1978, p. 91), are those, like the police, that represent "legitimated institutions with access to centralized information." Reporters rarely challenge the right of officials to make news; those in nonofficial positions, such as witnesses or advocates, must prove their legitimacy to reporters if they want to be included in a story.

In light of the importance of official sources, it is not surprising that most studies have found that the police are the primary source for crime reporters (Chermak, 1994a; Ericson, Baranek, & Chan, 1987; Fishman, 1978; Grabosky & Wilson, 1989; Humphries, 1981; Kasinsky, 1994; Meyers, 1997; Sherizen, 1978; Tunnell, 1998; Websdale & Alvarez, 1998; Welch, Fenwick, & Roberts, 1997). The advantages of using police as news sources are many. As "first responders," the police have already done their own investigation of the crime. This may have been followed up by detective and crime scene work that will emerge as a bureaucratic document (Fishman, 1980). Thus, reliance on a report created by the official source is a cost-effective way for any news organization to collect potential stories (Surette, 1998; Websdale, 1999). In addition, the police are highly credible in the eyes of the public, a fact that allows reporters to cloak themselves in objectivity (Chermak, 1994b; Ericson, Baranek, & Chan, 1987; Meyers, 1997).

The central drawback to such a heavy reliance on the police, as researchers note, is that news workers are reluctant to criticize the police out of fear of losing access to them in the future (Chermak, 1994a, 1995; Grabosky & Wilson, 1989; Welch, Fenswick, & Roberts, 1997). Any failures on the part of the police are unlikely to be reported; if reported, these are treated as isolated instances (Chermak, 1994a). Websdale and Alvarez (1998) refer to the media's reliance on the police as "forensic journalism." Because reporters are the "captives" of the police, news reports emphasize the details of the crime scene, to the exclusion of any patterns or causes in the broader social context. Perpetrators of domestic murder are discredited, but never are they as deeply stigmatized as serial killers. Details about victims are generally added to news stories in order to increase the "emotional hooks" that engage readers (Chermak, 1995; Ericson, Baranek, & Chan, 1987).

In homicide cases, sources present special problems. Websdale (1999) shows that domestic homicide reports rarely mention a family's history of violence. In the aftermath of such incidents, few people are available to answer reporters' questions. Survivors, coping with grave injury or the loss of a child, do not generally talk to reporters. Family and friends sometimes serve as surrogate sources but may be reluctant to expose their feelings in news reports. Louisell (1995) describes such exposure as the "commodification" of private experience. In the absence of victims and their social circles, reporters tap advocacy groups and other experts who have firsthand experience in dealing with the victims of domestic violence (Best, 1999; Meyers, 1997). Thus, reporters cite the "victim's perspective" without actually interviewing victims or their surrogates. Moreover, reporters rarely seek out victims, preferring police sources (Chermak, 1994a, 1994b, 1995). As Chermak notes, the process of news production excludes "unaffiliated sources" (e.g., crime victims, defendants, experts, and citizens) unless they can provide "newsworthy information" (Chermak, 1994b, p. 579). Although news reports cite experts and professionals (Welch, Fenwick, & Roberts, 1997), they tend to avoid victim advocates (Tunnell, 1998).

This chapter considers two news sources: official police sources and unaffiliated sources, including domestic violence professionals, counselors, and advocates as well as the family, friends, and co-workers of victims. It does so in the particular context of domestic homicides with multiple fatalities. These crimes tend to be excessively violent and are typically subject to sensationalism and extensive news coverage. The most common victims—women, children, and altruistic bystanders—contribute to the newsworthiness of these incidents (Buckler & Travis, 2005; Pritchard & Hughes, 1997). Additionally, due to the likelihood—or at least the likely speculation—of intimate partner violence in these cases, the contrast between official and unofficial sources may be amplified. As domestic crimes, however, they are less likely to be reported than public murders with multiple fatalities (Duwe, 2000; Petee, Padgett, & York, 1997). Nevertheless, news reports are numerous enough to allow us to examine the role of police and alternative news sources in constructing the images of the multiple victims of domestic homicides.

Research

The Lexis-Nexis database of newspapers was utilized to generate a sample of reports on domestic homicides with multiple fatalities. Although searches can be done by region of the country, the search terms yielded more cases (1000+) than Lexis-Nexis allowed, so each state had to be searched separately. News stories were collected during a 72–month period from January 1, 1994, to December 31, 1999. Using "domestic violence" and "murder" as search words, thousands of cases were pulled from the newspapers. Narrowing the search criterion to "multiple murders," we concentrated on cases where an intimate or ex-intimate murdered three or more victims, provided that at least one victim was the adult partner, ex-partner, or child of the perpetrator. This reduced the sample to 78 cases, most (71) of which involved male killers. Because the high proportion of male offenders is typical of such incidents (Duwe, 2000; Websdale & Alvarez, 1998), we excluded cases with female perpetrators for purposes of this chapter.[1] From the smaller pool of cases, we drew a purposive sample ($N=41$) that includes incidents from each year surveyed and from all regions of the country. The sample was small enough for qualitative analysis but still included a reasonable distribution of news stories.

The number of murders committed by male offenders ranged from 3 to 12, with the mean being 3.7. Twenty-seven of the cases involved four or more murder victims. These rampages also led to 46 injuries, many of which could easily have been deaths with slight changes in circumstances. In terms of outcome, 33 of the men were arrested, 28 committed suicide, 8 were killed by police, and 2 were still sought by police as the stories were being written. The sample underrepresents the suicidal intent of perpetrators in domestic homicides with multiple victims. For example, several of those arrested intended to commit suicide but failed or backed out at the last moment. Moreover, several of those who were killed by police seem to fall into the category of "suicide by police" in that they continued to fire at the police in the face of overwhelming odds against their surviving. Finally, a number of those who were arrested later tried to commit suicide while in custody. So, although suicide occurs in about 40% of our cases, it is actually more pervasive than the figure indicates.

In the context of our dataset, we address three issues: (1) the sources news reporters use to write their news stories, (2) how the sources cited influence the representation of domestic violence with multiple fatalities, and (3) how victims are characterized in news reports.

Results
Police and Other Official Sources

Reporters' commitment to presenting the "facts" was evident in the reliance on police sources. When incidents were followed by the death of the perpetrator by suicide (13 cases) or by police (5 cases), the news reports relied almost exclusively on police sources. At times, news reporters might interview neighbors or relatives who could serve as witnesses to events. However, these interviews added little; they tended to confirm police accounts.

The reliance on police sources can be problematic. In the case of a triple homicide in a small town in Kentucky, the police refused to provide reporters with information on a motive, results of a lie detector test, and other details. The net effect of the police refusal was to limit coverage to a few stories, though the triple murder would have seemed to be newsworthy on other grounds: It featured violence, white victims, a small-town setting, and some unusual crime details. In cases where little is known about what happened at a murder scene and where no witnesses are available for reporters to interview, the police view is so authoritative that police officials are free to speculate about unknowable events. For example, in several of the murder-suicides where there were no living witnesses, law enforcement offered as definitive their theory of how events unfolded. In addition, police officials sometimes provided reporters with predictions about alternative scenarios. In two separate cases, both in Colorado, police spokespersons opined that failures in the system of social control were *not* to blame for the deaths. Instead, the killers were seen as uncontrollable persons who could not be stopped. In the words of the police chief in one of these cases, where the offender's release from jail was followed quickly by the homicide, "I don't think there was a way to prevent this. If he'd spent more time in jail, it just would have been later."

When the offender survives the slaughter and the case goes to trial, other official sources emerge. Here the contending sides in the trial—the defense attorney and the prosecutor—are given their opportunity to argue their cases in the newspaper. Generally, reporters give the prosecution and defense "equal time," but in a few cases coverage leaned toward one side or the other. In the following example, news accounts tilted toward the alleged killer, a white, middle-aged Washington State man who had married a Filipino mail-order bride. Less than two weeks after their marriage, the bride claimed abuse and moved out. Convinced that his wife had married him to gain U.S. citizenship, the husband sought an annulment, which would have required her to return to the Philippines. She, in turn, wanted a divorce based on allegations of abuse, which would have allowed her to remain in the United States. During the divorce proceedings, the husband murdered his wife and two of her Filipino friends in a courthouse hallway. The resulting trial was heavily covered by the press; newspaper stories devoted the vast majority of space to the husband's life story and his complaints about his wife, while slighting evidence of his anger and abuse. Similarly, news stories concentrated on discrepancies between the victim's statements and behavior, thus undermining her credibility as a victim. The inequality implicit in devaluing the female victim is compounded by her devaluation based on her status as a foreigner (see Consalvo 1998).

Typically, however, news reports tended to side with victims and the prosecution case, especially when the case advanced by the defense could be ridiculed. For instance, a Massachusetts case involved a retired military man who had both a wife and a girlfriend, having had two children with the latter. When the girlfriend discovered that he was married, she threatened to go to his wife with the story of his other life. In response, the offender killed his girlfriend and their two small children. At trial, the defense argued for "diminished capacity" because the defendant, when threatened with exposure, went "into the zone" just as he might have in a military situation. In addition, the defense tried to shift blame to the victim by saying she had a "fatal attraction" for the killer and would not take "no" for an answer. The newspaper stories scoffed at the defense's claims, noting that the killer had been overheard bragging to friends that he was a "king" with the "prerogative" of having two women. In an accompanying article that underscored the skepticism about the defense, a reporter noted that the defense's case was built on "blaming the victim" and that its theory that the defendant was "in the zone" depended on a pop psychology that was not supported by scientific evidence.

Alternative Source: Domestic Violence Professionals and Advocates

Just under a quarter of the cases (10 of 41) cited alternative sources, including a variety of domestic violence workers, activists, and experts. Half of the articles with alternative sources appeared in 1999, with the rest spread over the years from 1995 to 1998, indicating an increasing reliance on nonpolice sources in cases. Typically, alternative sources would be quoted in lengthy overviews or feature stories about the multiple homicides, and they were likely to be published days or weeks after the event itself. In four instances, the news reports citing alternative sources followed a wave of domestic homicides. There appeared to be no regional or city-size pattern, with these articles occurring in small and large cities in the northeastern, northwestern, midwestern, southern, and western parts of the United States.

Important themes emerged in the news reports that cited alternative sources about domestic violence.

- Past abuse is the best predictor of future violence. Domestic violence precedes and predicts domestic homicide. Domestic homicides are a substantial percentage of all homicides.
- Domestic violence is pervasive but hidden from public view. Many families that are outwardly "perfect" are simply too embarrassed to seek outside help from social service or law enforcement agencies.
- Domestic violence is not taken seriously enough by police and courts. Abusers' threats to the safety of the family are often followed through with physically violent acts.
- Intimate partner violence can occur in any relationship, regardless of class or ethnicity.
- Abusers often come from violent homes. They are concerned with control and power in the intimate partner relationship and are intensely jealous and vengeful. Drug and alcohol use accentuates these issues.
- Domestic violence may have a lengthy course due to the cycle of vio-

lence that typically occurs. This cycle posits that periods of abuse alternate with contrition.

- Offenders do not suddenly "snap" and commit murder in the family. There is usually deliberate planning of the crime and careful choosing of methods and victims.
- Whatever choices they have made, victims cannot be blamed for the violence. Abusers and murderers must be held accountable for their crimes.

Domestic violence workers and advocates cited in the news repeat these same themes. They place domestic violence in a larger context, offer constructive insights, and present contrasts with official sources that blame victims or downplay offender responsibility. By pointing out the nature and seriousness of domestic conflict, domestic violence professionals take advantage of the opportunity given them by reporters to make the general public more aware of domestic abuse and more attentive to the signs of its escalation toward fatal outcomes.

The assertation of these themes by domestic violence professional's is overtly intended to counter commonly held beliefs about domestic abuse. This is especially true in cases where local beliefs make the situation worse. Following a family "annihilation" homicide that shocked a small Iowa community, a neighbor said, "I didn't know anything. That's practically typical of our lifestyle, though. You're supposed to keep everything inside. You're not supposed to reach out for help." In communities with centralized domestic violence units, such beliefs can be dispelled. In an Oklahoma case, an outwardly "perfect" family was murdered by the husband/father, and the local police were initially unable to find a motive. An official with Domestic Violence Intervention Services (DVIS), however, suggested that the family was probably hiding physical abuse, saying, "It wouldn't be a surprise if over the next weeks and months, a different picture emerges" than that of the perfect family. A few months later, the prosecutor announced that they had uncovered evidence that showed this to be true; ongoing physical abuse had led to the murder of the wife and children. The alternative source of DVIS had proven to be surprisingly accurate.

Newspaper reporters utilizing alternative sources encourage justice officials to take domestic violence more seriously by helping them to recognize that it is not an isolated tragedy and accept that it is an escalating conflict with the potential for fatalities. One case, which began with the workplace murder of an estranged wife, led to the killing of a sheriff's deputy. Another multiple murder, stemming from the familial and financial problems of the offender, began with the murder of three family members, but eventually it led to the murder of nine of the offender's business associates. Moreover, these reports demonstrate that inaction in the face of intimate partner violence can be deadly. In one case, an offender had choked and assaulted his wife and crashed the family car with her and the children in it. He was charged with simple misdemeanor domestic abuse and was released after posting a $130 bond. Although the misdemeanor charge did not require the offender to surrender his guns, he turned them over to police on his own. With the approach of pheasant season, the police unilaterally decided that he needed his guns back in order to go hunting. Within two weeks, the guns had been turned on his family. The local police chief explained away the failure to act and his neglect in returning the guns, claiming that the three murders were "not preventable." In this instance, the reporter consulted with the head of the statewide domestic violence coalition and wrote, "It is not helpful for law-enforcement officials to talk about such homicides as unpreventable." In another context, a domestic violence advocate noted that women who use the protective tools available to them (restraining orders, shelters, escape) still may be killed, but this should not lead to the pessimistic conclusion that nothing can be done.

Alternative sources point out that there are specific precursors to domestic homicide, such as, "I'll kill you and myself." Nonpolice sources understand that these threats are not idle and should not be ignored. Any diminution of an abuser's power or control over his family may lead him to carry through with the threat. When the ex-wife of one offender moved to another part of the state, the "loving father" killed his four children rather than let them go with her. Although he claimed to be saving them from a "hellish" future with their mother, a psychiatrist pointed out that this was the father's warped attempt to declare: "If I can't have them, then nobody can!" A similar outcome may emerge from a mix of separation, depression, and suicide. Whether the clinical depression or the separation comes first, they reinforce one another and may lead a perpetrator to plan suicide and murder, taking the family along with him into death. As an official with a statewide domestic violence coalition said, abusive suicidal men are dangerous.

An extraordinary effort using alternative news sources (domestic violence experts) is a 1999 series that was published by the *Tulsa World* following a multiple murder/suicide that took six lives (see *Tulsa World*, 1999a, 1999b). The articles present information on domestic violence, including characteristics of abusers, patterns in abusive relationships, and feelings experienced by both parties involved. Sources from Domestic Violence Intervention Services (DVIS) provide the criteria and procedures for getting a protection order and describe the range of relationships in which protection can and should be requested. A series of risk assessment questions allowed readers to consider whether they might be in need of assistance with respect to an abusive relationship. The series also encouraged those who might need assistance, providing plans for escape from a dangerous situation, a temporary place to stay, and the prospect that abusers can be stopped and even changed under some circumstances. Publication of the domestic violence series by the *Tulsa World* was most likely helped along by the Tulsa police department's Family Violence Unit (FVU). Established in 1993, the eight-officer unit assigns the same officer to respond to repeated calls, monitors domestic situations, and thereby helps ensure victim safety. The FVU is credited with being successful: From 1993 to 1999, no women who had filed orders of protection had been killed in Tulsa. In the aftermath of a rash of domestic fatalities that occurred in 1999, FVU was ready with information for the *Tulsa World* series.

Professionals and advocates with expertise in domestic violence provide a welcome contrast to police sources. Even when the focus is on the offender, alternative sources avoid explanations based on individual pathology; instead, they look at broader patterns of family violence across cases, the victim–offender relationship, how abuse affects victims, and where the responsibility for the crime necessarily lies. Although these sources can hardly be said to speak for the victims, many of whom are dead, what they say is informed by the domestic violence victims they have encountered in the course of their work. This "standpoint" on intimate partner violence is generally offered to the reading public in a helpful and educational manner.

Alternative Source: Friends, Family and Co-workers

The fullest and most direct account of the daily experience of victims in our sample is found in the recollections of their friends, family, and neighbors. In about one-third of the cases in our sample, there were fairly elaborate discussions in the news reports of the abusive treatment that eventuated in homicide. A New Jersey case illustrates the level of detail that friends, family, and neighbors can provide. A male offender, D. C., lived with his girlfriend and eventual victim, A. G., for two months before she asked him to move out and refused to see him any longer. In the six months leading up to the murder, D. C. smashed the windows of her car and her house, accosted her at her place of work, threatened her life, and stalked her. Increasingly fearful, A. G. started to park her car a mile from her house in order to sneak in without being seen by D. C. When she got one of her many restraining orders, he confronted her and ripped it up in her face. Being very jealous, D. C. spread rumors that A. G. had contracted AIDS, so that other men would not go out with her. A. G. had said to a friend, "I know he's going to kill me. I know it. I can just feel it." When the temporary restraining order became permanent, she went to the police for help in stopping his continuing harassment. A warrant was issued for his arrest at 10 p.m. Within five hours, A. G. and her mother had been murdered and D. C. began a crime spree that resulted in six more deaths, including his own in an exchange of gunfire with police. The last thing D. C. said to A. G. after shooting her was, "Why did you tell [the police]?"

Three Types of Victims

Examining all the victims in the sample of news reports about multiple murders we see that the victims are presented quite differently from one another. Some victims seem to be valued so little that they appear unworthy of much news space. For many victims of multiple domestic homicides, however, news descriptions are more elaborate, with some articles devoted solely to commemorating the lives of victims. Three categories of victims were identified based on how they came to be in the path of the murderers. The first type, "innocent victims," are not held responsible for their ultimate fate. The second, "heroic victims," died while altruistically trying to prevent the impending onslaught. Finally, "culpable victims" are portrayed as being responsible for the carnage or at least having some involvement in the events that took their lives.

As might be expected, the largest group of victims is composed of innocents. Here are included children killed in episodes of domestic homicide as well as the adults who by chance happened to be in the path of a murderous rampage. The children who were killed represent the largest group of victims. Their deaths are portrayed with poignancy. In one case, a Louisiana man burst into a church intent on killing his estranged wife. His two-year-old son saw him first and called out, "Daddy." The killer said, "Son, don't call me daddy now," and shot him in the face. In a Tennessee case, a divorced father had a scheduled visit with his four children to take them Christmas shopping. Instead, he took them to his auto shop and killed them. Investigators found a letter written by the killer's four-year-old daughter, asking for an Elmo doll, and a drawing showing the four children next to their father with "I love you, Daddy" written at the bottom of the picture. Several stories commented on the tragic irony that the children's murderers are the same fathers who had previously nurtured and protected them.

When child victims are older, news reports tend to single out their qualities and special talents. The children are noted for being bright, talented in athletics or the arts, cheerful, and having other qualities that register how much they will be missed. For example, two sisters from Washington State who were killed by their stepfather were described as excelling in academics and music. One sister, Amanda, was "funny and flamboyant" and was "adored for her kindness." To memorialize her murder, other students wore butterfly clips in their hair as the victim had done. Her older sister, Salome, wanted to be an oceanographer and had volunteered in a local political campaign. The legislator she worked for described her as an "intelligent, balanced person" who had "extremely good values." In an Iowa case, child victims had been active in several sports in the local schools. Ryan was described by a neighbor as a "sweet boy" who had gone out during a blizzard to shovel snow from driveways in the neighborhood. His sister, Lindsey, was taking confirmation classes at the Lutheran Church and had a favorite Bible passage from Matthew:

"Let the little children come unto me . . . for the kingdom of Heaven belongs to such as these."

Schools and classmates often have special ceremonies and establish memorials for these child victims, and these are described at length in news reports, demonstrating how much these children are missed. One Colorado school built a specially designed bench surrounded by three blue spruce trees to represent the three murdered sisters who had been students there. A Massachusetts school had a special assembly to debrief the students and offer counseling when one of their students was killed. What followed was an unexpected outpouring of student grief over the loss. About 15 students held a candlelight vigil for Kirthi, while others adorned her locker with flowers and "notes from the heart." Besides her cheerfulness, she was an honor student in every subject, and one teacher described her as "the kind of child who was the reason we all enter this profession." At the community level, there was strong public support for raising money for the children who survived a rampage that destroyed the rest of the family. In one case, three separate benefit concerts were given to raise money for a surviving child whose whole family was dead.

As a category, "innocent victims" also takes in adults who had had no prior contact with the killer and who had been caught in the line of fire. Included are a range of bystanders, from elevator passengers to taxi drivers and those who were simply too near an intended victim. In cases of innocent bystanders, reports similar to those commemorating child victims are published, detailing the victims' lives and the ways in which they will be missed. Less commonly, intimate partners killed in domestic homicide incidents are characterized as innocent. In these instances, news accounts attributed the killings to the perpetrators' mental condition (e.g., delusions or anxiety) and represented the killers' behavior as unprecedented and unpredicted and the intimate partner's actions as beyond reproach. In an Ohio case, a husband, who had no prior psychiatric problems, had voluntarily checked into a mental hospital for stress and panic symptoms. Four days later, he checked himself out again. His wife immediately took him back to the hospital and consulted with a doctor on his condition; the couple was given medication and a follow-up appointment. Within the next 12 hours, the husband killed five family members and himself. The reports regarded the murders as so unexpected that the reporter could find no fault with the wife in precipitating events.

In two other cases, news reports attributed the murders to mentally disturbed individuals, noting that the victims had had no contact with the perpetrator for a number of years. Responsibility for the homicidal outcome was attributed to the psychiatric illness, with the "partner" contributing nothing to it.

HEROIC VICTIMS

A second category of victims demonstrated acts of heroism in the midst of the homicidal rampage. Here are adult victims who tried to stop the killing. Some were murdered when offering shelter or assistance to a killer's intended victims. One, the mother of an offender, tried to convince her son to turn himself in, but he took her life. In three incidents, strangers intervened to help the primary victim—usually the wife or partner of the killer—who was under attack. News reports paid tribute to their sacrifices. For instance, a Colorado killer was confronted separately by two men who tried to stop him from killing his wife. He killed both of them, then his wife. The brother of one victim recounted how the victim had experienced gunfire before while serving as a conscientious objector in a medical unit in Vietnam. A brother of the second hero described him as a "courageous guy" with a "bigger heart than anybody's ever had." A police officer was also singled out as a heroic victim in one case; the news stories quoted family, friends, and fellow officers who expressed their feelings about sacrifice in the line of duty.

CULPABLE VICTIMS

Last among the victims represented in news stories about domestic violence with multiple fatalities are the "culpable victims." Generally, culpable victims are the partners and ex-partners of the perpetrators. In several cases, the wives were viewed as knowing about the perpetrator's past or as being responsible for finding out about it before beginning a relationship. In one Georgia case, the killer may actually have murdered a previous wife while the second one (and later also a murder victim) was having an affair with him. In a couple of instances, the wife or girlfriend met the offender when he was in prison on a previous offense that indicated his violent tendencies. One news story quoted the district attorney in a Colorado case: "We're talking about life choices. This woman married a man who spent six years in prison for child abuse and had a history of violence. . . . The bad choices begin there."

In other cases, the female partner was seen as responsible because she took the offender back after previous violent episodes, at times lying to the police about what actually happened. One DA is quoted as saying, "if only she hadn't vacillated on the restraining order," suggesting that this legal device offered protection when in fact it failed to do so in many other cases in this sample. Infidelity was implicated in a few instances, with the offender finding out about the infidelity while the first relationship was still intact. Finally, some female victims were seen as contributing to the killer's financial ruin. In two cases, the financial blow came through divorce settlements, but, whatever the context, the prospect of financial ruin was portrayed as having backed the killer into a corner.

Multiple Domestic Homicides: Discussion and Conclusions

With respect to the mass murders examined here, the news reports collectively become the authoritative account. With the accumulation of these news reports, a certain version of events becomes enshrined. It is necessarily a version of reality that emphasizes some things and omits others. In cases where the murder spree ends with the suicide or death of the perpetrator, the news stories published in the first few days after the event typically become the official story since little further investigation will occur. Where the killer survives and goes to trial, the final version awaits the judicial verdict. In either case, this story is distributed to thousands of readers curious to know what happened and why. The news story gives answers to these questions. It implicates certain contributing causes, apportions responsibility, and points toward possible preventive measures that can be taken. In short, the news story selects some details for recounting and then solidifies these elements into a relatively unchanging story.

Although this analysis is descriptive, it has provided some indication that representations of victims are related to the different kinds of news sources, police, domestic violence workers or advocates, and family or friends. Understandably, the police are the initial and centralized source of information on which reporters rely. Later, if there is a trial, the official view generally emanates from the prosecutor. However, the strength of official sources can be diminished. Those who work in shelters for abused women, intimate partner violence experts, and other victim advocates have been able to offer some countervailing perspectives within these media reports. In addition, some feature articles, written from a broadly feminist viewpoint, encompassed analysis and recommendations about prevention and policy. These domestic violence professionals tend to see such incidents as foreseeable problems that can be managed, as opposed to police, who are more likely to focus on victim blaming and the "random" or "inevitable" nature of the homicide.

The statements of friends, family, and neighbors detail victims' immediate experience; these sources add detail without much altering the police accounts. Recollections about victims include descriptions of personal qualities, accomplishments, hardships overcome, relevant details of the fatal relationship, and some account of the emotional life of the murder victim. Where feasible, reporters include accounts of the violence that victims endured, although these accounts tend to include speculation about victim responsibility, if the victim was an adult. Innocent victims are mourned. Victims that sacrificed themselves to help others are represented as heroic bystanders. Intimate partners are often represented as culpable targets of a killer's rampage.

In general, the emphasis on the female victim's role in triggering violence reflected police perspectives and the journalistic commitment to neutrality. Simply reporting what police sources indicate protects reporters from the criticism that they are biased. In some cases, reporters ignored this principle, taking one side or another when a case came to trial. Reporters were, for example, openly skeptical about defense attorney claims in one case and openly took the side of the killer in another. In other cases, however, news reports included the victim's viewpoint as told by domestic violence advocates or counselors or family/friends. In one case, the domestic violence unit within a police department was in a position to provide reporters with a victim's perspective that also carried the weight of an objective and authoritative account. The present shift in police perspective toward protecting the victim is a positive sign. In other cases, however, educating reporters about the value of alternative sources is a reasonable approach to correcting the tendency to blame victims.

NOTE

1. The women's cases seemed to be considerably different from the men's. In the women's cases, the main murder victims were their children. Few partner murders accompanied the child killings, and the common male pattern of killing outside the family was not found among the women's cases. Moreover, the motive or emotional situation for women was typically one of depression rather than the common pattern of control/revenge found among men. Guns were less likely to be used by the women than by the men. Although there are certainly some parallels to these female patterns among the male cases, these were not the patterns for *most* of the male killers in our sample.

REFERENCES

Best, J. (1999). *Random violence: How we talk about new crimes and new victims.* Berkeley: University of California Press.

Buckler, K., & Travis, L. (2005). Assessing the newsworthiness of homicide events: An analysis of coverage in the *Houston Chronicle. Journal of Criminal Justice and Popular Culture, 12* (2), n.p. Retrieved February 6, 2006, from http://www.albany.edu/scj/jcjpc/vol12is1/buckler.pdf.

Chermak, S. M. (1994a). Crime in the news media: A refined understanding of how crime becomes news. In G. Barak (Ed.), *Media, process, and the social construction of crime: Studies in newsmaking criminology* (pp. 95–125). New York: Garland.

———. (1994b). Body count news: How crime is presented in the news media. *Justice Quarterly, 11* (4), 561–582.

———. (1995). *Victims in the news: Crime and the American news media.* Boulder, CO: Westview Press.

Consalvo, M. (1998). 3 shot dead in courthouse: Examining news coverage of domestic violence and mail-order brides. *Women's Studies in Communication, 21,* 188–211.

Duwe, G. (2000). Body-count journalism: The presentation of mass murder in the news media. *Homicide Studies, 4,* 364–399.

Ericson, R. V., Baranek, P. M., & Chan, J. B. L. (1987). *Visualizing deviance: A study of news organization.* Toronto: University of Toronto Press.

Fishman, M. (1978). Crime waves as ideology. *Social Problems, 25,* 531–543.

———. (1980). *Manufacturing the news.* Austin: University of Texas Press.

Gans, H. (1979). *Deciding what's news: A study of CBS Evening News, NBC Nightly News, and Time.* New York: Vintage Books.

Grabosky, P., & Wilson, P. (1989). *Journalism and justice: How crime is reported.* Sydney: Pluto Press.

Humphries, D. (1981). Serious crime, news coverage, and ideology. *Crime and Delinquency, 27,* 191–205.

Kasinsky, R. G. (1994). Patrolling the fact: Media, cops, and crime. In G. Barak (Ed.),

Media, process, and the social construction of crime: Studies in newsmaking criminology (pp. 203–233). New York: Garland.

Louisell, R. (1995). Living the newsmaker story: A case history of emotionality. *Studies in Symbolic Interaction, 18*, 121–156.

Meyers, M. (1997). *New coverage of violence against women: Engendering blame.* Thousand Oaks, CA: Sage.

Petee, T. A., Padgett, K. G., & York, T. S. (1997). Debunking the stereotype: An examination of mass murder in public places. *Homicide Studies, 1*, 317–337.

Pritchard, D., & Hughes, K. D. (1997). Patterns of deviance in crime news. *Journal of Communication, 47*, 49–67.

Schudson, M. (1978). *Discovering the news: A social history of American newspapers.* New York: Basic Books.

Sherizen, S. (1978). Social creation of crime news: All the news fitted to print. In C. Winick (Ed.), *Deviance and mass media* (pp. 203–224). Beverly Hills, CA: Sage.

Surette, R. (1998). *Media, crime and criminal justice: Images and realities* (2nd ed.). Belmont, CA: Wadsworth.

Tuchman, G. (1972). Objectivity as strategic ritual: An examination of newsmen's notions of objectivity. *American Journal of Sociology, 77*, 660–679.

———. (1978). *Making News: A study in the construction of reality.* New York: Free Press.

Tulsa World. (1999a, April 11). Putting punch in protective orders (byline: Ashley Parrish).

———. (1999b, April 11). System's not perfect, but she's a believer (byline: Ashley Parrish).

Tunnell, K. D. (1998). Reflections on crime, criminals, and control in newsmagazine television programs. In F. Y. Bailey & D. C. Hale (Eds.), *Popular culture, crime, and justice* (pp. 111–122). Belmont, CA: West/Wadsworth.

Websdale, N. (1999). Police homicide files as situated media substrates: An exploratory essay. In J. Ferrell & N. Websdale (Eds.), *Making trouble: Cultural constructions of crime, deviance and control* (pp. 277–300). New York: Aldine de Gruyter.

Websdale, N., & Alvarez, A. (1998). Forensic journalism: The newspaper construction of homicide-suicide. In F. Y. Bailey & D. C. Hale (Eds.), *Popular culture, crime, and justice* (pp. 123–141). Belmont, CA: West/Wadsworth.

Welch, M., Fenwick, M., & Roberts, M. (1997). Primary definitions of crime and moral panic: A content analysis of expert's quotes in feature newspaper articles on crime. *Journal of Research in Crime and Delinquency, 34*, 474–494.

CHAPTER 10

RUNNING OUT OF OXYGEN

Is "Television for Women" Suffocating Women?

Emily Lenning and Darrin Kowitz

The social sciences have long wondered whether reality reflects television or whether television reflects reality (Baehr, 1980). That it is difficult to sort out the relationship tells us how ingrained television is in the structure of modern society and leads us, as feminist critics, to place the question of reflection at the center of our work. Do the images that flicker across our television screens incorporate masculine ideologies, reflecting a patriarchal reality? Alternatively, do such images offer an alternate reading that identifies feminine ideologies, opening rather than closing doors to women? What justifies our question is that television is simply unavoidable. In Dow's words, it is "part of life" (Dow, 1996, p. 5). In fact, 69.2% of all households had basic cable, and 72.8% of those households subscribed to pay channels, in 2001 (Wright, 2003). Moreover, 84.6 million Americans subscribed to the Lifetime channel, making the women's network one of the top 15 cable networks in the 2001–2002 period (Wright, 2003). Given the importance of women's cable networks, we focus on made-for-television movies—a staple feature of their programming—to work toward a feminist film critique.

Literature Review

Feminist Approaches to Film Criticism

Feminist film criticism that concerns this project entails debates over the interpretation of film images. On the one hand, feminist criticism focuses on the negative effects of masculine ideologies. Freeland (2002, p. 191) asserts that feminist criticism can essentially be summed up as ideology critique inasmuch as it functions to expose "a false or distorted belief system that sustains the interests of the dominant group, males, over the subordinate group, females." Feminist researchers, for instance, have argued that the negative or hostile gender stereotypes perpetuated by the media serve to restrict the interpersonal, social, and political advancement of women (Baehr, 1980; Gunter, Harrison, & Wykes, 2003).

On the other hand, an alternative approach to feminist criticism has emerged, as represented by the work of Freeland (2002) and Shaw (2002). Feminism is a belief system that seeks to change the interests of the dominant group. By ignoring the ideological framework of feminism, Freeland (2002) argues that feminist film critics succeed in pointing out the negative aspects of sexist ideology but fail to provide an alternative cinematic purpose. Moreover, "the negative critique of masculinist ideology" is "old hat in intellectual circles" (Shaw, 2002, p. 210). A more desirable approach involves "offering positive redescriptions of films" and promises to "do more to further the feminist cause" than prior criticism based on exposing masculinist ideology (Shaw, 2002, p. 210). Kozol (1995) claims that the media may not fail the feminist vision; they may set out positive gender representations. Films and television programming sometimes embrace the victim's standpoint and may be the basis for an audience to gain a broader understanding of victimization. Rapping points out that television movies that are concerned with social issues such as domestic violence (e.g., *The Burning Bed*) should be viewed in part as propaganda, made effective because "they combine a strong ideological component with an equally strong appeal to emotion" (Rapping, 1992, p. 88).[1]

In addition to the debate over critical standards, a second school of feminist thought, which bears on our project, focuses on films in relation to the gender of those who create them. According to feminist standpoint theory (Harstock, 1998; Smith, 1987), stories about women and for women must be told by women in order to be something other than a reproduction of traditional patriarchal ideology. The meaning of the term "by women" may have to give way to the realities of ownership and management as well as to gender variation in decision-making roles. Because corporate ownership is removed from day-to-day filmmaking, the gender mix of creative talent may influence films. For example, if the writer is a woman and the director and producer are men, we can ask whether the resulting film would necessarily reproduce patriarchal ideology. The answer would depend on the film's content.

Women's Cinema

Over the last decade, feminist researchers have analyzed the content of television and film (Cooper, 1999; Harris & Hill, 1998; Rapping, 1992; Rich, 1994). "Women's cinema" is an emerging arena for feminist criticism. Women play a substantial role in its production. Feminist critics argue that women's cinema exercises more favorable influences on the lives of women.[2] Rapping (1992, p. xi) notes that women's made-for-television movies have their own significance within feminist film criticism. They attract female audiences and may "play a role in determining . . . how we, as a nation, construct and conceptualize matters that affect us collectively." The three television networks known for female-oriented, made-for-television movies are Women's Entertainment (WE), Oxygen, and Lifetime. Beyond the fact that they claim to be women-focused in their programming, each network claims to be of great value to the personal and social growth of women. In fact, Lifetime has become widely known as not only a television channel but also an active advocate for the advancement and recognition of women. On its Website, Lifetime boasts affiliations with dozens of women's organizations, including the National Organization of Women (NOW), the National Women's Law Center, the National Coalition Against Domestic Violence, and the National Breast Cancer Coalition. The Website boldly states that:

> Lifetime is dedicated to using the power of the media to make a positive difference in the lives of women. Our Lifetime Commitment public outreach campaigns represent the network's ongoing efforts—on-air, online and in communities around the country—to support women on a range of issues affecting them and their families. (Lifetime, 2003b)

Interestingly enough, the Lifetime network was headed by male CEOs until 1999, when Carole Black became the president and CEO. The Walt Disney Company has owned Lifetime since 1994, and in 1995 the network officially became known as "Television for Women." The Oxygen and Women's Entertainment (WE) networks focus much less, if at all, on women's advocacy issues, concentrating instead on the entertainment value of their programming. The Oxygen network is "independently owned" and was founded in 1998 by current chairwoman and CEO Geraldine Laybourne, Oprah Winfrey, and the well-known television production team of Marcy Carsey, Tom Werner, and Caryn Mandabach (Oxygen, 2003b). Women's Entertainment is owned by Rainbow Media Holdings LLC (Rainbow, 2003), which is owned by the media conglomerate Cablevision (Cablevision, 2003). A quick scan of these two networks' homepages (Oxygen, 2003a; Women's Entertainment, 2003) in comparison with Lifetime's (Lifetime, 2003a) reveals that the former are concerned primarily with providing an entertaining escape for women, whereas Lifetime attempts to provide women with useful ways to escape social and health problems they may face. Whereas Oxygen and WE use their homepages to list entertainment programming, Lifetime has links to Websites on breast cancer, unsafe mastectomies, prosecuting rapists, and domestic violence.

Victimization and Movie Images

In the context of made-for-television movies, female characters represent a very specific slice of the public. Even in television films produced with a female audience in mind, female characters tend to promote a rigid conceptualization of typical female behavior and roles:

> Most TV movies (and other forms of TV narrative) lock women into a very traditional mold. No matter what happens in the movies, their ultimate message is still that women are predominantly—we may say essentially—represented as wives and mothers. Sexually unconventional women are invariably fated either to reform or to come to a bad end. (Rapping, 1992, p. 97)

When female characters are victimized, the biggest difficulty in representing victimization is the confusion over the meaning of violence. Violence is a far-reaching, even debatable term, which makes identifying a "victim" rather subjective (Slocum, 2001). Is verbal abuse a form of violence? On the other hand, does violence depend on physical attack? Verbal abuse may be coercive, but perhaps not everyone perceives it as violence. A physical attack crosses the line between coercive force and violence. According to Slocum (2001, p. 2), violence is complicated in part because of "the complex cultural processes by which some behaviors and actions are marked as 'violent' and others not. The classical sociological distinction . . . between violence and coercive force relies on a standard of legitimacy that has deep social roots" (Slocum, 2001, p. 2).

In studies that probe audience reactions, media scholars are free to examine perceptions of violence, but in content studies, media scholars have avoided problems of subjectivity by relying on legal definitions of personal violence: murder, aggravated assault, forcible rape, and robbery. The effects of violent victimization, however, go beyond the narrow definition of offenses; thus, their secondary effects are an essential consideration in feminist criticism. "The sexual assault victim has frequently been described as twice victimized: once by her assailant and once by the crime-processing system" (Belknap, 2001, p. 253). Putting the victim on trial is a standard defense ploy, but victim blaming extends well beyond the courtroom. Media researchers have documented victim blaming and other representations that justify and perpetuate women's subservience in society (Baehr, 1980). Rich argues that "the tradition of realism in the cinema" incorporates subordinating themes and concludes that realism "has never done well by women" (Rich, 1994, p. 40). Indeed, "extolling realism [read subservience] to women is rather like praising the criminal to the victim, so thoroughly have women been falsified under its banner" (Rich, 1994, p. 40).

Our research problem lies at the intersection of feminist film criticism, women's cinema, and media images of victimization. Is it possible that film criticism emphasizes what is helpful to women, offering a new way of thinking about media representations? Within this broader question, our more immediate concerns turn on how women's cinema may represent violent victimization and whether images of victimization vary depending on cable networks and gender differences among decision makers involved in writing, directing, and producing women's films.

Methods

This study explores gendered images of criminal victimization in the context of women's cinema and feminist criticism. Its aim is to identify patterns and to gain a sense of variation in woman-centered, made-for-television movies aired by Lifetime, WE, and Oxygen. Gendered differences refer to male–female differences among characters that play film roles as victims and perpetrators and male–female differences among decision makers in the production of films. Criminal victimization is a matter of law violation. Secondary victimization refers to consequences of criminal victimization; it is indicative of the victim's standpoint, as it captures the "hidden" cruelties that institutions impose on victims as well as systematic institutional violence against female characters.

In collecting data, we targeted primetime made-for-television movies on the Lifetime, WE, and Oxygen networks and recorded movies for a two-week period. Subsequently, we viewed movies from Monday, Wednesday, and Friday of the first week and Tuesday and Thursday of the second week. This procedure yielded 15 films, five from each cable network. To provide a systematic method for collecting gendered images, we developed a coding instrument that counted incidents of criminal victimization, identified the demographic characteristics of victims and perpetrators, and tapped into the broader context of victimization.

By coding single acts of illegal victimization, such as sexual assault or a character's initial attack, we were able to construct a measure of frequency for victimization. Coding victimization in this way, however, only captured one single act out of a potentially larger pattern of victimization. Subsequently, single acts of illegal victimization served as a rough proxy for the presence of those broader feminist understandings of victimization and were useful for pointing out where to begin looking for those larger patterns.

In addition to victimization, the coding instrument alerted coders to watch the films' credits for the names of directors, producers, and writers. We identified the gender of films' decision makers based on their first names.[3] Although this was a simple strategy, the resulting data enabled us to evaluate the impact of gender differences among staff on victimization in made-for-television movies.

In analyzing our data, we relied on descriptive statistics (i.e., relative frequencies and cross-tabulations) to shed some light on patterns and variations in the data. Such techniques are useful for identifying major patterns or variations in which we are interested. We report as findings cases in which two-thirds of the data cluster around a single value.

Findings

Table 10.1 reports findings for gender and criminal victimization (e.g., physical assault, rape, murder) as portrayed in our sample of 15 movies. In total, there were 37 instances of criminal victimization, involving 37

TABLE 10.1

Perpetrators and Victims by Gender, N = 74

| Role | GENDER | | | | |
| | Female | | Male | | |
	N	%	*N*	%	Totals
Perpetrators	16	36	21	72	37
Victims	29	64	8	28	37
Totals	45	100	29	100	74

Source: Table is based on 15 made-for-television films aired on Lifetime, Oxygen, and WE.

victims and 37 perpetrators. (There were no victimizations involving multiple perpetrators or single perpetrators targeting multiple victims.) Crime victims were overwhelmingly female: 64% of the victims were female, compared with only 28% for males. The findings for perpetrators were the reverse: 72% of the perpetrators were male, compared with 36% for females.

We examine the relationship between gender and criminal victimization separately for each of the three cable networks. Table 10.2 reports the percentages, although many cell frequencies fall below reportable levels. More than half (41%) of the incidents of criminal victimization that we reviewed for this study were shown in movies aired on the Lifetime network. The pattern of female victimization holds up for the Lifetime and WE cable networks. Of the females in Lifetime or WE films, 65% and 64% were victims, respectively, whereas males were cast too infrequently as victims to compare percentage figures. Of the males in Lifetime films, 73% were cast as perpetrators; of the females in Lifetime films, 35% were cast in perpetrator roles.

Findings associated with female characters and the consequences of victimization are qualitative. We note that victimized female characters tended to promote a rigid conceptualization of feminine behaviors and roles. They were sexually promiscuous or provocative. They were mediocre as parents or unfaithful as wives. In several of our movies, female characters were subject to secondary victimization; that is, they were vic-

TABLE 10.2

Perpetrators and Victims by Gender and Network, N = 74

| | GENDER | | | | |
| | Female | | Male | | |
Role	N	%	N	%	Totals
LIFETIME TELEVISION					
Perpetrators	9	35	11	73	20
Victims	17	65	4		21
Subtotal	26	100	15	100	41
OXYGEN					
Perpetrators	2		5	56	7
Victims	3		4		7
Subtotal	5		9	100	14
WOMEN'S ENTERTAINMENT					
Perpetrators	5	36	5	100	10
Victims	9	64	0		9
Subtotal	14	100	5	100	19

Source: Table is based on 15 made-for-television films aired on Lifetime, Oxygen, and WE.

timized in systematic ways that were not captured by simply counting the number of single acts of victimization. Our research indicates that there were clear differences between criminal and secondary victimizations. For example, in the movie *The Sure Thing* (Reiner, 1985), which was shown on the Oxygen network, a truck-driving stranger sexually assaulted the film's main female character, Allison. As a result, Allison's situation was coded as an incident of criminal victimization; however, the film omitted references to further victimization. Allison's assault was isolated, and in the movie she appeared to suffer no further distress because of the assault.

In contrast, the Lifetime channel seemed to link each act of criminal victimization to subsequent victimizations, broadening the understanding of crime. For example, in *Student Seduction* (Svatek, 2003), an original Lifetime movie, the main character, Christy, was assaulted by one of her students. Through the remainder of the movie, Christy struggled to prove to indifferent authorities that the incident had occurred. Told from Christy's point of view, the struggle has the potential for countering the idea that victimization is an isolated act and for broadening perceptions of victimization to include the cruelties imposed by institutional response.

Lifetime also surpassed the two other networks in fulfilling multidimensional victim descriptions. In *What Kind of Mother Are You?* (Nosseck, 1996), a single mother was faced with raising her rebellious teenage daughter, Kelly. Initially the film attributed Kelly's erratic behavior to deficient parenting, but her mother fought to get her out when Kelly was sent to a juvenile facility. The film invited viewers to rethink their earlier assessment of the mother as a bad parent and encouraged them to see the mother–daughter relationship against a background of structural problems over which they had no control. One might liken the shift in perception to resocialization: The audience goes beyond victim blaming to recognize multiple levels of victimization; that is, the hidden and sometimes violent consequences of divorce, inadequate schools, overwhelmed social services, and the general disdain society exerts toward single mothers.

Table 10.3 reports our findings regarding gender and decision makers (in producing, directing, and writing movies). In the films we reviewed, females were more likely than males to work as writers: 43% of the females, compared with 25% of the males. On the other hand, a negligible number of females directed films, compared with 19% of the males. For

TABLE 10.3

Creative Staff by Gender, N = 96

| | | | GENDER | | |
| | Female | | Male | | |
Creative Staff	N	%	N	%	Totals
Directors	3		14	19	17
Producers	10	43	41	56	51
Writers	10	43	18	25	28
Totals	23	100	73	100	96

Source: Table is based on 15 made-for-television films aired on Lifetime, Oxygen, and WE.

TABLE 10.4

Creative Staff by Gender and Network, N = 96

	GENDER				
	Female		Male		
Creative Staff	N	%	N	%	Totals
LIFETIME TELEVISION					
Directors	1		4		5
Producers	7	50	9	60	16
Writers	6	43	2		8
Totals	14	100	15	100	29
OXYGEN					
Directors	1		4		5
Producers	1		18	62	19
Writers	0		7	24	7
Totals	2		29	100	31
WOMEN'S ENTERTAINMENT					
Directors	1		6	21	7
Producers	2		14	48	16
Writers	4		9	31	13
Totals	7		29	100	36

Source: Table is based on 15 made-for-television films aired on Lifetime, Oxygen, and WE.

the films we studied, 43% of the women and 56% percent of the men were involved in producing films.

We also look at the relationship between gender and decision-making positions separately for each network. Table 10.4 summarizes reportable findings. The direction of findings supports a pattern of male decision making at all three cable networks, this being most pronounced at Oxygen, where 62% of the males work as producers. The exception may be Lifetime, where 50% of the women and 60% of the men worked as producers. In addition, 43% of the women associated with Lifetime films worked as writers, whereas too few men worked as writers to make a comparison.

In sum, the pattern of victimization that we found in made-for-television movies was gender-specific, although we should note that the male-perpetrator pattern had greater empirical support than the female-victimization pattern. Both patterns were characteristic of movies made by the Lifetime network. The female-victimization pattern characterized films developed by Lifetime and the Women's Entertainment network. Women's Entertainment and Oxygen tended to represent violence as isolated incidents, whereas Lifetime focused on secondary victimization, representing individuals against a background of social problems. Female participation in making films (as producers and writers) was greatest at the Lifetime network, suggesting a potential connection between female decision makers and original representations of secondary victimization.

Discussion and Conclusion

As an exploratory study, our findings are necessarily limited. External sources tend to support findings on the gender-specific patterns of victimization and offending, but our efforts to relate these patterns to networks and to male–female differences among decision makers fall short of conventional standards of proof. Instead, our research points to potential sources of variation.

One source of variation is the networks. Attention to the hidden cruelties of victimization may be consistent with the mission of Lifetime to "make a positive difference in the lives of women." Our "positive redescription" of the film *What Kind of Mother Are You?* (Nosseck, 1996) puts the mother in the context of difficulties facing single parents and invites film viewers to engage the film as a resocializing experience. Admittedly, this is one among alternative interpretations, but it demonstrates the positive potential of "redescription" as a form of feminist criticism.

The other source of variation concerned gender differences among the creative workers who make films. Findings are suggestive, but they point to the importance of the female voice in defining women's perspective (Harstock, 1998; Smith, 1987). If writers control film scripts, then the finding that women are clustered in writing positions might lend support to standpoint theory. If, however, writers work with directors and producers, then the issue has to be one of representation: The presence of women, perhaps among men, affects the content of women's films. We are not in a position, however, to sort out the effects of network and female staff. Even so, our findings are helpful in developing a feminist critique that goes beyond unmasking masculine ideologies.

Throughout the research process, we found ourselves returning to the same issue, namely whether made-for-television movies and the networks we examined portrayed women in a positive light. Ultimately, the questions that we were forced to ask ourselves were, "What should feminist critics or researchers consider to be positive representation?" and "How should feminists redescribe women's cinema in a way that will complement a feminist ideology?"

On the one hand, one might argue that the best way to improve the way women are perceived in the "real world" is to eliminate female victimization from films or television. One could counter that wholesale elimination belittles the female experience and enables the larger society to ignore what feminist researchers recognize (i.e., that women are continuously victimized in our culture). On the other hand, one might argue that the best way to improve the response women elicit is to maximize female victimization. Magnifying the images of victimization, however, risks increasing the levels of tolerance for violence against women.

The dilemma over whether to maximize or minimize victimization defines two opposing standards for criticism. We could applaud WE and Oxygen for showing movies that minimize victimization or, conversely, we could applaud Lifetime for revealing the true multidimensionality of the victimization of women. Instead, we have chosen to focus on the positives presented by the three networks and, as Shaw (2002) suggests, offer a redescription of what feminists should expect of women's cinema. Accordingly, we propose the following three points of reference for feminist film critics interested in the questions of violence, media, and women.

First, we insist that victimization be portrayed as a multidimensional experience. The experiences of women provide us with the knowledge that victimization is not simple, but rather one instance of victimization often leads to another. For example, a woman who has been raped also has the potential to be victimized by medical personnel who treat her indifferently, police officers who question her culpability, and a legal system that places minimal urgency on seeking justice for her. If the general public is not constantly reminded of the far-reaching consequences of violence against women, then women will continue to be objectified and seen as one-dimensional beings.

Second, in order to genuinely speak to a female audience, we feel that television content needs to be created by women. According to feminist standpoint theory (Harstock, 1998; Smith, 1987), when men create cinematic portrayals of women, and particularly women as victims, they recreate oppressive patriarchal cultural patterns. As our findings suggest, the more women serve in decision-making capacities in the production of films, such as writers, directors, and producers, the better are the chances of creating new, liberating cultural forms in support of a feminist ideology.

Finally, we suggest that it is not only beneficial but necessary that feminist critical standards cross over into and engage nongendered media productions. Feminist film critics and researchers should be on the alert for multiple layers in images of victimization as well as for female writers, noting their presence as positive change and noting their absence as negative. In contrast to the other networks, Lifetime has done an acceptable job of giving victimization multidimensional descriptions. Still Lifetime can be seen as "preaching to the choir." That Lifetime is a gendered network, however, has to be considered in light of the rise of male networks such as Spike TV, which caters to the tastes of a male audience. The division of networks and audiences along gender lines creates obstacles for the proliferation of a feminist critique. Nonetheless, as long as the goal of feminism is to replace the dominant ideology with a new one, women's victimization needs to become a concern to everyone, not just women.

Let us be clear that these suggestions are not meant for those in the television or film industries, but rather feminist researchers questioning film. Although we would hope that this text might fall into the laps of film executives and be a catalyst for new cinematic visions, the realistic notion is that feminist researchers will use this framework as a tool for change in feminist film critique. These proposals are a beginning step toward redescribing women's cinema and analyzing film from a feminist ideology, as opposed to a critique of male-dominated media. Rather than continuing to point out the negative representations that we as feminists know are ingrained in television, it is time that we start formulating our own expectations and start recognizing when they are met. A new feminist discourse must discuss what is acceptable, desirable, and necessary in films, as opposed to remaining stagnantly focused on the unacceptable, undesirable, and unnecessary representations that we have so avidly criticized.

Because the reality of television is that it helps shape how the public perceives the "real world," feminists need to react to claims that networks offer representations that advance the cause of women. Some, like the Lifetime network, do; others do not. With the rise of male-centered television (i.e., Spike TV), female-centered networks (and those networks that are not for women only) play a potentially vital role in how women view themselves and how they are viewed by others, if not only because of the sheer magnitude of their audiences. Although it is surely frustrating to watch a battery of programs that depict women as victims of fate, one must consider how such programming does or does not reflect real life. Our study has shown that Lifetime movies consistently show female characters that were not only victims but (as in real life) victims on several levels. Rather than minimizing the consequences of victimization, Lifetime explored each woman's long-standing struggle against her initial victimization. Although visibly harsh, the Lifetime programming clearly strives to envelop the entirety of the female experience, which reflects the mission statement of the channel. The feminist community and feminist researchers in particular should encourage these efforts as they evolve to meet the changing needs of women and further as they cross over into the mainstream media.

NOTES

1. This observation becomes particularly important to the findings of this work, as starkly different conclusions are drawn about the made-for-television movies we viewed versus those Hollywood films that are reaired on women's television.

2. Women's cinema is, however, an ill-defined medium. As Butler (2002, p. 1) notes, "Women's cinema is a notoriously difficult concept to define. It suggests, without clarity, films that might be made by, addressed to, or concerned with women, or all three." Nonetheless, others find the definition less problematic, establishing precedent for accepting all of Butler's identifications (Doerner & Lab, 1995; Harstock, 1998).

3. We searched Internet sources for biographical information and photos to clarify gender when first names (e.g., Dale) where ambiguous.

REFERENCES

Baehr, H. (1980). The 'liberated woman' in television drama. In H. Baehr (Ed.), *Women and Media* (pp. 29–39). Oxford: Pergamon.

Belknap, J. (2001). *The invisible woman: Gender, crime, and justice* (2nd ed.). Belmont: Wadsworth.

Butler, A. (2002). *Women's cinema*. London: Wallflower Press.

Cablevision. (2003). Cablevision. Retrieved July 29, 2003, from http://www.cablevision.com/index.html.

Cooper, B. (1999). The relevancy and gender identity in spectators' interpretations of Thelma & Louise. *Critical Studies in Mass Communication, 16*, 20–41.

Doerner, W. G., & Lab, S. P. (1995). *Victimology*. Cincinnati: Anderson Publishing.

Dow, B. (1996). *Prime-time feminism: Television, media culture, and the women's movement since 1970*. Philadelphia: University of Pennsylvania Press.

Freeland, C. A. (2002). Feminist film theory as ideology critique. In K. L. Stoehr (Ed.), *Film and knowledge: Essays on the integration of images and ideas* (pp. 191–204). Jefferson, NC: McFarland.

Gunter, B., Harrison, J., & Wykes, M. (2003). *Violence on television: Distribution, form, context, and themes*. Mahwah, NJ: Erlbaum.

Harris, T., & Hill, P. (1998). "Waiting to exhale" or "breath(ing) again": A search for identity, empowerment, and love in the 1990's. *Women and Language, 21*, 9–20.

Harstock, N. C. (1998). *The feminist standpoint revisited and other essays*. Boulder, CO: Westview Press.

Kozol, W. (1995). Fracturing domesticity: Media, nationalism, and the question of feminist influence. *Journal of Women in Culture and Society, 20*, 646–667.

Lifetime. (2003a). Lifetime: Television for women. Retrieved July 29, 2003, from http://www.lifetimetv.com.

———. (2003b). About us. Retrieved July 29, 2003, from http://www.Lifetimetv.com/about/index.html.

Nosseck, N. (director). (1996). *What kind of mother are you?* A Lifetime original movie. New York: Lifetime.

Oxygen. (2003a). The Oxygen network. Retrieved July 29, 2003, from http://www.oxygen.com.

———. (2003b). About us. Retrieved July 29, 2003, from http://www.oxygen.com/basics/about/.

Rainbow. (2003). About rainbow. Retrieved July 29, 2003, from http://www.rainbow-media.com/about/index.html.

Rapping, E. (1992). *The movie of the week: Private stories, public events*. Minneapolis: University of Minnesota Press.

Reiner, R. (director). (1985). *The sure thing*. An Embassy Pictures production. New York: Nelson Entertainment.

Rich, B. R. (1994). In the name of feminist film criticism. In D. Carson, L. Dittmar, & J. Welsch (Eds.), *Multiple voices in feminist film criticism* (pp. 27–47). Minneapolis: University of Minnesota Press.

Shaw, D. (2002). It's all ideology, isn't it? In K. L. Stoehr (Ed.), *Film and knowledge: Essays on the integration of images and ideas* (pp. 205–213). Jefferson, NC: McFarland.

Slocum, J. D. (2001). *Violence and American cinema.* New York: Routledge.

Smith, D. (1987). *The everyday world as problematic: A feminist sociology.* Boston: Northeastern University Press.

Svatek, P. (director). (2003). *Student seduction.* A Lifetime original movie. New York: Lifetime.

Women's Entertainment. (2003). WE: Women's Entertainment. Retrieved July 29, 2003, from www.wewomensentertainment.com.

Wright, J. (Ed.). (2003). *The New York Times almanac: The almanac of record.* New York: Penguin.

MAKING SENSE OF A FEMALE MALADY
Fear of Crime, Hysteria, and Women *Watching* Crimewatch UK

Deborah Jermyn

From the mid-1980s to the mid-1990s, the British media became ab-sorbed in debates about the damaging effects of television in producing fear of crime. Although in a broad sense the problem was initially envis-aged as a condition detrimental to society as a whole, as it progressed it became increasingly evident that women were being positioned as partic-ularly prone to these "irrational" fears. In 1984, the British National Crime Survey had questioned the public about its fear of crime. The re-sponse was startling: A third of survey respondents felt "fairly unsafe" or "very unsafe" walking around in their own neighborhoods after dark (Gunter, 1987, pp. 2, 3). In the debates that followed, media coverage of the rise of reality-based television crime shows and an accumulation of re-search into the issue of fear of crime played a key role in rendering this problem as a particularly female one. Real-life crime shows came to prominence in TV schedules in the 1980s. In the United States, these shows have been called "reality-based entertainment" (e.g., *America's Most Wanted*), while in Britain this format is known as "crime reconstruction" programming. An early British version, *Crimewatch UK*, made its debut on the respected public service channel BBC1 in 1984 and featured real crime reconstructions followed by police appeals for information to assist in their investigations. It quickly achieved popularity, prompting a flurry of other "real-crime" programming in its wake,[1] and indeed it has con-tinued to be a steadfast feature in the BBC schedule since then, typically being broadcast once a month.

Rather than helping to alleviate criminal activity, however, these pro-grames were soon suspected of contributing to rising fears about crime.[2] Subsequently some of the shows were quietly withdrawn, but a full-blown debate about their effects on fear, and their questionable taste, eventually centered on the television show *Michael Winner's True Crime*.

The former chief executive of Channel Four, Michael Grade, led the attack, accusing the show's creative team of blurring the boundaries between real life and entertainment and sensationalizing terrifying crimes (Connet, 1994, p. 7). Defending *True Crime* was Michael Winner, onetime film director and host for the show's reconstructions, who dismissed claims that the show sensationalized crime. The public, he claimed, were "far from being terrified by the non-revelation that crime actually exists," and he warned that cancellation would amount to censorship (Campbell, 1994a, p. 16). A rather different critique was carved out by the *Guardian's* crime correspondent, Duncan Campbell. In a climate of heightened governmental concern about crime, Campbell cautioned that all the crime reconstruction shows were being used as a scapegoat, becoming "the latest handy excuse for worries about crime" (Campbell, 1994a, p. 16). Campbell found *True Crime's* reconstructions formulaic and "remarkably unthreatening," commenting that other programs, such as *Crimewatch UK* and *Crime Limited*, were "much more likely to make people fearful of crime because they deal with identifiably real events and identifiable unhappy victims" (Campbell, 1994a, p.16). Ultimately, Michael Winner's defense of *True Crime* failed, and the show was canceled "on grounds of taste" (Campbell, 1994b, p. 13).

A growing body of work began increasingly to connect women, fear of crime, and crime-reconstruction programs. Findings from the second British National Crime Survey had indicated that women were far more likely (48%) than men (13%) to describe themselves as feeling unsafe (Gunter, 1987, p. 3). Shortly after this, a BBC report on audience responses to *Crimewatch UK* stressed gender: "Some of the women, but none of the men, said they had been frightened by [the] program. Some subjects mentioned that elderly viewers were frightened" (BBC Broadcasting Research, 1988, p. 18). Wober and Gunter's subsequent (1990) research paper for the Independent Broadcast Authority found that although "fear of crime is a very real social problem in itself" and "crime reconstruction programs could be significant in shaping the public's perception of crime" (Wober & Gunter, 1990, p.1), once again women (along with the elderly) were particularly vulnerable since "where fear of crime was exacerbated by the [crime-reconstruction] programs, women and the elderly were most likely to be those whose fears had been heightened" (Wober & Gunter, 1990, p. 1).[3]

Elsewhere, when the Broadcasting Standards Council set out to study female audiences and their experience of watching violence in television and film, resulting in *Women Viewing Violence* (Schlesinger, Dobash, Dobash, & Weaver, 1992), the research included the reception of an episode of *Crimewatch UK*. Their analyses revealed not merely instances of fear of crime, however, but the kinds of active and discerning viewing practices some female viewers were engaged in; for example, when they criticized *Crimewatch UK* for lingering gratuitously over the details of the murder of a young female hitchhiker. The study concluded that prior reports "may not have tapped adequately into some of the complex anxieties about personal safety that we have uncovered among women" (Schlesinger, Dobash, Dobash, & Weaver, 1992, p. 46).

Although fear of crime was sometimes recognized as having broader social implications, its actual sufferers were recurrently envisaged as vulnerable females,[4] whose heightened fears were understood to be disproportionate to their statistically low risks of victimization. In this, their image comes to parallel another historical "female malady," that of hysteria, a medicalized condition used to trivialize and dismiss women in the nineteenth century (Showalter, 1987). In this chapter, I probe the cultural roots of this gendered "irrationality" in order to better understand the testimonies of modern women about their experiences in viewing *Crimewatch UK*. I use the analogy between nineteenth-century hysteria and contemporary female fear of crime to build a case that, just as these historical female "hysterics" have been revisited and recast as having enacted resistance to the very real social constraints under which they lived, modern women's fears are by no means simply unreasonable. Rather, many women can instead be understood as resilient in using the media to explore, and perhaps even manage, their fear of crime. To make this case, I have marshaled evidence from several different kinds of sources. I draw on documentary evidence about women's fear of crime, including public-opinion surveys (Gunter, 1987), audience research projects that featured *Crimewatch UK* (BBC Broadcasting Research, 1988; Schlesinger, Dobash, Dobash, & Weaver, 1992), first-person accounts of writers and journalists about viewing the program (Graham, 1994; Ross, 1992; Toynbee, 1994), and interviews with producers[5] involved with *Crimewatch UK*.

The crime reconstructions described in this chapter are taken from a six-month sample of *Crimewatch UK* episodes broadcast in 2000. In part, these sources yield a set of examples drawn from individual experience, anecdotes if you like. But it is precisely within the kinds of conversational exchanges revealed by the testimonies of the women I quote that much of our experience of television takes place. Similarly, John Tulloch also has endorsed "a qualitative approach" to examining "micro-narratives" of "lay-knowledge" in his work on fear of crime (Tulloch, 2000, p. 186). Although none of the examples prove anything by themselves, together with other press reports, producer's accounts, and existing audience research, they build a picture that suggests how potent *Crimewatch UK* is in British women's experiences of fear of crime and their television viewing preferences.

The analogy between the nineteenth century notion of hysteria and fear of crime in the twentieth century deepens our understanding of modern claims about female irrationality. By the end of the nineteenth century, hysteria, the "quintessential female malady," had assumed a central role in psychiatric discourse (Showalter, 1987, p. 129), with its unstable, physically and mentally vulnerable sufferers often leaving the (male) psychiatric profession frustrated and perplexed. As a metaphor for female irrationality, hysteria has much in common with twentieth century women's fears about crime. If we understand fear of crime to be a condition in which the subject becomes introspective and undergoes ill-judged or unfathomable confusion and anxiety (in this instance about the real likelihood of becoming a victim), we can begin to see how it mirrors aspects of hysteria. For the sake of clarity, I have summarized the three main elements of the analogy here.

The first element concerns some of the symptoms of irrationality. Victorian society (1880s–1890s) "perceived women as childlike, irrational" (Showalter, 1987, p. 73). Psychiatrists, who diagnosed troubled and restless women as hysterics, were troubled themselves by their psychosomatic symptoms (e.g., fits, fainting, choking, sobbing, paralysis, and hysteria), which lacked an organic basis (Showalter, 1987, pp. 129–130). A century later, female fears of crime were often described in much the same manner, as having prompted trembling, paralysis, and sleeplessness. Experts were again troubled by "illogically" high levels of female fear that were unsupported by their actual statistical risk of being attacked.

The second element involves the significance of the home to accounts of both female hysteria and women's fear of crime.[6] Here Gothic literature serves as a vivid counterpoint to fear-of-crime testimonies; both discourses describe the home as part of a powerful matrix for experiencing menace and expressing fear. Fred Botting desribes how, in Victorian culture, the home and family were seen as "the last refuge" from the forces of the era that threatened social relations (Botting, 1996, p. 128). At the same time, in Gothic literature, the home can also become a prison (Gilbert & Gubar, 1984, p. 85), an uncanny space in which a malignant presence recurrently threatens the heroine's safety or sanity. For example, in *The Yellow Wallpaper*, Charlotte Perkins Gilman's celebrated Gothic tale (1892), shadowy figures that lurk in the yellow wallpaper are the source of madness for a woman confined to the home by her husband. The modern home adds television to the mix, bringing menacing crime reconstructions to play directly into it. In watching crime reconstruction shows, the testimonies of female viewers recurrently suggest a potent preoccupation with fears about intruders, safety, and danger within the confines of the home.

A multifaceted feminist project is the last element of the analogy. Feminists from a range of disciplines have sought to *reclaim* rather than condemn nineteenth century hysterics, Gothic heroines, and "madwomen," to see them as having resisted patterns of conventional femininity. Within feminist critiques, these women can be understood as "failed but heroic rebels" and as "champions of a defiant womanhood" (Gilbert & Gubar, 1984; Showalter, 1987, pp. 4–5).[7] Similarly, I seek to reclaim women from the vision of irrationality and paralysis imposed by the fear-of-crime debate, suggesting that their fears can be seen as reasonable, and further, that women can critically explore their fears even in the context of a medium that disseminates frightening and violent images of crime against them.

Testimonies of Women Watching *Crimewatch UK*

Crimewatch UK's reconstructions and viewers' testimonies about watching them often parallel the Gothic novels and their heroines. Like the female hysterics of the Victorian era, women watching *Crimewatch UK* describe experiencing physical symptoms of anxiety, including insomnia, pounding hearts, and flinching and huddling motionless. Interestingly, one intention of Gothic literature was to produce physiological responses to fear, "to get to the body itself" (Moers, 1986, p. 90). In testimony drawn from the BBC's audience research, one woman described her distress when watching a *Crimewatch UK* crime reconstruction in which "two little old ladies" were attacked in their remote country house. "When you saw them, to think that someone could do that to them. You start cracking. It makes me cry" (BBC Broadcasting Research, 1988, p. 18a). The image of "cracking" here is a painfully striking one: The body literally gives up under the stress wrought by the program.

Fear, menace, and the absence of safety in the home are all themes common to Victorian novels. Botting captures the significance of the home in nineteenth century Gothic novels:

> As the privileged site of Victorian culture, home and family were seen as the last refuge from the sense of loss and the forces threatening social relations. The home, however, could be a prison as well as a refuge. . . . the home is the site of both internal and external pressures, uncanny and terrifying at the same time. (Botting, 1996, p. 128)

In *Crimewatch UK*, "external pressures" take form as threatening strangers penetrate the internal world of the home, making it both familiar and foreign, safe and terrifying, longed for and repellant. After watching *Crimewatch UK*, British women frequently describe their fears of intruders, being anxious when alone in their homes and feeling unsafe there. Consider the following account from a participant in the *Women Viewing Violence* study:

> When I have watched it [*Crimewatch UK*] in the past, it's made me nervous, like when I've had to go upstairs thinking 'God I'm not safe,' because they have shown a lot of scenes where things have happened within your own home. When people have come when you could be in bed. . . . (Schlesinger, Dobash, Dobash, & Weaver, 1992, p. 51)

Such fears are a recurring theme in women's descriptions. The act of watching television at home, and in so doing watching reconstructions of other women being attacked *also* while in their homes, becomes an acutely disturbing experience. What was once safe and familiar about the home is rendered both unsafe and unfamiliar; that is, the home is "defamiliarized." The following account from Polly Graham, writing in the *Guardian*, further explores the experiences that defamiliarize the home:

> Babysitting for friends in a creaking Victorian house, I mistakenly watched *Crimewatch*. For the rest of the night I huddled motionless on the sofa,

flinching at every noise. It got darker, but I couldn't draw the curtains for fear of the phantom in the shrubbery. I sat like this until my friends came home. (Graham, 1994, p.13)

Here, though one suspects Graham of a certain irony. The passage evokes the stereotype of female paranoia and Gothic foreboding, where the home is made "uncanny."

Likewise, Jean Ross confesses that her "over-voracious imagination" is such that for her "thrillers are out, as are programmes such as *Crimewatch [UK]*," since they transform the home from a domestic haven to a night-time site of terror:

But what was that? I sit bolt upright in bed. I surely heard a door opening? I slide noiselessly out of bed and tiptoe across the landing, my heart pounding, my ears straining for further evidence of intrusion. I sit on the top step of the stairs and resume my lonely vigil. It is 4 a.m. and I am home alone. By day I am an eminently sensible woman. But turn the clock round to midnight, remove my husband to foreign climes and you will see before you a neurotic wreck, whose nerves explode at the slightest creak of a central heating pipe. (Ross, 1992, p. 19)

What these "hysterical" responses indicate and what Gothic literature characteristically suggests is that there is no space, public or private, clearly defined as safe for women.[8] Other respondents in the *Women Watching Violence* study describe watching the show in spite of being frightened:

I think [*Crimewatch UK*] still frightens you, really. But I do watch it. I mean my husband's on nights when I watched it this week . . . and my alarm is on. That's the only thing that reassures me, I've got real brilliant alarms in the house. That's the only way I feel safe in my house. (Schlesinger, Dobash, Dobash, & Weaver, 1992, pp. 69–70)

Those dangers, both "real" and perceived, also enable us to see another parallel between the fear of crime and Gothic sensibilities. The menace that threatens women in the modern home sends them looking for family or friends, so that just like the nineteenth-century sense of menace, it places the "hapless female at the mercy of ominous patriarchal authorities" (Kilgour, 1995, p. 9). Men are envisioned as protectors of women, as alleviators of paranoia about crime, and especially as saviors for lone, defenseless women. This is a vision (some) women share; hence, in writing about her at-home-alone experience, Jean Ross describes being especially prone to fears when her husband was away (Ross, 1992, p. 19). Polly Graham reports being too scared to move until her "friends came home" (Graham, 1994, p. 13). The BBC's respondents speculate, "I think if I was on my own I wouldn't watch it" and "It might make people a bit nervous if on their own" (BBC Broadcasting Research, 1988, p. 18). The implication is that women can expect to be safer in the care of male partners or friends, a notion that encourages women to seek solace and security in the conventional social spaces of family and heterosexual relationships, where actually "danger" is most likely to occur.

Reimagining Female Viewers

Even though these testimonies seem at one level to substantiate claims that fear of crime is an irrational and debilitating condition among women, it can be argued that their fears can be understood as a reasonable reaction to a barrage of cues about vulnerability experienced by women in their daily lives. Here it becomes necessary to interrogate standards of rationality and to reconsider narrow definitions of danger and risk. If women's fear of crime has been constructed as an irrational response, then we must first ask how "irrationality" is defined. As criminologist Sandra Walklate has noted, it is imperative to ask, "Whose standards are being used as the markers of a reasonable or a rational fear? Whose standards are being used as a marker . . . connecting that reasonable or rational fear to risk?" (Walklate, 1995, p. 68). Presumably, not women's. Indeed, for Walklate, the standards for rationality and for defining risk and danger are inherently masculine and can be found throughout criminology (Walklate, 1995, p. 76).

In the simplest terms, the masculine standard for rationality is based on a male–female dichotomy. Men are thought to possess rational knowledge: They weigh benefits and risks and thereby chart reasonable courses of action. Women, however, are typically thought to lack rationality: They respond emotionally and disproportionately to external events. Accepting masculine rules about rationality carries with it the implication that much of what are considered feminine behavioral traits will be construed as irrational, and it is from this vantage point that the testimonies quoted above might be said to appear "irrational."

Even in accepting masculine standards of risk and danger, public information about women's risks of victimization is often contradictory. For example, in an attempt to reassure the public that their fear of crime was unwarranted, the BBC announced new crime-reporting guidelines in June 1994. By way of explanation, Polly Toynbee, cited in the *Guardian*, informed women, "Most attacks are domestic, men attacking their lovers and wives. Yet women and old people live in growing irrational fear of attack by a stranger on the street" (Toynbee, 1994, p. 20). Toynbee's words arguably endorse a number of worrying assumptions. By seeking to "reassure" women that most attacks are domestic, her statement makes domestic violence appear as if it were the lesser crime. Moreover, Toynbee repeats the view that fear of crime is a problem for certain "vulnerable" groups, namely women and the elderly, without acknowledging that the view rests on masculine assumptions about rationality.

Feminists in criminology who have challenged such masculine interpretations have argued that women are better placed than men to understand female experiences, including the risks and dangers they face. Central to those experiences are "the routinized daily threats to personal security which characterize many women's lives" (Walklate, 1995, p. 67). According to John Tulloch, whose work concerns risks posed by the environment, any conceptualization of women's experience would have to include a "whole spectrum of cues to fear—the man across the carriage staring fixedly at you, the man in the seat next to you whose knee nestles into yours each time the train lurches," a continuum that brings the rationality of women's fears into focus (Tulloch, 2000, p. 187). Because men do not experience the same "spectrum of cues to fear" that women do, male assessments of risk and danger very often omit critical female experiences. Including these experiences in the equation means that women's fears become more proportional to their experience of male aggression. Moreover, the risk assessments neglect to consider the coverage of attacks on women that saturate the media. *Crimewatch UK's* preoccupation with stranger assaults on women is difficult to reconcile with its announcements that women's fears are "for the most part unwarranted" and that "attacks by strangers [are] very rare" (March 2000). In fact, one of the participants in the *Women Viewing Violence* study tackled this very inconsistency:

> I didn't like the bit where she says the cases are rarer than—what? Because it's not really [true]. Because you lift the papers, you get it in the papers

day in and day out. You get it on the 'telly', day in and day out. (Schlesinger, Dobash, Dobash, & Weaver, 1992, p. 69)

A closer look at some of the violent attacks on women featured in *Crimewatch UK* crime reconstructions validates this woman's concerns; hence, in what follows, I briefly examine two examples of crime reconstructions aired by *Crimewatch UK*.

In February 2000, *Crimewatch UK* broadcast an appeal asking the public for help in identifying a leather fetishist who had broken into women's homes, viciously assaulted some of them, and demanded their leather purses or gloves. The reconstruction opens with scenes of a woman at home and alone watching BBC1's *EastEnders*, a popular British soap opera that airs in the evenings. She goes to the door to answer a knock. When she opens it, a man with a bag over his head grabs her by the throat, places his hand over her mouth, and drags her back inside her home as she shrieks and struggles in blind panic. In a few short seconds, then, we see the precariousness of the sanctity of the home and women's safety there. An initially everyday scene, which the lone female viewer will be replicating at home as she watches *Crimewatch UK*, becomes a nightmare. She watches her own fears materialize onscreen.

In addition, *Crimewatch UK* reconstructions are designed to heighten viewers' anticipation, tension, and suspense, and disconcerting camera shots, scene changes, soundtracks, and lighting are just some of the dramatic devices drawn on to make such reconstructions especially chilling. The June 2000 episode featured the reconstruction of a series of sex attacks in Chichester that featured prolonged interior shots of the rapist with his victims after he broke into their bedrooms. Twice during the reconstruction we see the intruder watch his victims as they lay sleeping, unaware of his presence in their darkened bedrooms. He stands over his victims, waking them with a hand over their mouths, only to tie them up before threatening them. Two highly potent scenes are used to stage one of the attacks. In the first sequence, the mundane details of everyday life are evoked as the victim gets ready for bed. Her room is shot in conventional, naturalistic light as she tells in voiceover how she'd just made herself a cup of tea. Moments later, the same space is transformed, however, as the attack itself takes place. It is now shot in shadowy and evocative blue tones that recall the aesthetics of Hollywood thrillers.[9] The victim explains, "I was absolutely petrified. My heart was beating really hard and really fast. From then on I thought I was dead. I really did." We see her frightened face as the rapist binds her hands together, telling her not to scream in a lengthy and disturbing exchange. The audience also hears the brave and inspirational testimony of the victim, now a rape survivor, as she comments, "He's really picked the wrong girl 'cos I'm such a strong person." But rather than the victim's pluck, what is focused on and what the audience is most likely to remember is the mounting tension, suspense, and anticipation as the attacker moves around his victims' bedrooms, invading this most private of spaces.

Viewing Violence and Managing Fear

Television is a medium characterized by its qualities of intimacy and familiarity (Auslander, 1999; Ellis, 1994) and as a characteristically domestic object,[10] it has also historically been constructed as feminized. *Crimewatch UK* undeniably holds a powerful place in its female audience's experience of crime and television, as evidenced by the women's responses described above and indeed in comments made by *Crimewatch UK*'s producers during my interviews with them. In a 2002 personal interview with assistant producer Belinda Phillips, for example, she described how, "I spoke to a woman last year, when I was answering the phones, and she said she'd watched every single *Crimewatch* since 1984," and on another occasion, "A policewoman on the programme said she'd watched since she was a little girl and that's what inspired her to join the police."

Rather than only reflecting on the damaging implications of fear of crime, however, we might seek to understand how some viewers use *Crimewatch UK* constructively.[11] Watching real-crime television may actually fulfill a kind of cathartic function for women; that is, watching and processing the program may allow them both to experience fear and to release an accumulation of associated anxieties. Indeed, Tulloch refers to strategies such as this as "adaptive coping" (Tulloch, 2000, pp. 186–187) and sees them as adaptations to a culture where women are continually reminded of their vulnerability. For example, in his Australian fear-of-crime research project, female respondents who reported feeling nervous about using public transportation in Sydney discussed how they carried an apple to legitimate possessing a knife or sat in a particular part of the train (Tulloch, 2000). Watching *Crimewatch UK*, then, may also be a form of "adaptive coping" for some of its female viewers similarly bound up in a culture where they are continually reminded of their vulnerability.

After all, the largely female audiences that watch *Crimewatch UK* (and *America's Most Wanted*) must reap some kind of reward for the time they spend. Arguably, one such reward is the opportunity to experience the fears evoked by seeing violence enacted within a controlled environment. By controlled environment, I refer here not to the home but instead to the formulaic character of crime reconstructions, which provide a familiar and safe generic arena for experiencing such fear. Columnist Polly Graham acknowledges this when she writes:

> These programmes are as formulaic as Mills and Boon [publishers of highly standardized romance novels]. First the reconstruction of the crime—the practised voice-over reminds us that 'actors play the main parts' while the reconstruction shows how easily everyday life is turned upside down. Next they wheel on the camera-shy officer in charge with the all important and usually quite comical description of the attacker. . . . And so it goes on. (Graham, 1994, p.13)

The formula imposes a measure of predictability on violence, thus providing an environment in which women may explore and consolidate their responses to such crimes. Indeed, Graham is able to appropriate the formula to such an extent that she imagines herself as a homicide victim. She writes,

> Sometimes, walking home alone at night I imagine a reconstruction of my own murder. The echoes of my footsteps fade-out as *Crimewatch's* Nick Ross says: "Two days later her body was found by a woman walking her dog."(Graham, 1994, p. 13)

The passage offers a fascinating reflection on Graham's engagement with the show. She ticks off the formula's dramatic devices: being alone at night, the echoing footsteps, the discovery of the body. She uses the formula, then, as a controlled environment in which to play out her worst fears in self-conscious fashion, almost as if she were watching them or herself in a Hollywood movie.

Conclusion

Showalter describes how the Victorian hysterics proved a particularly unpopular and irksome breed among the male psychiatric profession, "disagreeable and disliked for their uncooperative ways" (Showalter, 1987, p. 134). Although we should exercise caution in romanticizing or endorsing their actions, it is, nevertheless, gratifying to think of them vexing their nineteenth century psychiatrists, figureheads of a patriarchal culture that repressed and constrained women. By becoming "a problem," they won attention in a hostile culture and made women's rage visible even as its causes remained unspoken or suppressed. They became "powerful antagonists" (Showalter, 1987, p. 33). Female sufferers of fear of crime might be seen in some ways as their descendants, for although the full nature of women's engagement with the threat of violent crime and the role of television within that is still far from being properly understood or addressed, these women have also, at the very least, made these issues a necessary and significant part of our cultural agendas. When we consider the conflictual, sensationalistic, and misleading nature of the media's representation of crime against women, when we reimagine the female viewer of *Crimewatch UK* as *using* the program in order to confront and explore her fear of crime, the notion of the hysterical female viewer loses its legitimacy. Rather, the true source of hysteria in all of this—thriving on emotional outbursts, trading in frenzy and anxiety—is arguably the media itself.

NOTES

1. These programs included *Crimestoppers* (ITV, 1988–1995), *Crime Monthly* (1989–1996), *Crime Stalker* (ITV, 1993–1997), *Crime Limited* (BBC, 1992–1994), and *Michael Winner's True Crimes* (ITV, 1991–1994), all of them responding to the public's (or perhaps the broadcasters') escalating taste for the genre with varying degrees of explicitness and sensationalism. For a summary of the critiques these programs have provoked, see Jermyn (2005).

2. The link between fear of crime and television programming had already been established, notably by Gerbner and Gross (1976): Those who watched the most television were most likely to substantially overestimate the likelihood of their being involved in violence.

3. See also the report published by the Home Office Standing Conference on Crime Prevention (1989, December 11) based on the work of an independent working group on the fear of crime chaired by Michael Grade.

4. Although the discourse addresses women per se, I do not mean to suggest that women are a homogeneous group either in their role as an audience for television programs or as the victims represented within them. Class, age, sexuality, and race all play a part in the way *Crimewatch UK* constructs its female victims and in the way different women experience fear of crime, but limited space prohibits me from examining these issues of identity.

5. On January 22, 2002, I interviewed Katie Thomson, series producer of *Crimewatch UK*, and on February 19, 2002, I interviewed Belinda Philips, assistant producer of *Crimewatch UK*, both at the BBC TV offices, Wood Lane, London.

6. As corollary to the home's interior, women have been encouraged by patriarchy to view the outside world as a place that leaves them vulnerable, a place where they should seek to be escorted and chaperoned, thus enabling male authority to police their sex(uality). That women are at greater risk of violence and abuse within the home than outside it is the contradiction that patriarchal culture struggles to contain. Even though *Crimewatch UK* represents women as vulnerable in the *home*, C. Kay Weaver argues that "crime reconstructions help promote the power of a gendered hegemony by reinforcing women's fears for their safety in public spaces" (Weaver, 1998, p. 248). On the use of the term domestic violence, see Carter (1998, p. 8), who argues that it is unhelpful in differentiating violence within and outside the home. In *Crimewatch UK*, violence within the home is overwhelmingly perpetrated by strangers, not intimates, so violence committed by intimates within the home is rendered virtually absent.

7. Showalter warns caution here also, however, since efforts to reclaim the figure of the female hysteric run the risk of "endorsing madness as a desirable form of rebellion rather than seeing it as the desperate communication of the powerless" (Showalter, 1987, p. 5).

8. Cavender, Bond-Maupin, and Jurik make the same point in their study of *America's Most Wanted*: Whatever measures crime victims adopted to circumvent crime, "The world is a dangerous place for women" (Cavender, Bond-Maupin, & Jurik, 1999, p. 660).

9. The aesthetic shift recalls images from Hollywood thrillers, the territory of *Jagged Edge* (U.S., Marquant, 1985) or *Manhunter* (U.S., Mann, 1986).

10. Because there are now multichannel, multiset households, the notion that the audience can be likened to a family is less tenable than it once was.

11. Cavender, Bond-Maupin, and Jurik took issue with the claim that *America's Most Wanted* empowers women to talk about their victimizations (1999, p. 643) on the grounds that the show "creates a portrait of peril and disseminates subordinating images of women" (1999, p. 659). Although the evidence I have produced suggests that the same ideologically conservative constructs are present in *Crimewatch UK*, this observation is not a bar to considering that women may use the program for empowering ends.

REFERENCES

Auslander, P. (1999). *Liveness: Performance in a Mediatized Culture*. London: Routledge.

BBC Broadcasting Research. (1988, October). *Crimewatch UK*, BBC Special Projects Report SP.88/45/88/16.

Botting, F. (1996). *Gothic*. London: Routledge.

Campbell, D. (1994a, August 31). Who stabbed Michael Winner in the back? *Guardian*, p. 16.

———. (1994b, September 19). Sky tries to make crime pay. *Guardian*, p. 13.

Carter, C. (1998). News of sexual violence against women and girls in the British daily national press. Unpublished doctoral dissertation, Cardiff University.

Cavender, G., Bond-Maupin, L., & Jurik, N. C. (1999). The construction of gender in reality crime TV. *Gender and Society, 13*, 643–663.

Connet, D. (1994, August 30). Winner's crime show loses out to its critics. *Daily Mail*, p. 7.

Ellis, J. (1994). *Visible fictions* (2nd ed.). London: Routledge.

Gerbner, G., & Gross, L. (1976). Living with television: The violence profile *Journal of Communication, 26*, 173–199.

Gilbert, S. M., & Gubar, S. (1984). *The madwoman in the attic: The woman writer and the nineteenth century literary imagination*. New Haven, CT: Yale University Press.

Graham, P. (1994, August 19). Double barrel; the column that gives vitriol a bad name. *Guardian*, p. 13.

Gunter, B. (1987). *Television and the fear of crime*. London: Libbey.

Home Office Standing Conference on Crime Prevention. (1989, December 11). Report on the working group on the fear of crime. London: Home Office.

Jermyn, D. (2005). Fact, fiction and everything in between: Negotiating boundaries in *Crimewatch UK*. In J. Furby & K. Randell (Eds.), *Screen method: Comparative readings in screen studies* (pp. 145–156). London: Wallflower Press.

Kilgour, M. (1995). *The rise of the Gothic novel*. London: Routledge.

Mann, M. (Director). (1986). *Manhunter* [film].

Marquant, R. (Director). (1985). *Jagged edge* [film].

Moers, E. (1986). *Literary women*. London: The Women's Press.

Perkins Gilman, C. ([1892], 1980). *The yellow wallpaper*. In A. J. Lane (Ed.), *The Charlotte Perkins Gilman reader*. London: The Women's Press.

Ross, J. (1992, February 26). First person: Home alone. *Guardian*, p. 13.

Schlesinger, P., Dobash, R. E., Dobash, R. P. & Weaver, C. K. (1992). *Women viewing violence*. London: British Film Institute.

Showalter, E. (1987). *The female malady*. London: Virago.

Toynbee, P. (1994, June 3). The channels of fear. *Guardian*, p. 20.

Tulloch, J. (2000). Landscapes of fear: Public places, fear of crime and the media. In S. Allan, B. Adam, & C. Carter (Eds.), *Environmental risks and the media* (pp. 184–197). London: Routledge.

Walklate, S. (1995). *Gender and crime: An introduction*. Hemel Hempstead: Prentice-Hall.

Weaver, C. K. (1998). *Crimewatch UK*: Keeping women off the streets. In C. Carter, G. Branston, & S. Allan (Eds.), *News, gender and power* (pp. 248–262). London: Routledge.

Wober, J. M., & Gunter, B. (1990, August). Crime reconstruction programmes: Viewing experience in three regions, linked with perceptions of and reactions to crime. IBA Research Paper GPC/03977.

CHAPTER 12

VICTIM BLAMING THROUGH HIGH-PROFILE CRIMES

An Analysis of Unintended Consequences

Lynn S. Chancer

For many scholars interested in cultural studies, the high-profile crime cases of the last several decades provide a striking source of information. Some have concentrated on how "popular trials" affect our awareness of rape, domestic violence, or police brutality; others have analyzed trial transcripts to get at dominant cultural constructs or to understand legal dynamics that underlie celebrated cases. What strikes me as important about high-profile cases is that they appear to operate on two levels. Culturally, they serve as vehicles for debating unresolved issues related to crime, and they lend themselves to analysis that focuses on the cultural conventions that structure debate. At the social-psychological level, high-profile cases generate individual and group reactions among those who follow the cases, and these reactions in particular merit examination.

In this chapter, I draw on my study *High-Profile Crimes: When Cases Become Causes* (Chancer, 2005) to consider victim blaming and other responses to high-profile cases. I begin by describing my research and considering the origin and characteristics of high-profile cases that I call "provoking assaults." Next, I draw on interview material to illustrate two defense mechanisms used by people in responding to high-profile cases, "reversing" and "substituting." Last, I reflect on the implications of my argument for changing the cultural environment that too often holds men and women responsible for events over which they have little control.

Doing Research on Provoking Assaults

In the late 1980s, a group of men sexually assaulted a woman on a pool table in New Bedford, Massachusetts. The incident's mix of sex, violence, and publicity led me to investigate what became known as the New Bedford rape case. In its aftermath, a number of other highly politicized cases exhibited similar and seemingly distinctive traits, and I discuss these later. I undertook a detailed study of seven cases that involved both crime incidents and highly publicized trials,[1] and conducted a wide range of interviews with people involved in those cases. The interviewees included editors and reporters from the media; jurors, lawyers, and judges from the law; and community and social movement activists and ordinary people who responded passionately to the cases. All told, over 200 interviews were conducted.

I focused on a particular kind of high-profile case, provoking assaults, that seemed to be a vehicle for negotiating, arguing, and incorporating issues related to many of the problems that had remained unresolved since the social movements of the 1960s. I use the term "provoking assault" in a special sense: These are cases that involve terrible acts of violence, but by revealing racial injustice or gender inequality, they raise stakes that are much higher than for ordinary crimes. In using the term, I do not mean to suggest that someone has provoked an assault; instead, I use it in the sense that some highly symbolic assaults provoke debate.

In addition, the symbolic value of many high-profile cases was rooted in the social movements of the 1960s. Thirty years later, ongoing resistance to racial discrimination attests to the lasting influence of the civil rights and Black Nationalist movements. Likewise, legal reform in the area of sexual violence (e.g., rape, domestic violence, stalking) is the product of U.S. feminism. Nonetheless, by the late 1980s and into the 1990s, these movements found themselves on the defensive (Beckett, 1997). In 1991, journalist Susan Faludi described the antifeminist "backlash" as undermining gains women had made in the workplace, in and outside diversifying families, and in the general quality of their lives (Faludi, 1991). Affirmative action programs and other measures aimed at combating the historical legacies of race discrimination were vulnerable to retrenchment (Steinberg, 1995). If contending groups could not agree about feminism, race-based legislation, or gay rights, then they could agree about the heinous nature of assault, homicide, and rape. Of course, some crimes would emerge as very public symbols of gender injustice and racial discrimination.

Because this was a new phenomenon, I had to wonder about where these cases came from and what made them distinctive. As far as their origins were concerned, high-profile cases of the 1980s and 1990s appeared to grow out of and reflect America's preoccupation with violent crime and the festering issues of social justice and discrimination. Opinion polls and surveys confirmed that Americans' concerns about crime, especially violent crime, were on the rise. In 1988, 2% of Americans had identified crime and violence as "the most important problem facing this country today." The figure had jumped to 37% by 1994 (Maguire & Pastore, 2002, Table 2.1, p. 108).[2] Concerns, however, did not match reality. Reported violent crime rates had actually declined. [3] More Americans died from the violent consequences of corporate crime than from interpersonal violence (see Hills, 1987). People were more likely to be outraged by the 1989 rape of the Central Park jogger than to care about corporate criminals.

In addition, violent crimes between individuals (i.e., assaults, rapes, and homicides) had made their way into emerging public policies. Beginning in the late 1980s, states passed mandatory sentencing and "three strikes and you're out" laws. Just as the O. J. Simpson murder case hit the news in 1994, Congress passed the Omnibus Crime Bill, calling for an additional 100,000 police officers and using federal funds for new prison construction. Efforts to reinstitute capital punishment started to take hold in many states. Thus, high-profile crimes emerged and reflected public concerns about violent crime and "tough on crime" laws (Tonry, 2004).[4]

Finally, changes in the media made high-profile cases possible. As these cases emerged in the 1980s and 1990s, the number of news venues increased, and competition within and between news venues intensified (Schudson, 1995). Not only were newspapers and television vying for an audience, but cable networks and Internet news services had entered the mix as well. Once a criminal incident evoked interest, it could be picked up and moved faster through more outlets than ever before in an infrastructure of mass-mediated communication: When the Central Park jogger and Bensonhurst cases exploded into the news, four daily newspapers competed for readership in New York City, and cable's Court TV emerged to compete with network news shows.

Provoking assaults have at least three defining traits. First, they are crime incidents or cases that come to symbolize one or two social problems. Second, in high-profile cases of the provoking assault variety, cases become causes and the resulting debates unfold in the context of "partialization." Third, provoking assault cases engender debate about whether alleged victims are as innocent as they appear and, as a corollary, whether accused parties are as culpable as they seem.

Cases may become causes, as illustrated by the O. J. Simpson case. The O. J. Simpson case came to symbolize racial injustice and gender equality, two problems to which were attached recognized social movements: feminism and civil rights. In addition, key to my argument is that cases and causes refer to cultural phenomena. Legal cases involve two-sided debate: The prosecution is pitted against the defense in a contest the outcome of which determines whether the accused is guilty or not guilty. The two-sided structure of debate is suited to sorting out factual questions such as guilt, but it is ill suited for assessing social problems, which often have more than two sides, and for sorting out complex arguments involved in symbolic causes. Jury verdicts, for example, do not resolve social problems, nor do jury verdicts address the concerns of social movements seeking fundamental change. Racism, gender biases, and class inequities are so ingrained in institutions and so deeply felt by individuals that it would be foolish to think that a jury's verdict would induce much change.

When cases and causes merge, so do terms of debate. By this, I mean that the symbolic issues raised by provoking assaults are formulated through a process of partialization. The issues are squeezed into the same two-sided framework that regulates adjudication. Just as lawyers marshal arguments for and against the defendant, the people I interviewed started to take sides, feeling partial to the defendant or partial to the prosecution. Recurring arguments solidified the two sides, leaving little room for anyone to acknowledge the validity of the other's (or another's) position. Alternative perspectives went unheard or unnoticed; third or fourth interpretations were discarded as irrelevant or unrealistic. More nuanced understandings took a back seat to a simplistic understanding of the issues.

The two-sided framework that structures debate appears natural and inevitable. For most people only two sides of debate seemed valid. On one side of this framework, concerns about domestic violence were clearly justified by O. J. Simpson's previous arrest record; the Los Angeles Police Department's history of past brutality and misconduct validated worries about racially motivated improprieties. When feminists aligned themselves with the prosecution and civil rights advocates lined up with the defense team, it seemed to exhaust the range of possible positions. Consider evidence of the social pressures on people to take one side or the other. Millions of people waiting around television sets to hear the final verdict were compelled to take one side or the other. People who did not take a side felt guilty, or they faced social recriminations from others who disagreed or felt betrayed. People who had gotten friendly during the trial felt the pressure to stick together, but they also reported feeling alienated from former acquaintances who took the other side. People organized themselves into groups, which in turn exacerbated differences between them. As I have argued elsewhere, the result was, rather insidiously, to "play gender against race" (Chancer, 1998).

Victim blaming, among other responses, is the third characteristic of provoking assault. On the one hand, the cases often engendered debate over whether alleged victims were as innocent as they appeared and, as a corollary, whether accused parties were as culpable as they seemed (indeed, perhaps they were innocent altogether). In the Mike Tyson case,[5] for example, local residents asked why young Desiree Washington, the rape victim, would have accompanied the famous boxer to his Indianapolis hotel room. She must have been looking for trouble, or hoping to procure a book contract. On the other hand, cases also recycled questions about social responsibility; they offered a way for some people to express, and others to challenge, individualistic propensities in American culture. Feminists used the Mike Tyson case, for example, to raise questions about social responsibility, linking the incident to social codes of masculinity that condone violence against women. They struggled to redefine rape as an act of violence, not sex, and group-based feminist arguments about "victim blaming" have influenced the adoption of rape shield laws in many states (Fairstein, 1993).[6]

Victim blaming is one response to high-profile cases. I use the term *substituting* to describe victim blaming. Essentially, the party substitutes the victim for the defendant, who would normally be blamed, and then blames the victim. The dynamic resembles the Freudian concept of displacement, although substituting is rooted in, and tends to emerge from, groups in addition to individuals. In addition to victim blaming, people or groups may take the side of the defendant. *Reversing* is a defense mechanism in which a party focuses on the defendant's situation, recasting the alleged victimizer as the victim. As the case progresses, indignation gives way to feelings of sympathy toward the accused. Because this defense mechanism entails asserting the opposite of what appears to be true, it recalls the Freudian concept of reaction formation, but again it applies to patterns of response to high-profile cases, not psychological mechanisms.

Reacting to High-Profile Crimes: Substituting and Reversing

As the interviews show, parties involved in high-profile cases tend to focus on personal, not social, responsibility. In the context of the O. J. Simpson case, comments made by a woman interviewed outside a church in South Central Los Angeles illustrate substituting: "You know, the media painted her [Nicole Simpson] as a saint, and she was not, she was close to a (pause). . . . She's dead now and no one wants to make her look awful but she wasn't a saint and she had a temper." Another young woman described hearing others call murder victim Nicole Simpson "bad names" during the O. J. Simpson trial:

> They say she wasn't the angel that the Browns are making her out to be. And wasn't a proper mother that people are trying to make her to be. . . . But, yeah, they called her a lot of names. . . . I've heard [that she was promiscuous] hundreds and hundreds of times. (Anonymous, interview outside courtroom, September 20, 1995)

Substituting was not confined to the O. J. Simpson case. Questions were raised about other victims.[7] Why, for example, was the rape victim in the Central Park jogger case running alone in the park late at night? Some people insisted that the young woman who returned with William Kennedy Smith to the Kennedy compound was responsible for whatever happened, including being raped. Although she was not the victim, Gina Feliciano was blamed for turf fights that led to the killing of Yusef Hawkins, a young African American man in Bensonhurst, an all-white section of Brooklyn. In one woman's opinion, "She [Feliciano] provoked the whole thing! It's a sin." And several Glen Ridge residents referred to a rape victim, a developmentally impaired young woman, as "promiscuous," thereby diverting attention from the accused high school football players who had brutally exploited a vulnerable girl.

Group identification is a consideration in substituting. For instance, Candace Kim, an assistant to Asian American activist Angela Oh based in Los Angeles, identified with the Korean community. She felt that Korean storekeepers had been unjustly blamed in the aftermath of the trial that acquitted police officers accused of beating Rodney King in 1991. The verdict was unfair, she thought, but so were some people's reactions to the Korean community. In her words:

> It [the Los Angeles riot] was a wake-up call; it raised our level of consciousness. We're not taking racism for granted anymore like it will disappear if we leave it alone. Korean-Americans were blamed: many Korean-Americans had businesses in predominantly Latino and African-American communities where there was a lot of resentment. . . . If you look at the area where the riots occurred, there was a history of neglect, but who was to blame for it? It became Koreans and, in this sense, we were scapegoats. (Chancer, 2005, pp. 239–340)

According to Oh herself, when people blamed Koreans and not African Americans, the effect was to depoliticize whatever claim black rioters had to being protesters. As Oh put it:

> Many storekeepers didn't even know who Rodney King was. You always blame the weak but why wouldn't you burn down City Hall? If you make a political statement, make a political statement—don't go after poor immigrants. (Chancer, 2005, pp. 239–240)

In contrast to substituting (victim blaming), reversing describes a tendency to defend the defendant. Reversing focuses on the defendant's situation. As the case evolves, parties recast the defendant as a victim, not a victimizer, and they relinquish their moral indignation, adopting a more sympathetic stance toward the defendant. Because reversals often entail asserting the opposite (victimized) of what appears to be the case (victimizer), reversing recalls the Freudian concept of reaction formation.

In the Rodney King case, for instance, a party who preferred to remain anonymous told me that King had "brought on his own beating." Taking an additional step, another observer said that he believed the police officers who beat Rodney King had been defending themselves and further that the officers were now being victimized by "anti-police forces." In the William Kennedy Smith rape case, numerous people I interviewed thought that "Willie" was basically a "nice guy" from "a good family." Mike Tyson was believed by some to have been unfairly treated by the criminal justice system and by the media, both of which were overly eager to see him convicted on rape charges. Many believed that the young men accused of murdering Yusef Hawkins in the Bensonhurst section of Brooklyn had been "railroaded." Also, several people felt that prosecutors, influenced by the Central Park case, were overly zealous in pursuing indictments against the well-to-do, white football players accused of sexually assaulting a young girl in Glen Ridge, New Jersey.[8]

It is difficult to imagine that victim blaming (substituting) could be anything other than destructive. However, I argue that in some instances, reversing gives voice to the legitimate possibility that a particular defendant is innocent. In the 1989 Central Park jogger case, community activists believed the young men who had been arrested on rape charges were not victimizers; rather, many activists saw them as victims who had been "railroaded" by frenzied media coverage and by overzealous prosecutors. In the end, the activists were legally vindicated. In 2002, a convicted felon named Mathias Reyes admitted to having brutally raped the Central Park jogger. A single individual admitted to the rape that the media had described as "gang rape," a designation that remained even though no forensic evidence ever linked the young men accused of rape to the Central Park jogger. A decade and a half later, lab tests matched Reyes's DNA to a semen sample taken from the original rape kit. Reactions to the case based on reversing were constructive and prescient.

When the evidence is strong that a defendant is guilty, reversing and substituting are more likely to come into play.[9] In the William Kennedy Smith and Mike Tyson cases, and in the Bensonhurst and Glen Ridge cases parties who followed these trials both blamed victims and defended the defendants. Why might this be the case? One answer is that, in tandem, the mechanisms add up to a stronger argument. This is so in a legal sense: By shifting responsibility onto the victims *and* recasting victimizers as victims, defense attorneys are in a better position to defend clients. It is also true in a collective sense. By blaming victims and defending the accused, persons who may be arguing their case in the informal court of public opinion bolster their causes.

Again, group identification is an important factor in responding to defendants disparaged by the media. Groups include racial and/or ethnic groups, neighborhoods, and symbols traditionally endowed with authority, such as a celebrity or politically powerful dynasties like the Kennedy family. People who belong to or identify with a group feel demeaned when a member of that group comes under attack. In the following example, a young man I have already quoted responded more to the way the media stereotyped African Americans than to the question of O. J. Simpson's guilt per se. The young man said, "Do you know what? Sometimes I think that whether or not O. J. is guilty, I can't afford for him to be guilty. Where would that leave me given everything else that's happened?" Similarly, working-class whites in the Bensonhurst section of Brooklyn may not have felt they could afford that the young men who killed Yusef Hawkins be guilty: A guilty verdict would mark Bensonhurst as a racist community. In Glen Ridge, the media exposed more than the rape of a girl with Down's Syndrome; they also threatened a community's sense of propriety and exclusivity.

People may have a well-founded cause for anger. Media outlets can be careless in the way they link defendants and groups with whom individuals may identify. And good reasons exist for objecting to historical mistreatment of minority groups by local criminal justice systems, especially in Los Angeles or New York City. And yet, collective anger at institutional sources of discrimination can be reshaped by partialized debate and turned into specious victim blaming or unfounded attempts to exonerate victimizers. Although triggered by social problems, the defensive reactions I call substituting and reversing can displace troubling emotions about institutions or groups onto individuals. Unfortunately, what this means is that a victim may be the undeserving brunt of someone's displaced anger or a defendant may receive the unjustifiable benefit of sympathy as a victim of oppression. And all this can happen unconsciously, consistent with and perhaps reinforcing individualistic propensities that are themselves highly characteristic of American culture.

Furthermore, the failure to clearly distinguish between social cause and the facts of a case may undermine social criticisms offered by activists or protesters. The 1988 case involving a young African American woman, Tawana Brawley, is a telling illustration. Tawana Brawley claimed that white police officers had kidnapped and raped her over a period of several days. Activist Reverend Al Sharpton took on her case, building it into a vehicle for protest designed to expose racial injustice and advance the cause of equality. It had all the hallmarks of a provoking assault case. But the case never came to trial because no evidence was ever produced validating Brawley's claim that she was raped. In the end, the case exposed the risks that can sometimes accompany the use of symbolic incidents of this kind (i.e., provoking assaults) to make larger political points. The public responded with cynicism. Some people joined in caricaturing Sharpton, ridiculing Brawley, and doubting claims made in other cases concerning discrimination.

Discussion and Conclusion

When we step back from all of this, what can we say about victim blaming? I have suggested that one reason victims may be blamed for their own victimization has to do with conventions of debate that straitjacket—and one might say impoverish—the complexity of discourse within American culture, limiting discussion to a two-sided framework of debate. Moreover, high-profile crimes of the provoking assault variety are not the only cultural form through which restricted debate is played out. These cases are shaped by other analogously two-sided cultural conventions, which both the media and the law share. As a result, the two-sided debate also structures public debate, squeezing it too often into simplistic choices between blaming victims or defending defendants.

How do anger and injustice fit into this discussion? Provoking assaults are crimes that at the same time involve terrible acts of violence committed by and against individuals and larger social institutions of which the cases become symbolic. Because the violence is brutal and cruel, these cases carry far broader and more general ramifications than ordinary crime. Something larger is at stake, whether rapes that women too often experience or police brutality that minorities too often suffer. And although this chapter may lack clear-cut policy ramifications, it does suggest the importance of looking for the roots of victim blaming in larger cultural habits and structured social inequities. For high-profile crimes of the provoking assault variety reflect a deeply embedded cultural tendency to individualize and oversimplify social problems.

Last but not least, social activists should be cautious when dealing with provoking assault cases. On the one hand, the cases help to publicize causes that have symbolic value. Admittedly, they do this through the narrative opportunities offered by individual cases. On the other hand, legal verdicts are only capable of resolving one case, not the general social problem for which that case came to stand. Moreover, high-profile crimes offer certain ambiguous pleasures that may include arguing about who did or did not commit a particular crime and using these cases to "talk politics" about gender biases and racial discrimination. The social distance provided by reading about or hearing about crimes that affect other people makes these pleasures both safe and intimate. For these reasons, the cases are often experienced as engaging. But for the reasons discussed in this chapter, they can also be problematic. They both engage and distract us from seeing the patterns of crime, the systematic character of injustice, and structural solutions that may alleviate social problems. The challenge for us all is to learn how to draw on the considerable potential of these cases to advance social causes while at the same time learning to take them with a grain of salt.

NOTES

1. In New York City, I studied the Central Park jogger and Bensonhurst cases. (Both of these crimes were committed in 1989 and tried in 1990; the Central Park jogger case allegedly involved a gang rape, and the Bensonhurst case involved the murder of a young black man who was set upon by a group of mostly white youths in Bensonhurst, Brooklyn.) In Indianapolis and Palm Beach, respectively, I studied the Mike Tyson and William Kennedy Smith cases involving allegations of rape. (Both alleged incidents took place in 1991; while the Kennedy Smith case was tried and an acquittal was obtained in late 1991, a conviction was obtained in the trial of Mike Tyson in early 1992.) Finally, in Los Angeles, I studied the Rodney King, Reginald Denny, and O. J. Simpson cases. (The highly publicized beating of Rodney King took place in March 1991, though the infamous acquittal of police officers in Simi Valley, California, occurred in April 1992, precisely the time and day when an assault on truck driver Reginald Denny occurred. The Denny case was tried in 1993, while the dual homicides attributed to O. J. Simpson occurred in 1994 and the criminal trial of Simpson resulted in a 1995 acquittal.)

2. Kathleen Maguire and Ann L. Pastore (2002). *Sourcebook of criminal justice statistics* (Table 2.1). Retrieved June 9, 2004, from http://www.albany.edu/sourcebook/. More specifically, with regard to New York City, around the time that the Central Park and Bensonhurst cases exploded into press coverage; see, for example, Rex Smith, "Survey: Crime fear high," *Newsweek*, January 6, 1989, p. 9, and "Living in Fear: 1 of 2 is a victim of crime," first in a City on the Brink series, *Newsday*, August 13, 1989, p. 5.

3. As Kathleen Beckett writes in *Making crime pay: Law and order in contemporary American politics* (New York: Oxford, 1997), "The most recent anticrime campaign (1993–1994) occurred as the reported crime rate plummeted and in the absence of widespread unrest" (p. 27).

4. An excellent description of this 'toughening' criminal justice environment can be

found in Chapter 2 of Michael Tonry's *Thinking about crime: Sense and sensibility in American penal culture* (New York: Oxford University Press, 2004).

5. See note 1 for details on this and other cases.

6. For example, see the account of changes in rape laws that resulted from feminist intervention in Linda A. Fairstein, *Sexual violence: Our war against rape* (New York: William Morrow, 1993).

7. Common to the Rodney King, Abner Louima, and Amadiou Diallo cases, the first symbolizing police brutality in Los Angeles and the latter two New York City, was that some parties on the "side" of police officers questioned whether apparent victims might have brought about their own victimization. Perhaps it wasn't the officers' fault but Rodney King himself, who menaced the police on that now notorious night in Los Angeles that George Halliday, unnoticed, captured on videotape. Perhaps it was Abner Louima, who picked a fight with Officer Justin Volpe one evening, years later, when serious abuse resulted in a Flatbush, Brooklyn, police station. Perhaps Amadiou Diallo was flashing something threatening in the Bronx before he was shot to death in an apartment building entranceway.

8. More specifically, this viewpoint suggests that indictments in the Glen Ridge case were used to compensate for media and criminal justice biases against minority and lower-class young defendants, about which many people had protested in the April 1989 Central Park case. Attention coming as it did to Glen Ridge soon thereafter, in May 1989, these parties felt the media, as well as prosecutors, were "picking on" rich white kids to show that the system was not prejudiced after all.

9. These social-psychic dynamics often, but not necessarily, appeared together in interviews I conducted. Some parties concentrated more on one than the other. For instance, some people in the O. J. Simpson case were concerned that the defendant had been framed (therefore seeing O. J. Simpson as a sympathetic figure) but drew back from in any way blaming Nicole Brown Simpson and Ronald Gold for the brutal murders they suffered. Similarly, some people who emphasized that Nicole Brown Simpson was not as "pure" as her media image suggested also said that, still, perhaps O. J. Simpson was guilty. Clearly, this emphasis on one dynamic and not the other can (and did sometimes) happen in other cases as well.

REFERENCE

Anonymous. (1994, September 20). Interview outside courtroom [of O. J. Simpson trial].

Beckett, K. (1997). *Making crime pay: Law and order in contemporary American politics.* New York: Oxford University Press.

Chancer, L. S. (1998). Playing gender against race through high profile crimes. *Violence Against Women, 4,* 100–113.

Chancer, L. S. (2005). *High-profile crimes: When legal cases become social causes.* Chicago: University of Chicago Press.

Fairstein, L. A. (1993). *Sexual violence: Our war against rape.* New York: William Morrow.

Faludi, S. (1991). Backlash: The undeclared war against women. New York: Crown Books.

Hills, S. (1987). *Corporate violence*. Lanhan, MD.: Rowman and Littlefield.

Maguire, K., & Pastore, A. L. (Eds.). (2002). *Sourcebook of criminal justice online*. Retrieved June 9, 2004, from http://www.albany.edu/sourcebook.

Schudson, M. (1995). *The power of news*. Cambridge, MA: Harvard University Press.

Smith, R. (1989, January 6). Survey: Crime fear high. *Newsweek*, p. 9.

Smith, R. (1989, August 13). Living in fear: 1 of 2 is a victim of crime, City on the brink [series], *Newsday*, p. 5.

Steinberg, S. (1995). *Turning back: The retreat from radical justice in American thought and policy*. Boston: Beacon Press.

Tonry, M. (2004). *Thinking about crime: Sense and sensibility*. New York: Oxford University Press.

SELECTED READINGS

Women, violence, and the media is a fast-paced area of study, and for this reason, the reading list that follows is intended to convey to interested readers a few of the emerging and continuing themes that characterize the field. Postfeminist work and responses to it mark a trend (see Bean, 2007; Chesney-Lind, 2006; Chunn, Boyd, & Lessard, 2007; Cole & Daniel, 2005; Dow & Wood, 2006). Postfeminism, new feminism, and third-wave feminism are themes explored by several edited collections on media topics (see Cuklanz & Moorti, 2006; Johnson, 2007a; Projansky, 2001; Tasker & Negra, 2007). The study of masculinities generates distinctive treatments of media representations, and one recent study, *Media and Violence* (Boyle, 2005), builds on earlier work on masculinities (Cuklanz, 2000; Ghoussoub & Sinclair-Webb, 2000). Moreover, terrorism and the wars in Iraq and Afghanistan have inspired new media research on domestic terror (Cohler, 2006), domestic stabilization (Cohler, 2006), the sexing of war (Herbst, 2005), militarized femininity (Sjoberg, 2007), the exploitation of women in time of war (Sarikakis, 2002), and women as weapons of war (Oliver, 2007). On a final note, scholarship on girls as producers of media (Kearney, 2006) and as participating feminists (Labaton & Martin, 2004) defines a new audience in a field that tends to address adult, female audiences (Boyle, 2005; Jermyn, 2007).

Globalization, intersectionality, and transgressive women continue to inspire feminist media scholarship. News studies based on the media in Turkey, the Netherlands, New Zealand, and the Middle East signal movement away from the Western press (Alat, 2006; de Leeuw & Van Wichelen, 2005; Gavey & Gow, 2001; Ghoussoub & Sinclair-Webb, 2000; Kogacioglu, 2004), as do edited collections organized around the global village or international perspectives (Kamalipour & Rampal, 2001; Ross & Byerly, 2004). A few of these sources are responsive to criticisms leveled at first-world feminists by third-world and postcolonial feminists.

Intersectionality continues to drive theory and research (see Collins, 2004; Arrighi, 2007; hooks, 2006). African American (Meyers, 2004) and Italian American women (Johnson, 2007b; Quinn, 2004) are specifically featured in three studies. Several titles deal with intersections of gender, race, and/or class in the context of media (Collins, 2004; Dines & Humez, 2003; hooks, 2006), audience and producers (Lind, 2004), and crime and justice (Cavender & Jurik, 2007; Markowitz & Jones-Brown, 2001; Moorti, 2002; Projanksy, 2001). As for transgressive women, their deviations from heterosexual femininity have inspired studies on Medea (Barnett, 2006; Caputi, 2004), *Buffy the Vampire Slayer* (Levine & Parks, 2007), bad girls (Chesney-Lind & Irwin, 2008; Owen, Vande Berg, & Stein, 2007); television's female warriors (Early & Kennedy, 2003), outlaw culture (hooks, 2006), lesbian serial killers (Pearson, 2007), mean girls (Ringrose, 2006), and violent women (Hendin, 2004; White, 2007).

The reading list also reflects a continuing interest in rape as the iconic form of violence against women (Bevacqua, 2000; Cuklanz, 2000; Franisk, Seafelt, Cepress, & Vanello, 2008; Gavey & Gow, 2001; Horeck, 2004; Projansky, 2001; Read, 2000; for domestic violence, see Berns, 2004) and in high-profile criminal trials (Chancer, 2005; Chermak & Bailey, 2007; Franisk, Seafelt, Cepress, & Vanello, 2008). It also indicates scholars' preferences for examining gendered crime in film and television (Burfoot & Lord, 2006; Cavender & Jurik, 2007; Cuklanz, 2000; Cuklanz & Moorti, 2006; Early & Kennedy, 2003; Horeck, 2004; Jermyn, 2007; Johnson 2007a, 2007b; Levine & Parks, 2007; Moorti, 2002; Projanksy, 2001; Quinn, 2004; Rafter, 2006; Rapping, 2003).

Alat, Z. (2006). News coverage of violence against women: The Turkish case. *Feminist Media Studies, 6,* 295–314.

Arrighi, B. A. (2007). *Understanding inequality: The intersection of race/ethnicity, class and gender.* Lanham, MD: Rowman and Littlefield.

Barnett, B. (2006). Medea in the media: Narrative and myth in newspaper coverage of women who kill their children. *Journalism, 7,* 411–432.

Bean, K. (2007). *Post-backlash feminism: Women and the media since Reagan/Bush.* Jefferson, NC: McFarland.

Berns, N. (2004). *Framing the victim: Domestic violence, media and social problems.* Hawthorne, NY: Aldine de Gruyter.

Bevacqua, M. (2000). *Rape on the public agenda: Feminism and the politics of sexual assault.* Boston: Northeastern University Press.

Boyle, K. (2005). *Media and violence: Gendering the debates.* London: Sage.

Burfoot, A., & Lord, S. (Eds.) (2006). *Killing women: The visual culture of gender and violence.* Waterloo: Wilfred Laurier University Press.

Caputi, J. (2004). *Goddesses and monsters: Women, myth, power and popular culture.* Madison: University of Wisconsin Press/Popular Press.

Cavender, G., & Jurik, N. C. (2007). Scene composition and justice for women. *Feminist Criminology, 2,* 227–303.

Chancer, L. S. (2005). *High-profile crimes: When legal cases become social causes.* Chicago: University of Chicago Press.

Chermak, S., & Bailey, F. Y. (Eds.). (2007). *Crimes and trials of the century.* Westport, CT: Greenwood Press.

Chesney-Lind, M. (2006). Patriarchy, crime and justice: Feminist criminology in an era of backlash. *Feminist Criminology, 1,* 1–26.

Chesney-Lind, M., & Irwin, K. (2008). *Beyond bad girls: Gender, violence and hype.* New York: Routledge.

Chunn, D. E., Boyd, S. B., & Lessard, H. (Eds.). (2007). *Reaction and resistance: Feminism, law and social change.* Vancouver: UBC Press.

Cohler, D. (2006). Keeping the home fires burning: Renegotiating gender and sexuality in US mass media after September 11. *Feminist Media Studies, 6,* 245–261.

Cole, E., & Daniel, J. H. (2005). *Featuring females: Feminist analysis of media.* Washington, DC: American Psychological Association.

Collins, P. H. (2004). *Black sexual politics: African Americans, gender and the new racism.* London: Routledge.

Cuklanz, L. M. (2000). *Rape on prime time: Television, masculinity, and sexual violence.* Philadelphia: University of Pennsylvania Press.

Cuklanz, L. M., & Moorti, S. (2006). Television's "new" feminism: Prime-time representations of women and victims. *Critical Studies in Media Communication, 23,* 302–321.

de Leeuw, M., & Van Wichelen, S. (2005). "Please go wake up!": Submission, Hirsi Ali, and the "War on Terror" in the Netherlands. *Feminist Media Studies, 5,* 325–340.

Dines, G., & Humez, J. M. (Eds.). (2003). *Gender, race, and class in the media: A text reader.* Thousand Oaks, CA: Sage.

Dow, B. J., & Wood, J. T. (2006). *The SAGE handbook of gender and communication.* Thousand Oaks, CA: Sage.

Early, F., & Kennedy, K. (Eds.). (2003). *Athena's daughters: Television's new women warriors.* Syracuse, NY: Syracuse University Press.

Franisk, R., Seafelt, J. L., Cepress, S. L., & Vanello, J. A. (2008). Prevalence and effects of rape myths in print journalism: The Kobe Bryant case. *Journal of Violence Against Women, 14,* 287–309.

Gavey, N. J., & Gow, V. (2001). 'Cry wolf,' cried the wolf: Constructing the issue of false rape allegations in New Zealand media texts. *Feminism and Psychology, 11,* 341–360.

Ghoussoub, M., & Sinclair-Webb, E. (Eds.). (2000). *Imagined masculinities: Male identity and culture in the modern Middle East.* London: Sagi.

Hendin, J. (2004). *Heartbreakers: Women and violence in contemporary culture and literature.* New York: Palgrave Macmillan.

Herbst, C. (2005). Virtual females and the sexing of war. *Feminist Media Studies, 5*, 311–324.

hooks, b. (2006). *Outlaw culture: Resisting representations*. New York: Routledge.

Horeck, T. (2004). *Public rape: Representing violation in fiction and film*. London: Routledge.

Jermyn, D. (2007). *Crime watching: Investigating real TV*. London and New York: I. B. Tauris and Palgrave Macmillan.

Johnson, M. L. (Ed.). (2007a). *Third wave feminism and television: Jane puts it in the box*. London: I. B. Tauris.

Johnson, M. L. (2007b). Gangster feminism: The feminist cultural work of HBO's "The Sopranos." *Feminist Studies, 33*, 269–296.

Kamalipour, Y. R., & Rampal, K. R. (Eds). (2001). *Media, sex, violence and drugs in the global village*. Lanham, MD: Rowman and Littlefield.

Kearney, M. C. (2006). *Girls make media*. New York: Routledge.

Kogacioglu, D. (2004). The tradition effect: Framing honor crimes in Turkey. *Differences, 15*, 118–151.

Labaton, V., & Martin, D. L. (Eds.). (2004). *The fire this time: Young activities and the new feminism*. New York: Anchor Books.

Levine, E., & Parks, L. (2007). *Undead TV: Essays on Buffy the vampire slayer*. Durham, NC: Duke University Press.

Lind, R. A. (2004). *Race, gender, media: Considering diversity across audiences, content and producers*. Boston: Pearson/Allyn and Bacon.

Markowitz, M. W., & Jones-Brown, D. D. (Eds.). (2001) *The system in black and white: Exploring the connection between race, crime and justice*. Westport, CT: Praeger.

Meyers, M. (2004). African American women and violence: Gender, race and class in the news. *Critical Studies in Media Communication, 21* (2), 95–118.

Moorti, S. (2002). *Color of rape: Gender and race in television's public space*. Albany: State University of New York Press.

Oliver, K. (2007). *Women as weapons of war: Iraq, sex and the media*. New York: Columbia University Press.

Owen, A. S., Vande Berg, L. R., & Stein, S. R. (2007). *Bad girls: Cultural politics and media representations of transgressive women*. New York: Peter Lang.

Pearson, K. (2007). The trouble with Aileen Wuornos: Feminism's "first serial killer." *Communications and Critical/Cultural Studies, 4*, 256–275.

Projansky, S. (2001). *Watching rape: Film and television in postfeminist culture*. New York: New York University Press.

Quinn, R. G. (2004). Mothers, molls and misogynists: Resisting Italian American womanhood in "The Sopranos." *Journal of American Culture, 27*, 166–174.

Rafter, N. H. (2006). *Shots in the mirror: Crime films and society*. Oxford: Oxford University Press.

Rapping, E. (2003). *Law and justice as seen on TV*. New York: New York University Press.

Read, J. (2000). *The new avengers: Feminism, femininity and the rape–revenge cycle*. Manchester and New York: Manchester University Press and St. Martin's Press.

Ringrose, J. (2006). A new universal mean girl: Examining the discursive construction and social regulation of a new feminine psychology. *Feminism and Psychology, 16*, 405–424.

Ross, R., & Byerly, C. M. (Eds.). (2004). *Women and media: International perspectives*. Malden, MA: Blackwell.

Sarikakis, K. (2002). Violence, militarism, terrorism: Faces of masculine order and the exploitation of women. *Feminist Media Studies, 2,* 151–154.

Sjoberg, L. (2007). Agency, militarized femininity and enemy others: Observations from the war in Iraq. *International Feminist Journal of Politics, 9*, 82–101.

Tasker, Y., & Negra, D. (Eds.). (2007). *Interrogating postfeminism: Gender and the politics of popular culture*. Durham, NC: Duke University Press.

White, R. (2007). *Violent femmes: Women as spies in popular culture*. London: Routledge.

CONTRIBUTORS

Madelaine Adelman is an associate professor in the School of Justice and Social Inquiry at Arizona State University in Tempe. Her ethnographic research centers on the politics of domestic violence and the contested relationship between national identity and religion. She is completing a monograph based on this research entitled *Battering States*. She is also editing the volume *Jerusalem Across the Disciplines* with Miriam Elman.

Frankie Y. Bailey is an associate professor in the School of Criminal Justice at the University at Albany (SUNY), Albany, New York. She and Steven Chermak coedited *Crimes and Trials of the Century* (2007), published by Praeger Press. Overmountain Press (Silver Dagger Mysteries) published her latest murder mystery, *You Should Have Died on Monday*, in 2007.

Melissa H. Barlow is professor in the Department of Criminal Justice and Director of the Institute for Community Justice at Fayetteville State University, Fayetteville, North Carolina. She is coauthor of *Police in a Multicultural Society: An American Story* (Waveland, 2000) and has published articles on the history and political economy of crime control policy, crime and justice in the news media, and race and class issues in criminal justice. Her article "The Ideological Nature of Crime News" was published by Vita e Pensiero in 2005 as part of Gabrio Forti and Marta Bertolini's edited volume *La televisione del crimine*, roughly translated as *Television's Representations of Crime*.

Janine Bower is acting assistant professor in the Department of Criminology and Criminal Justice at Keuka College, Keuka Park, New York. Her research has considered human rights in a global context: torture at Abu Ghraib prison and ethnic cleansing in the former Yugoslavia and Rwanda.

Gray Cavender is professor in the School of Social Justice and Social Inquiry at Arizona State University in Tempe. His research interests involve the study of media, crime, and culture. He has written extensively on the *Prime Suspect* series. With Nancy C. Jurik, he published the 2004 article "Policing Race and Gender: An Analysis of Prime Suspect 2 in *Women's Studies Quarterly*.

Lynn S. Chancer is professor of sociology at Hunter College and the Graduate Center of the City University of New York. Her research interests include culture, feminist theory, criminology, media, and social movements. Her publications include *Gender, Race and Class: An Overview* (Blackwell, 2006) and *High Profile Crimes: When Legal Cases Become Social Causes* (University of Chicago Press, 2005) from which parts of chapter 12 (this volume) have been drawn.

Janice E. Clifford is an associate professor in the Department of Sociology at Auburn University in Auburn, Alabama. Her areas of teaching and research include family studies, violent crime, juvenile deviance, victimization, and violence against women. She has published in the *Journal of Contemporary Criminal Justice, Journal of Quantitative Criminology, The Journal of Homicide Studies*, and *The American Sociologist*. She is a member of Alpha Kappa Delta, the International Sociology Honor Society, and she serves as an advisor for the local chapter.

John W. Heeren recently retired as a professor in the Department of Sociology at California State University in San Bernardino. His major interests are in the mass media and crime and religion. With Jill Theresa Messing, he published in 2004 "Another Side of Multiple Murder: Women Killers in the Domestic Context" in *Homicide Studies*.

Drew Humphries is a professor in the Department of Sociology, Anthropology, and Criminal Justice at Rutgers University in Camden, New Jersey. Her research areas are women, drugs, violence, and the media. Her 1999 book *Crack Mothers: Pregnancy, Drugs, and the Media* was published by Ohio State University Press.

Carl J. Jensen III joined the Legal Studies faculty at the University of Mississippi in 2007. Prior to that, he served as a special agent in the FBI for 22 years, where he was assigned to various field offices, the FBI Laboratory, and the Behavioral Science Unit. Upon his retirement from the FBI in 2006, he joined the RAND Corporation as a senior behavioral scientist, a position he continues to hold in addition to his faculty appointment.

Deborah Jermyn is a senior lecturer in film and TV at Roehampton University. She has written a number of articles on the representation of women and crime in popular film and television and is coeditor of *Understanding Reality TV* (2003) and author of *Crime Watching: Investigating Real Crime TV* (2007) from which parts of chapter 11 (this volume) have been drawn.

Nancy C. Jurik is professor in the School of Social Justice and Social Inquiry at Arizona State University in Tempe. Her interests include gender, work, work organization, and economic justice. Her 2005 book *Bootstrap Dreams: U.S. Microenterprise Development in an Era of Welfare Reform* was published by Cornell University (ILR) Press.

Mahfuzul I. Khondaker is an assistant professor of criminal justice at Kutztown University in Kutztown, Pennsylvania. His research interests include juvenile delinquency, crime and delinquency prevention, crime and perceptions of crime among South Asian immigrants, women and victimization, and crime in third world countries. His most recent peer-reviewed publication is "Immigrant Bangladeshi Communities and Intergenerational Conflict: The Need for Multicultural Education," which appeared in 2008 in the *PAACE Journal of Lifelong Learning.*

Darrin Kowitz is a doctoral candidate in the Department of Sociology at the University of New Mexico, where he teaches Introduction to Sociology, Society and Personality, and Military Sociology. His research combines ethnographic and quantitative methods to examine the intersection of politics, culture, and society.

Emily Lenning is an assistant professor in the Criminal Justice Department at Fayetteville State University in Fayetteville, North Carolina. Her research focuses on crimes of the state, issues surrounding the implementation and problematic nature of international law as it is currently constituted, and the challenges facing transgendered individuals and their significant others.

Michelle L. Meloy is an associate professor in the Department of Sociology, Anthropology, and Criminal Justice at Rutgers University in

Camden, New Jersey. Her areas of research include victimology, sex offenders, policy, and legal reform. Her 2006 book *Sex Offenses and the Men Who Commit Them: An Assessment of Sex Offenders on Probation* was published by Northeastern University Press.

Jill Theresa Messing is an assistant professor in the School of Social Work at Arizona State University. She spent the last year as a National Institute of Mental Health postdoctoral fellow in interdisciplinary violence research at the Johns Hopkins Medical Institutions (T32–MH20014). Her main interests are intimate partner violence, domestic homicide, risk assessment, and the intersection of the social service and criminal justice systems. Most recently, she was the principal investigator on an intimate partner violence supplement to an examination of workplace violence funded by the National Institute of Occupational Safety and Health (#R01 OH007953-01A2).

Susan L. Miller is professor in the Department of Sociology and Criminal Justice at the University of Delaware in Newark. Her areas of interest include gender and criminal justice policy, domestic violence, and victimology. Her 2007 edited collection *Criminal Justice Research and Practices: Diverse Voices from the Field*, was published by the University Press of New England/Northeastern University Press. Her forthcoming book on restorative justice and violent crimes will be published by New York University Press.

Thomas A. Petee is affiliated with the Center for Governmental and Public Affairs at Auburn University in Montgomery, Alabama. His areas of interest include homicide, public mass murder, and serial offending. His article "Analyzing Violent Serial Offending," coauthored with J. Jarvis, appeared in *Homicide Studies* in 2000.

Zoann K. Snyder is an associate professor in the Department of Sociology and Criminal Justice at Western Michigan University in Kalamazoo. Her research and publications have focused on incarcerated women and their children. In a forthcoming collection edited by Muraskin, Joseph, Sharp, and Inderbitzin, her "Voices from the Inside: Incarcerated Women Speak Out" will be published by Roxbury Publishing Company.

Yaschica Williams is an assistant professor in the Department of Criminology and Criminal Justice at the University of Memphis, Memphis, Tennessee. Her research interests are in the areas of parenting and delinquency, gender and crime, and the intersections of race, class, and gender within the criminal justice system.